# Twenty-first-century capital

MANCHESTER
1824

Manchester University Press

Geopolitical Economy

*Series Editors*
Radhika Desai and Alan Freeman

Geopolitical Economy promotes fresh inter- and multi-disciplinary perspectives on the most pressing new realities of the twenty-first century: the multipolar world and the renewed economic centrality of states in it. From a range of disciplines, works in the series account for these new realities historically. They explore the problems and contradictions, domestic and international, of capitalism. They reconstruct the struggles of classes and nations, and state actions in response to them, which have shaped capitalism, and track the growth of the public and de-commodified spheres these dialectical interactions have given rise to. Finally, they map the new terrain on which political forces must now act to orient national and the international economies in equitable and ecological, cultural and creative directions.

**Previously published**

The US vs China: Asia's new Cold War? *Jude Woodward*

Flight MH17, Ukraine and the new Cold War *Kees van der Pijl*

Karl Polanyi and twenty-first-century capitalism *Edited by Radhika Desai and Kari Polanyi Levitt*

The capitalist mode of destruction: Austerity, ecological crisis and the hollowing out of democracy *Costas Panayotakis*

# Twenty-first-century capital

## Critical post-Soviet
## Marxist reflections

Aleksander Buzgalin and Andrey Kolganov

MANCHESTER UNIVERSITY PRESS

Published by Manchester University Press
Oxford Road, Manchester M13 9PL

www.manchesteruniversitypress.co.uk

British Library Cataloguing-in-Publication Data
A catalogue record for this book is available from the
British Library

ISBN   978 1 5261 3145 4   hardback

First published 2021

Typeset
by New Best-set Typesetters Ltd

# Contents

### Part I: Methodology matters

### Part II: The market, money, and capital in the twenty-first century

# Figures

# Tables

# Acknowledgements

This English-language edition owes a great deal to the weighty critical remarks and advice of several colleagues. Above all, the authors would like to express their profound gratitude to Radhika Desai, editor of the series Geopolitical Economy and Professor at the Department of Political Studies at the University of Manitoba, who performed a huge and systematic labour in editing and making corrections to our book, as well as in adapting the text for English-language readers. Her contribution is difficult to overstate.

Another critically important contribution to the work on the book was made by our young colleague Olga Barashkova. Without her help in the selection and presentation of the materials in the book, and also her valuable advice, this work would not have taken on its pleasing appearance and would not have contained an adequate range of sources and data. We extend our sincere and profound gratitude to them all. Special thanks are also due to Renfrey Clarke, our comrade and translator for close to thirty years.

Dialogues over the past quarter-century with foreign colleagues from the countries of Western and Eastern Europe, North and South America, and Asia (above all, China and Japan) have provided a significant impulse for our work. We are grateful to our friends Samir Amin, Elizabeth Bowman, Michael Brie, Galina Dubrovskaya, Cheng Enfu, Alan Freeman, James Galbraith, Chen Hong, David Kotz, Tamas Krausz, David Laibman, David Lane, Rut Stolyarova, Robert Stone, Yuzo Tanaka, and Immanuel Wallerstein (some of whom, sadly, are no longer with us). We also express our thanks to colleagues from the World Association for Political Economy, the International Initiative for Promoting Political Economy, the Radical Philosophy Association, the Union for Radical Political Economy of the USA, and Left Forum, as well as to all the social movements, organisations, and foundations that have helped us to assimilate foreign thinking on social topics and to present our ideas to the court of the international scholarly community.

The authors were trained in the Department of Political Economy of the Faculty of Economics of Lomonosov Moscow State University, working in close collaboration with the Institute of Comparative Studies of Socio-Economic

Systems of the Faculty of Economics. The leaders of this collective over the decades have included the founder of the university's school of political economy, Nikolay Tsagolov; Valery Radaev, who continued Tsagolov's tradition; and the present head of the department, Anatoly Porokhovsky, who is further developing the main achievements of the school in our difficult times. They turned us into researchers oriented above all towards resolving fundamental theoretical questions. We have also gained a great deal from numerous dialogues with scholars from a range of Russian centres of research and education. In recent years, these people have included our colleagues from the International Political Economy Association of the Post-Soviet Countries and the Free Economic Society of Russia, led by the author of the new theory of 'Noonomy', Professor Sergey Bodrunov.

We cannot fail to express our gratitude to all those who, in the course of the past years, have aided in the preparation of this book. Above all, these include our comrades who during various periods have been members of the editorial boards of the journals *Al'ternativy* (Alternatives) and *Voprosy politicheskoj ekonomii* (Problems in politial economy), some of whom also belong to the post-Soviet school of critical Marxism: Urak Aliev, Vadim Belov, Lyudmila Bulavka-Buzgalina, Vasily Chekmarev, Ruslan Dzarasov, Rafkat Gaysin, Ruslan Grinberg, Leonid Istyagin, Kaysyn Khubiev, Aleksandr Khudokormov, Petr Lemeshchenko, Vladimir Mironov, Karen Momdzhyan, Aleksandr Nekipelov, Viktor Ryazanov, Viktor Tarasevich, Sergey Tolkachev, and especially our close friends Mikhail Pavlov, Emil Rudyk, Boris Slavin, Andrey Sorokin, Mikhail Voeikov, and Natalya Yakovleva. An enormous contribution was also made by now-departed comrades who worked on *Al'ternativy* (Alternatives): the great Soviet authority on foreign Marxism Mily Gretsky, the outstanding philosopher of culture Nahl Zlobin, and the theoretician and activist of the social liberation struggle of the peoples of Latin America Kiva Maydanik.

We have discussed the main arguments put forward in this book extensively over twenty years in seminars of the post-Soviet school of critical Marxism operating under the patronage of the First Deputy Chairperson of the Committee on Education of the State Duma, our old friend Professor Oleg Smolin, and in the meetings and conferences of the Centre for Modern Marxist Studies of the Faculty of Philosophy of Lomonosov Moscow State University.

Our book also owes its existence to the help of our young colleagues who are representatives of the new generation of the post-Soviet school of critical Marxism, Olga Barashkova, Olga Lemeshonok, Gleb Maslov, Tamara Stepanova, and Natalya Yakovleva, and also of other young people sympathetic to our ideas who at various times have participated in our dialogues and helped with our work. These latter include Gulnara Aitova, Dmitry

Khromov, Larisa Ozhogina, and many, many other young assistants. We also extend our gratitude to the students of Lomonosov Moscow State University, discussions with whom helped give rise to a considerable number of the ideas put forward in our text.

To a great degree, the authors of this book were able to write it thanks to the fact that their young colleagues and students worked in dialogue with them. Of these young people, only a handful have chosen the path of critical Marxism, but we are sure they will become outstanding scholars whose works will advance scholarship. We are grateful to them for their rigorous criticism, and we hope they will surpass their teachers in the near future.

We would also add that we wrote *Twenty-first-century capital* not so much in the quiet of our studies (indeed, in the strict sense of the word, we do not have any) as in the pauses between constant social and political activity. The 'Alternatives' movement; the networks 'Education for Everybody' and 'Congress of Workers in Education, Science and Culture'; the constant initiatives of the alterglobalists; and informational and other assistance to independent left organisations in Russia and abroad have all been, and will remain, no less important for us than theoretical and scholarly work. Further, it is precisely and exclusively thanks to our involvement in the practice of social creativity that we are able to delve directly into the relationships of alienation and to analyse them. Our analyses are not based on generalisations derived from books but flow from our own experience, and from that of our comrades in the struggle for social liberation.

Now to our very closest and most important assistants, comrades, critics, and sources of inspiration. This book has come into being because we were raised by our attentive, communist-minded parents: Nina Buzgalina and Vladimir Buzgalin and Energiya Kolganova and Ivan Kolganov. It is also due to the fact that at the sources of our work stood our teachers – our instructor and research supervisor Nikolay Khessin and the great scholar and militant Ernest Mandel.

And one thing more: one of the authors of this book, Aleksandr Buzgalin, has been fortunate enough in his life to have met Lyudmila Bulavka-Buzgalina, an outstanding scholar (professor at Lomonosov Moscow State University, author of more than 100 academic works published in many languages), and incomparable human being. With her, he lives, works, and creates. For this he is boundlessly thankful to her. The other author of the book, Andrey Kolganov, is endlessly grateful to his wife, without whose untiring care his work on this book would not have been possible.

# Foreword to the English edition

Although between us we have published more than 400 works in many languages, this book is unusually important for us. In it we take a definite step towards achieving the supreme task of contemporary Marxism: laying the basis for a *Capital* of the modern epoch. Raymond Aron long ago reproached Marxists for lacking a *Capital* for the twentieth century (Aron 1969), and our work addresses that lack for the twenty-first. The questions it asks are: *what method* should be adopted for studying commodities, money, and capital in the epoch of late capitalism, and *what should the corresponding theory be*?

While this task may seem exceedingly ambitious, we stand on the shoulders of giants and aim to develop further what they accomplished. Those who have undertaken this methodological task include Vladimir Lenin, Rosa Luxemburg, Karl Kautsky, Nikolay Bukharin, Aleksandr Bogdanov, and Leon Trotsky; Soviet and Western Marxists of the mid-twentieth century; and in recent decades, a diverse range of neo-Marxists, post-Marxists, and analytical Marxists, as well as orthodox thinkers. A great wealth of ideas is also contained in the works of Russian thinkers, whose works are represented, in particular, in the journals *Voprosy politicheskoj ekonomii* (Problems in political economy; www.interpolitec.su) and *Al'ternativy* (AlternativesAl'ternativy; www.alternativy.ru). Between them, these rich contributions have laid the foundations for a new, integral Marxist theory that can address the challenges of the modern world. However, such a theory is yet to emerge. In this work, we seek to open the way to such a theory and methodology.

We are well aware of the difficulties that attend such ambitious attempts in an age in which it is almost bad form to attempt fundamental research, and most confine themselves to specialised works on narrow topics. The very few works in recent decades that have attempted an integral rethinking of the main arguments of *Capital* can be divided into two unequal groups: a small number of fundamental works by very well-known authors (Ernest Mandel, Paul Sweezy, and István Mészáros, for instance) and a considerably longer list of less well-known works whose content is not especially profound.

In a field staked out by such works, researchers who live and work in semi-peripheral countries, cut off from Western scholarship by linguistic and organisational barriers, have little chance of being accepted as serious scholars. They are far more likely to be viewed as graphomaniacs. Have we managed to escape this 'periphery trap'? Have we been able to take our place, to the degree required, in the context of the world Marxist thought of recent decades? To be honest, if we have succeeded in this, it is in nothing like full measure. Our work has been conducted mainly in the context of Russian thought. This is certainly our great shortcoming, but it is also an advantage. By comparison with our foreign colleagues, we are the legatees of the heritage of Soviet critical Marxism, a heritage that is little known outside our country. Its methodological and theoretical importance, we are convinced, is comparable to the legacy of Marxist thought elsewhere in the world. Further, we have not worked alone; the authors of this book are only two members of a post-Soviet school of critical Marxism whose members and works are more fully discussed later in this book.

This book is also significant to us for purely personal reasons. In it, we sum up a crucially important part of our work over the past few decades. It was probably no accident that the first Russian edition of this work appeared shortly before our fiftieth birthdays, while the third edition, in two volumes, coincided with our reaching our sixties. The fifth edition of the book was published in autumn 2019.

The point, of course, lies not in the dates as such but in the fact that, while we were still students, we set ourselves the task of investigating the origins and emergence of the 'realm of freedom' that is replacing, in however incomplete, haphazard, and contradictory a manner, the 'realm of necessity', the world of alienation. If this seems rather an odd way to describe the process of creating a *Capital* for the twenty-first century, let us explain.

The experience of the revolutionary changes of twentieth century, especially in our country, gave us critical insights into the complexity of progress. Progress in the USSR combined undoubted achievements with horrible crimes, and great hopes, which seemed quite reasonable, with great disappointments. This experience led us to reject a linear view of historical progress and explore the problems of the combination of progress and regress, evolution and involution, dead ends, stagnation and prematurity, and revolutions followed by setbacks.

At the same time, this experience confirmed for us the principle of the development of society through contradictions, in which revolutions which transform the old method of production into a new, more progressive one, are practically inevitably followed by regression, restoration, and rollback.

Equally inevitably, however, they eventually lead to progress and the possibility of breakthroughs in the future.

We devoted the first decades of our research primarily to studying the fresh shoots of a new society and its economy. Important way stations in the progress of this work were our doctoral dissertations, which we defended on the eve of the dissolution of the USSR, and three monographs, entitled *After the Market*, *The Political Economy of a Non-Existent Socialism*, and *The Key to the Economy of the Twenty-First Century*, that were prepared for publication in 1991 but never appeared. The years that followed saw us turn to the anatomy of late (twenty-first-century) capitalism, without, however, abandoning our concern with the study of new manifestations of the 'realm of freedom'. We wrote a good many texts on this topic. Some of these writings have been published, while others are still to appear. For us, the present book is thus the result of long years of work.

Now for a few words on the sources, the subject, the method, and the structure of our book.

## Subject and method

*Twenty-first-century capital* is devoted to studying the system of production relations of modern capitalism. It is, therefore, a text of a primarily methodological and theoretical character. The authors did not set themselves the task of analysing and summarising the immense masses of empirical information that can be and is gathered about the functioning of the modern world economy. This is not because such a task is beyond our powers. It is because a great deal of this work of analysing and summarising the immense masses of empirical information has already been performed by our predecessors. We have sought to make the greatest possible use of these results of earlier studies, while approaching them, naturally, from a critical post-Soviet Marxist standpoint.

Achieving this has been easier than it might have been because we have previously made an extensive comparative analysis of economic systems, and have written at length on the problems of 'globalisation'. Moreover, as professors in the graduate school of the Faculty of Economics at Lomonosov Moscow State University, we have covered the ground every year, teaching our students to analyse international statistical data in our course on comparing economies. Where, however, statistical information is important to our argument, we have included it.

The theoretical sources on which our book rests will be discussed later. Here we would merely like to clarify that we have relied above all on the works of classical and modern Marxists – on the books and manuscripts of Karl Marx himself, and on the works of Friedrich Engels, Vladimir Lenin, Rosa Luxemburg, György Lukács (who subjected classical Marxism to rethinking and substantial development in the fields both of the ontology of social being, and of analysis of the forms of social consciousness), Antonio Gramsci (whose theory of hegemony is especially important for us), and Jean-Paul Sartre (on the questions of alienation and the individual). All of these thinkers are present in the book in sublated form, their ideas having been 'digested' and reworked by the authors, even though direct references to their works are relatively few.

While the central topic of our book – the production relations of late capitalism – is clear, a couple of important clarifications may be made. Firstly, we do not study the production relations of any particular country. What we understand by 'twenty-first-century capital' are the transformations that the production relations of capitalism undergo *as the process of the 'sunset'* of the bourgeois mode of production unfolds. Accordingly, the immediate topic of our research is precisely these systemic transformations and how they change commodities, money, capital, and reproduction. These transformations, as we shall see, have a systemic character and logically condition one another. While the market is transformed into a totality dominated by what we call network structures and simulacra, this development is amplified by the transformation of money into virtual, fictitious capital. This leads to the formation of a complex system of relations that subordinates not only human labour power but also individuals' personal qualities to capital.

Secondly, although the immediate topic of our study is late capitalism, the authors also stress the fundamental importance of the 'sunset' of the realm of (economic) necessity that forms its context. Here it is necessary to concretise what we understand by 'late capitalism'. The concept of 'late capitalism' entered into academic circulation mainly from the second half of the twentieth century onwards, although it appeared earlier. 'Late capitalism' is the stage of development of the capitalist mode of production at which the latter's further progress is possible only through the controversial inclusion of post-capitalist elements (and, in particular, post-market elements, such as planning) relationships. The authors' position is closest to those of Mandel (1987) and Jameson (1991). So although we use the term 'twenty-first-century capitalism' most often, it is practically synonymous with late capitalism as defined above. This is important for understanding the logic of our book. The characteristics and contradictions of late capitalism are examined in detail in Chapter 5. As is readily apparent to those who have perused the table of contents, our work broadly follows the course of the argument of *Capital*, going from a discussion of stages of development through markets, money, and capital to reproduction. This is no accident;

as stated earlier, we set ourselves the task of investigating the transformations that the production relations studied by Marx a century and a half ago have undergone in today's world.

Our book has evolved over many years and, inevitably, in a somewhat unsystematic fashion. The text was conceived as an integral, systematic study with a tight structure based on the methodology that we reveal in the first chapter of the book. However, it actually grew more like a tree than a building and, moreover, like a tree tended by a gardener who was not particularly neat, and who was distracted by a variety of experiments. The result is that some branches of this 'tree' have grown to an unusual size, in the process taking on an an untidy and occasionally even unkempt appearance. Some of the branches, or sections, began to appear only when the book was on the point of being completed, and finished up as offshoots that may not be particularly sturdy, but which seem to us to have an indubitable vitality. Others, by contrast, ceased to engage the close attention of the authors, grew sickly, and remained as small, partly withered limbs extending from the main trunk of the work. In a number of cases, texts that were not related directly to its problematic were 'grafted' onto the book; these were ones that supplemented the strict course of the research or that showed how the methodology and theory set forward in the book 'functioned' in resolving important problems of the modern age.

As a result, this book has turned out to be something between logically structured research and a collection of preludes, postscripts, and digressions. Meanwhile, readers who are interested primarily in the present-day implications of theoretical constructs may turn their attention largely to the postscripts, where various results of our theoretical analysis that are important for understanding current problems come to light.

Finally, while we have aimed to maximise clarity and logic, experienced readers will notice that we have, like Marx, 'flirted' to a degree with Hegelian triads.

## The plan of the book

This book integrates key sections of the fifth Russian edition of the two-volume work *Global'nyy capital* (Global capital) and has two main parts – the methodological and the theoretical. Part I, 'Methodology matters', includes four chapters. In Chapter 1, 'The methodology of *Capital*: Karl Marx, Evald Ilyenkov, and the dialectics of the twenty-first century', we stress that methodology is important (just as 'institutions matter' in contemporary 'new institutionalism'). Unlike many contemporary scholars, including Marxists, we make our case not only on empirical but also on methodological arguments.

In the present work, these require on the one hand a critical analysis of works by Hegel, Marx, and other dialecticians, and on the other, of works by such theoreticians of postmodernism as Derrida (Derrida 1994) and Foucault (Foucault 1980, 2000, 2005).

We separate the elements in the methodology of Karl Marx that remain valid and require re-actualisation from those elements that are obsolete and require critical updating. The systematisation of these provisions, together with a discussion of the main directions of research in post-Soviet Marxism, provides a starting point for the post-Soviet school of critical Marxism (in post-Soviet left circles this legacy is referred to more and more often as 'Ilenkovist').

The proposed methodology re-actualises key provisions of the method of ascent from the abstract to the concrete and of the historical-genetic approach. It distinguishes the book fundamentally from all other studies of the market and of capital that have appeared in recent decades.

Chapter 2, 'From orthodoxy to the post-Soviet school of critical Marxism', provides an original 'portrait' of different trends in Soviet and post-Soviet Marxism, opening up for the English-language reader a previously unknown world of research. Special emphasis is placed on describing specific features of the post-Soviet school of critical Marxism, of which the authors are among the leaders. This school has become the object of special analysis in China, Germany, Italy, and other countries, where research articles and other publications have been devoted to it.

Unlike most modern works of social analysis that assume as self-evident a reliance on the methodology of positivism and postmodernism, our book sets out to show that these methods do not permit an understanding of the modern market and capital, and doom scholars to achieving no more than descriptions of external forms. In Chapter 3, 'Obsolete postmodernism: the dialectics of non-linear, multi-scenario social transformations', we argue their position with the help of an analysis of the causes and consequences of the dominance of positivism and postmodernism in the modern social sciences, and on this basis, make a constructive criticism of these trends.

The next section of Chapter 3 is devoted to criticism of the general expansion of economics and of its continuation, so-called 'economic imperialism'. We reveal the causes of its emergence and spread (the increasing subordination of not only economic but also all other spheres of human life to the market), as well as the negative consequences of this expansion for the development of economic theory and economic practice.

Continuing in this vein, and building on our innovations in the field of the dialectics of transformation, progress, and regression, in Chapter 4, 'What drives the development of technology and the economy: production relations vs. productive forces, social creativity vs. activism', we combine the original provisions that characterise the socio-economic transformations with issues of the socio-spatial (and not just the socio-temporal – the theory of formations) measurement of social being. This allows us, in particular, to hypothesise a possible succession of stages (genesis, developed state, 'sunset') and models (mutations) of a single pre-bourgeois mode of production (a curious detail: this is a hypothesis of Aleksander Buzgalin, not fully shared by Andrey Kolganov), explaining the diversity of historical forms of the latter. These conclusions emerged from a critical dialogue with 'world-system' analysis. These classic and new provisions of the social philosophy of Marxism allow us to make a constructive criticism of the 'civilisational approach' (for more details see (Buzgalin 2014) and to show that today's key issues, and in particular the specifics of Russian society, may be adequately explained without the use of this methodology.

In this chapter, we set out the socio-philosophical arguments underlying our proof of the main propositions put forward in the second part. The starting point for our argumentation consists of showing the difference between the Marxist periodisation of history and the well-known 'five-term formula' (this is a concept that is typical of Soviet textbooks on Marxism, according to which Marx distinguished five successive modes of production in history: primitive communism, slavery, feudalism, capitalism, socialism (or communism)), and the importance of understanding the nature of the world of (social) alienation (in Marx's terminology, pre-history, 'the realm of (economic) necessity') as a whole.

Part II, 'The market, money, and capital in the twenty-first century', includes five chapters. In Chapter 5, '"Late capitalism": stages of development' we show, on the basis of critical analysis of a broad range of sources and statistical comparisons, the development of the capitalist economy that brought it to the late capitalist stage, indicating the degree to which the market and capital have been replaced by post-market and post-capitalist relations. This permits an identification of the historical place and character of late capitalism as the space-time of the 'sunset' of the system of capitalist production relations. This allows us to define the nature of 'late capitalism' as a space-time negation of capitalist production relations within the framework of this system, and to provide a theoretically and historically grounded periodisation of this era. It runs as follows:

(1) The late nineteenth and early twentieth centuries witnessed the 'undermining' of the basics of capitalism (the appearance of national market regulation and its manipulation by major corporations), which has been identified as monopoly capitalism (imperialism).
(2) The decades of the mid-twentieth century (characterised by social reformism and its alter ego, fascism), the hallmark of which was the development of a system of social limitations on the market, can be

classified in theoretical terms as the period of the undermining of the power of money.

(3) The era of neoliberal revenge, globalisation, and financialisation, understood as 'the negation of the negation', followed. During it, the usury and merchant capital that prevailed in the period of the initial accumulation of capital re-emerged, making this a period of 'accumulation through deprivation' (or 'accumulation through dispossession' in David Harvey's phrase (2004)).

(4) Finally, we have before us today the increasing development of forms of negative withdrawal of classic capitalist exploitation in the form of the mass use of 'human' and 'social' capital and assignments of intellectual rent arising from the exploitation by capital of all the cultural wealth of humanity.

The determining resources of progress become *cultural phenomena that in their essence are unlimited* (in particular, knowledge), and the space of creative activity (to denote this space we use the term 'creatosphere', which is explored in more detail in Chapter 9). Nature, meanwhile, should serve as an asset rather than as a source of raw materials. With this understanding, we explore new forms of goods, money, and exploitation, and their relation to the global problems of humankind.

In Chapter 6, 'The totalitarian market: networks and simulacra', we characterise the market of twenty-first-century capitalism by reference to English-language and Russian-language works and through our analysis of data.

In Chapter 7, 'Money in the twenty-first century: financialisation as a product of virtual fictitious financial capital', we demonstrate our conclusions through data that characterise the contradictions and the new quality of the modern financial market, and also through a critical and comparative analysis of major works on finance capital and financialisation.

Chapter 8, 'Capital of the twenty-first century', proposes a historical-genetic system, ascending from the abstract to the specific, conditioned by socio-spatial contradictions of the forms and methods of exploitation of the worker by capital that are inherent in the global economy of the twenty-first century. From slave-like forms of personal dependence, the development of this system proceeds via the 'classical' forms of capitalist exploitation of the industrial worker, to the use of methods of generating and assigning monopolistic profits (as well as imperialist profits, based on the exploitation of the periphery), giving rise to significantly new relationships involving the exploitation of creative activity. In the latter case, we propose a hypothesis revealing the new nature of this relationship. We argue that the exploitation of the creative worker involves not merely the appropriation of the surplus value that he or she creates, but also the exploitation of a certain amount of the *universal creative effort of mankind*, of universal cultural wealth.

This result, associated as a rule not with a (creative) worker but with a subject of intellectual property (the corporation), has no value, but has a certain price. This situation allows the owner of a creative corporation to obtain so-called *intellectual rent*.

On this basis, we demonstrate changes in the relationships of formal and real subordination by capital not only of the workforce, but also of *the human individual*, in particular of her or his *free time*. This study permits a constructive criticism of the categories *of human and social 'capital', which in perverse form reflect* real changes in the role of human beings and in their social relations within the modern economy. We show that the basis for these phenomena is the subordination of the personal qualities of a creative employee, and of solidarity relations, to the overall process of the reproduction of capital.

The conclusions of Part II are based on the analysis of data characterising the structure of the labour market in different countries, the dynamics of salaries of different social groups in comparison with the dynamics of corporate profits, as well as the generalisation of a number of existing studies on this subject.

Chapter 9, 'Twenty-first-century reproduction: inequality and the "useless economy"', describes the new trends in the process of reproduction of capitalist production relations, based on contemporary development of productive forces of capitalism. As in all phases of capitalism, the processes of capital accumulation and of reproduction of capitalist production relations in twenty-first-century capitalism also remain arenas where contradictory class interests clash. However, today, capitalism cannot reproduce itself without the introduction of more and more non-capitalist elements into the system of reproduction of capital. Under the pressure of the needs of new productive forces, especially in the creatosphere, and of class struggle, from the first half of the twentieth century onwards capital started to participate (albeit only partially) in the reproduction of the labour force. At the same time, it also sought to displace the most part of expenditure on the formation of a highly skilled labour force onto the state budget and onto working people themselves.

Well before the onset of the current stage, capital, seeking new sources of expansion, was starting to use the savings of working people (through pension funds, the stock market, insurance system, bank deposits and loans, etc.) as the basis and source of capital accumulation. Where the balance of forces between labour and capital was not in favour of the working class, these tendencies resulted in higher levels of social inequality and, thus, in the growth of social costs, increasing the social problems confronting working people and their families. At the same time, the attempts of capital to utilise the possibilities of the creative economy is resulting in the growth of the 'useless sector' of the economy. This tendency is most openly manifested in financialisation, in the overdevelopment of financial transactions, and in the growth of financial instability.

In the Conclusion, we return to our point of departure, the argument that methodology does indeed matter in criticising positivism and postmodernism for 'overloading' the dialectical method. We also elaborate the hypothesis of nonlinear transformations and of regression of economic systems. We then show the main results of our development of classic Marxist definitions of market, money, and capital. We show that twenty-first-century capital is characterised by the genesis of the totalitarian market of networks and simulacra. Another transformation is transformation of money: financialisation leads to the domination in modern economy of virtual fictitious financial capital. Finally, we conclude that now the 'classical' exploitation of the industrial worker is multiplied through the appropriation of intellectual rent: the new quality of the general law of capitalist accumulation and the growth of the useless sector of the economy.

At the end of the end, in a Postscript to the book entitled 'Limits of the market and capital', we have decided to provide a short intensive summary of our view on the self-negation of capitalism. Whereas in the Conclusion we stress the importance of a critique of the market-centric model of economic theory and show that the new technological revolution grows out of social contradictions and leads necessarily to post-market economic relations, in the Postscript we propose that theoretical innovations are required for an adequate investigation of the new world of creative work and of the knowledge-based society. These innovations are, in particular, new proofs of the antagonism between market and creativity.

The present English-language book is a product of co-authorship. This does not mean that all its chapters were written as 'compositions for four hands'. Most arose out of joint discussions, the results of which one or the other of us wrote up as a text that we then repeatedly discussed and corrected or which, in some cases, one of us rewrote anew. The book consists of excerpts from the fifth edition of our two-volume *Global'nyy capital* (Global capital; vol. 1: *Methodology: Beyond Positivism, Postmodernism and Economic Imperialism (Marx Re-Loaded)*; vol. 2: *Theory: The Global Hegemony of Capital and its Limits ('Capital' Re–Loaded)*), which appeared in Russian in 2019 and has had a broad resonance among readers of that language. Since the release of the third edition in 2014–15, the book has received wide publicity in Russia, and has been reviewed in seven leading scholarly journals were published. The main ideas of *Global'nyy capital* were presented at international seminars, conferences, and forums in Beijing, Berlin, Cambridge, Helsinki, New York, Stockholm, and Vienna. Courses for students of master's and PhD programmes at the University of Cambridge, Beijing University, Lomonosov Moscow State University, New York University, and the University of Massachusetts (Amherst) have been based on the book.

Various sections of the book have been translated into English, Chinese, and other languages, and have appeared as articles. In Russia, Europe, the US, China, and elsewhere, a great deal of constructive, critical discussion of the main positions advanced in our book has led to important clarifications and elaborations on various points, which appeared in the form of articles (included in the list of references below). On the other hand, the book has also been radically abridged to less than a quarter of its original length, and citations of Russian-language sources have been curtailed to make our arguments more accessible to readers of English. At the same time, we have significantly reworked the text in many sections, not only adapting it to readers of English, but also expanding the argumentation, updating factual data, and introducing various new arguments.

A number of excerpts from the present edition have appeared previously in English, including:

Buzgalin, A.V., and Kolganov, A.I., 2011. 'Re-Actualising Marxism in Russia: The Dialectic of Transformation and Social Creativity', *International Critical Thought*, vol. 1, no. 3, pp. 305–23.

Buzgalin, A.V., 2012. review of *Freedom and Justice: The Temptations for Russia of a False Choice* by Ruslan S. Grinberg, *World Review of Political Economy*, vol. 3, no. 2, pp. 218–39.

Buzgalin, A.V., and Kolganov, A.I., 2013. 'The Anatomy of Twenty-First Century Exploitation: From Traditional Extraction of Surplus Value to Exploitation of Creative Activity', *Science and Society*, vol. 77, no. 4, pp. 486–511.

Buzgalin, A.V., and Kolganov, A.I., 2013. 'Marx Re-Loaded: il dibattito russo' [Marx re-loaded: the Russian debate], *Ponte*, vol. 69, no. 5–6, pp. 8–33.

Buzgalin, A.V., and Kolganov, A.I., 2014. 'Political Economy of the Human Being: Prolegomena', *MANEKO (Journal of Corporate Management and Economics)*, vol. 1, pp. 26–33.

Buzgalin, A.I., and Kolganov, A.V., 2016. 'Critical Political Economy: The "Market-Centric" Model of Economic Theory must Remain in the Past – Notes of the Post-Soviet School of Critical Marxism', *Cambridge Journal of Economics*, vol. 40, no. 2, pp. 575–98.

Kolganov, A.I., and Buzgalin, A.V., 2010. 'Economic Crisis: Scenarios of Post-Crisis Development', *Science and Society*, vol. 74, no. 4, pp. 538–46.

The texts concerned appear in the present book in reworked form, adapted to the requirements of a single monograph.

In bringing this extensive foreword to a close, we acknowledge that this work has had a difficult birth. There are dozens of different drafts, plans, and concepts of the book stored in our archives. Even now, we are dissatisfied with the state of many sections of it. We were unable to include hundreds of prepared extracts from sources, as well as important explanations and remarks connected with the contributions made by our predecessors and colleagues. Dozens of books that we selected but have not yet read are gathering dust on our shelves. On reflection, however, we have decided that we have to stop somewhere, and to present our colleagues with a result, since 'the best is the enemy of the good'.

This is the result that you, our respected readers, have before you. We await your critical comments.

# I

## Methodology matters

# 1

# The methodology of *Capital*: Karl Marx, Evald Ilyenkov, and the dialectics of the twenty-first century

As we noted in the Foreword to the English Edition, the best proof of the correctness of Marxism has to be its ability to answer the challenges of the modern epoch.[1] What have Marxists achieved in the past half-century in the quest for *a new Capital*, and what have they not achieved? What needs to be done if such a work is to emerge?

While positivism and postmodernism, which do not even recognise the challenge of developing Marxism, have dominated the modern social sciences in general and Marxism in particular, many texts have been written since the mid-twentieth century on the problematic of Marx's *Capital*, including the question of refashioning crucial categories of Marx's key work. These include books by foreign scholars of recent decades (see Arthur 2002; Harvey 2001, 2003, 2014; Mészáros 1970, 1995; Ollman 1976, 2003; Sayers 1985; Kotz et al. 2010; Kotz 2015; and others), as well as studies conducted within the framework of the Soviet political economy of imperialism (see for example Rudakova 1983; Chibrikov 1979; Inozemtsev et al. 1975; Porokhovsky 1985), and a number of works of the post-Soviet school of critical Marxism.

Collectively, these works have identified a number of ways in which contemporary capitalism differs from that which formed the subject of Marx's *Capital*. A brief and incomplete list of these would include changes in the characteristics of commodity production associated with the well-known concept of the undermining of commodity production (and particularly with the diffusion of value; for more on the concept of the undermining of commodity production see Chapter 5); the transformation of the nature of money under the conditions of twenty-first-century capitalism, making it a product of virtual financial capital; new forms of exploitation; capitalist forms of the 'knowledge economy'; the peculiarities of the modern capitalist cycle; the new role of financial capital; and changes in the role of the state.

While these works no doubt have value in themselves and as contributions to the development of a *Capital* for our times, we are not aware of any works that feature the dialectical development of a system of categories that integrally reflect the present-day state of the system of capitalist production relations, using the method of ascent from the abstract to the concrete. For instance, there is István Mészáros's *Beyond Capital: Toward a Theory of Transition* (1995).[2] This is not the place to analyse its content. For the purposes of this chapter, it is important to mention that Mészáros gives a systematic presentation of the contradictory trends that characterise the transformations of the capitalist system of production relations at the present stage of its development.

For his part, the well-known geographer and sociologist David Harvey, in his book *The Limits to Capital* (1982),[3] explores the contradictory dynamics of capitalism as they express themselves spatially in the centre and on the periphery, and they determine the spatial movement of capital and the fate of the global labour force while shaping the competition between capitalist powers in the world economy.

Andre Gorz (2010) develops the concept of cognitive capitalism, in which capital has increasingly appropriated the power of human knowledge, deepening the exploitation of labour by capital. Cognitive capitalism subordinates to itself the creative powers of the human individual, along with her or his activity during not only work hours but also leisure time. These processes create the preconditions for the rise of communist social relations, initially in the sphere of intellectual production. This concept has become widely disseminated in scholarly literature (see for example Corsani 2007).

A similar but distinct position is put forward by Wolfgang Fritz Haug, who stresses not only the production of knowledge and information, as asserted by Gorz and his colleagues, but also the totality of the shifts in productive forces that are changing the face of modern capitalism, leading to the rise of new forms of exploitation and mechanisms for ensuring the extraction of profit. The sum of these new phenomena he terms 'high-tech capitalism' (Haug 2003, 2012; see also Haug 2008). Most recently, Thomas Piketty's sensational *Capital in the Twenty-First Century* (2014) has confirmed the correctness of Marx's main theses concerning the laws of capitalist accumulation from a non-Marxist standpoint.

In one respect, nevertheless, these works differ fundamentally from *Capital*. The dialectical method employed by Marx requires that categories be examined with regard for their mutual interconnection and as parts of a *system*. Moreover, this system is constructed on the basis of the ascent from the abstract to the concrete – that is, as the dialectical reflection of the natural aspects of the real historical development of the objectively existing system of relations of a particular mode of production.

The outstanding Soviet Marxist Evald Ilyenkov developed this understanding of the method of *Capital* in an extremely sophisticated form. Unlike many Soviet creative Marxists of the mid-twentieth century, Ilyenkov became known outside Russia thanks to the translation of some of his works into English (Ilyenkov 1982), and to the activity of scholars who critically developed and popularised his legacy both in Russia (Mareev 1984) and abroad (Oittinen and Levant 2013). Moreover, as has been shown in works by Russian scholars, this method and the works written by Soviet political economists on its basis have a good deal in common with the output of the Cambridge school of researchers who developed the method of *critical realism* (Dzarasov 2010).

Let us recall here the main features of the method of ascent from the abstract to the concrete as applied in *Capital*. English readers may acquire a good overview of the ascent from the abstract to the concrete from the books of Fredric Jameson (2011) and Christopher J. Arthur (2002) and from Lange's polemics with Arthur (Lange 2016). First, the object of investigation is not a particular fact or tendency, but the entire system of production relations that constitutes a particular mode of production, in this case a capitalist one. At the same time, this system is viewed as undergoing development, requiring us to define (at least in theoretical terms) its point of departure and limits and the fundamental instabilities that drive its movement from its point of departure to its end(s). This systemic quality therefore encompasses the initial genetically universal relationship of the system to its contradiction(s); this relationship can be compared to an acorn, from which all the diverse elements of the oak grows and which, in this sense, contains all the oak in the bud, in potential; that is, the acorn is the genetic-universal of the oak.

Given this, it is practically axiomatic that the system of production relations grows ever more complex, proceeding historically and in logical terms from its most simple state to an ever more complex one. In *Capital* this development is reflected as the process of resolving the contradictions of the commodity in money, and of money in capital. The contradictions of the latter give rise to the whole totality of the phenomena and forms of capitalism. Further, these contradictions, in their full development, create the bases for the self-negation of capitalism, and for its replacement by a new mode of production.

Second, this process of the actual unfolding of the relations of capitalism in social time and space is reflected in the corresponding system of categories that follows the movement from the abstract to the concrete, as represented in particular in *Capital*. In this process each subsequent category 'sublates' the preceding one, dialectically negating it but at the same time preserving and enriching its content. Hence, the category of the 'commodity' described in the first chapter of volume I of *Capital* develops from the simple to the money form of value, and the result of this is the appearance of the category of 'money', reflecting the real relations of the money economy.

The category of 'money' synthesises in itself the whole content of the category of the 'commodity', as well as something far greater. We remind the reader that Marx, in the third paragraph of the first chapter of volume I of *Capital*, a chapter devoted to the analysis of the form of value, begins with an analysis of the simple form of value, where two commodities are exchanged for each other. He only gradually derives the objective necessity of the appearance of money, moving from the simple or random form of value to its expanded form in a moneyless exchange of a mass of commodities for each other. Only then does he arrive at the universal form of value, a monetary form, where money, and not an 'ordinary', non-monetary commodity with its own use value, acts as an equivalent and a 'mirror' of value. So money is not simply a commodity, but a commodity that acts as a universal equivalent, fulfilling a series of specific functions beyond the power of the 'ordinary' commodity. In this sense, the category of 'money' is more concrete (i.e. rich in content) than the category of the 'commodity', acting in relation to money as the abstract (something simpler and less rich in content) in relation to the concrete.

Capital is money, but not simply money; it is money that brings in *more* money. As such, capital comes to represent a relationship far richer and more complex than money. Capital embodies both the content of money and the relationship between hired labour and capital, including the relationship of exploitation in the process of production. In relation to capital, money is now something abstract (less developed, less rich in content), while capital is concrete (a more developed, richer relationship, reflected in a more concrete category).

The most subtle and important element in this method of the constant enrichment of theoretical knowledge is that *the outcome of this ascent, the concrete*, is not its end point. The end point, rather, is the *entire system of categories*, including the simplest and most abstract as well as the richest and most concrete, that is constructed on the basis of the ascent from the abstract to the concrete. As Georg Wilhelm Friedrich Hegel observed, 'Nor is the result which is reached the actual whole itself; rather, the whole is the result together with the way the result comes to be' (Hegel 2018: 5). This is why it is only the entire system of categories of *Capital* that yields concrete, genuine knowledge of classical capitalism, and to be truthful, in less than full measure (as we know, Marx's work on *Capital* was unfinished; the second and third volumes were prepared for publication by Engels).

Third, this whole system of categories was not just derived theoretically, 'sucked by Marx out of his thumb', but was constructed as the logical representation (in a system of categories) of the laws of the process of the birth and development of capitalism. At each stage of the ascent from the abstract to the concrete the researcher turns to practice, investigating how the contradictions displayed by a particular category may be resolved. How, for example, can one resolve the contradiction of money that is implicit in its quality of being limitless (in principle, *everything* can be bought for money) at the same time as it is limited in quantity (there is always *too little* money)? As Marx wrote in volume I of *Capital*:

> In its qualitative aspect, or formally considered, money has no bounds to its efficacy, i.e., it is the universal representative of material wealth, because it is directly convertible into any other commodity. But, at the same time, every actual sum of money is limited in amount, and, therefore, as a means of purchasing, has only a limited efficacy. This antagonism between the quantitative limits of money and its qualitative boundlessness, continually acts as a spur to the hoarder in his Sisyphus-like labour of accumulating. It is with him as it is with a conqueror who sees in every new country annexed, only a new boundary. (Marx 1867/1996: 143–4)

Theoretically, this can be resolved on the basis that the quantity of money must always increase. But in practice? In practice, we must abstract from the 'zigzags' of history. For instance, while capital was accumulated through plantation slavery in British colonies in North and Central America and then in the US in the eighteenth and nineteenth centuries, or through serf labour in factories in Russia from the eighteenth to the mid-nineteenth centuries, it came to be accumulated on a constant and stable basis only by employing the labour of hired workers. The contradictions of money cannot be solved inside the frameworks of money itself. They must be resolved only through the transition to capital, which can provide a permanent increase of value by exploiting hired labour.

Actual practice thus impels us to take a new theoretical step: towards investigating the interaction of labour and capital, an investigation that must show how value can be increased without violating the principles of equivalent exchange. Thus the researcher who, in the process of logically depicting the historical development of practice, ascends from the abstract to the concrete is obliged to abstract from the numerous zigzags of actual history those economic phenomena that are not reproduced by the economic system in the mature state. At the same time, the structure of a system of production relations that has 'grown up' and become mature reproduces the legitimate, theoretically relevant natural or concrete points (though not all the actual zigzags) of history. The legitimate natural points are those points which are inherited from the genesis into the mature system. For example, commodity and money were the categories, inherited from the genesis of capitalism, which were retained in the mature state of capitalism. Moreover, the reproduction of particular relationships by the developed whole also confirms the fact that these relationships were not historically fortuitous. Opponents of Ilyenkov (including Viktor Vazyulin, Konstantin Tronev, and Vladimir Shkredov) set out to show that the methodology of *Capital* is of a purely logical character, rather than arising from the historical development of the system of production relations of capitalism. A critique of this position and a proof of Ilyenkov's correctness may be found in the works by the outstanding Soviet political economist Nikolay Khessin (1975a). Like many Soviet political economists, he pointed out that the genesis and development of capitalism resemble the development of an acorn into an oak, where the acorn is the initial, extremely abstract form of the oak, its genetic-universal (and also its general essence).

This development is a complex process, and unfavourable external circumstances may cause the tree to grow crooked or slanting, or to die altogether. In actual history, capitalist relations grew out of the initial relationship of capitalism – generalised commodity production – in a painful and drawn-out process which required the system to break through the 'undergrowth' of feudalism. In some countries (for example, Britain and the US) this occurred relatively quickly, over one or two centuries. Elsewhere, as in Russia, the process remains uncompleted even now, despite the fact that capitalism has existed for more than five hundred years.

We can now turn to our task of constructing a system of categories that reflects the system of production relations of twenty-first-century capitalism. Let us stress that, in order to fulfil this task, it is not sufficient to distinguish the various modifications of particular categories that characterise the present stage of the involution of the capitalist economy. It is necessary to develop a system of categories that reproduces the system of *Capital* at a *new level* of the development of capitalism. We are obliged to ascend from the abstract to the concrete, just as this was done in Marx's *Capital*.

This method, we repeat, presupposes that each successive category will not appear in the researcher's field of vision arbitrarily, but as a reflection of the sublation of the contradictions of the preceding production relation, as reflected by the previous category. Each turn in the spiral of the sublation and reproduction of contradictions enriches the academic categories with a new content that also ensures the movement from abstract, simple, one-sided, and relatively incomplete knowledge to a knowledge that is new, richer, and more concrete. As the famous Soviet philosopher Evald Ilyenkov wrote:

> Analysis of commodity, this elementary economic concreteness, yields universal (and in this sense abstract) definitions pertaining to any other particular form of economic relations. The whole point is, however, that commodity is the kind of particular that simultaneously is a universal condition of the existence of the other particulars recorded in other categories. That is a particular entity

whose whole specificity lies in being the universal and the abstract, that is, undeveloped, elementary, 'cellular' formation, developing through contradictions immanently inherent in it into other, more complex and well-developed formations.

The dialectics of the abstract and the concrete in the concept reflects quite precisely the objective dialectics of the development of one kind of actual (historically defined) relations between men into other kinds of relations, just as actual, mediated by things. The entire movement of thought from the abstract to the concrete is therefore at the same time absolutely strict movement of thought from fact to fact, transition from considering one fact to considering another fact, rather than movement 'from concept to concept'. (Ilyenkov 1982: 39–40)[4]

It was of this method that Marx stated 'The latter is obviously the correct scientific method' (Marx 1857–58/1986: 38). Only in this way is it possible to trace and represent in theoretical form the actual evolution of capitalism's production relations under the influence of the development of productive forces and the unfolding of the contradictions of capitalist production relations.

Constructing *just such a system,* on the basis of the achievements of our aforementioned predecessors and original research, is our task here: how fully we achieve it is for our reader to judge. For the present, let us be clear that the work of the Ilyenkov school is indispensable for our task, but also insufficient. The complexity of the topic requires a renewal and development of methodology. The problem is that the methodology of *Capital* was aimed at fulfilling the task of investigating the emergence of the system of capitalist production relations, and at reflecting the structure of this system in its established, mature state. Now, however, we face the task of studying the process of dialectical self-negation of capitalism, of its 'sunset' and transformation into a new quality. For the present, however, this is occurring within the same old, but still living and changing, capitalist system. Twenty-first-century (involuting) capitalism is living and changing, but not developing in the genuine sense of term. Capitalism is changing by incorporating into itself those elements which are non-capitalist in nature. Therefore twenty-first-century capitalism is changing in order to survive in what is to a certain extent a process of self-negation. This is not development (evolution), but involution.

We believe that the most important and complex element of our task is establishing not simply that capitalism is now in its 'sunset' phase, but that it is undergoing a transformation into a qualitatively new state. This fundamentally important conclusion was drawn by Lenin, though it is now forgotten almost completely, even by Marxists. Lenin was clear that

'Imperialism is a specific historical stage of capitalism. Its specific character is threefold: imperialism is (1) monopoly capitalism; (2) parasitic, or decaying capitalism; and (3) moribund capitalism' (Lenin 1916/1964a: 105). Moreover,

> Imperialism emerged as the development and direct continuation of the fundamental characteristics of capitalism in general. But capitalism only became capitalist imperialism at a definite and very high stage of its development, when certain of its fundamental characteristics began to change into their opposites, when the features of the epoch of transition from capitalism to a higher social and economic system had taken shape and revealed themselves in all spheres. (Lenin 1916/1964b: 265)

Lenin stressed further, 'From all that has been said in this book on the economic essence of imperialism, it follows that we must define it as capitalism in transition, or, more precisely, as moribund capitalism' (Lenin 1916/1964b: 302).

One of the consequences that follow is that the classical Marxist dialectic must be able to deal not merely with progress but also with regression, and not only with *evolution*, but also with *involution*. These elaborations take into account not just reforms and revolutions, but also *counter*-reforms and *counter*revolutions as attributes of transformational processes; they deal with the periods of the genesis and 'sunset' of socio-economic systems. We shall argue further that these conditions and phenomena are dominant in historical time.

A second consequence is that transformational conditions of any economic system have come to display a mosaic-like character in terms of social time and space. Within the bounds of one and the same country, fragments of systems in transformation may both co-exist and 'intermingle', both 'cleave apart' and 'cling together'. A classic example is provided by the multi-systemic nature of the economy and society of the USSR during the period of the New Economic Policy.

A third consequence lies in the fact that under the conditions of qualitative transformation the social dynamic is fundamentally *nonlinear*, and that this non-linearity is not accidental, but is conditioned by the specific nature of the contradictions that give rise to the non-linearity of transformations.

These contradictions not only lend the process of transformation a multi-scenario character, but also mean that the realisation of one or another 'scenario' has a definite dependence on the 'subjective factor'. To put it more simply, during periods of the 'sunset' of an old system and the birth of a new one, how this process plays out, whether more rapidly or more slowly, and with greater or lesser deviations from the 'classic line' of history, will depend to a certain degree on political and cultural factors, including the role of great social creator-revolutionaries. The reason for this is relatively simple. During these periods, the basic forces of socio-economic determination are weakened; the old system is already dying, while the new has not yet been born ...

This, so to speak, is our 'advance notice' of the questions to be addressed. In the next chapter, we will add some explanations concerning the theoretical and methodological circumstances in Russia in which our ideas developed.

## Notes

1 The main sources on which this chapter rests, and in relation to which we propose qualitatively new ways of resolving the questions under examination, are works by Arthur (2002), Ilyenkov (1982), Mareev (1984), Ollman (2003), and Sayers (1985).
2 See also Mészáros 1998, 2000.
3 In this work Harvey in many ways anticipated the conflicts that have been inherent in capitalism since the fall of the world socialist system and the new turn shown by globalisation. The book was deservedly republished in 1999 and 2006. See also Harvey 2014.
4 For a more detailed treatment see Ilyenkov 1960.

# 2

# From orthodoxy to the post-Soviet school of critical Marxism

In this chapter we situate the post-Soviet school of critical Marxism, from which our work arises, in the contemporary Russian intellectual milieu. Despite the collapse of the USSR, and the incursion of Western social sciences into Russia, the topic of Marxism remains very widely discussed in Russia.[1] Indeed, Marxist works have been appearing with increasing frequency in the twenty-first century. Moreover, they appear regularly even in mainstream academic journals such as *Voprosy filosofii* (Problems in philosophy), *Voprosy ekonomiki* (Problems in economy), and *Svobodnaya mysl'* (Free thought). A post-Soviet school of critical Marxism has regularly been represented by articles published in the journal *Voprosy politicheskoj ekonomii* (Problems in political economy) and in almost every issue of the journal *Al'ternativy* (Alternatives) over the past twenty-five years. As a result, social scientists have defined themselves quite precisely in relation to Marxism. Several groups can be distinguished in terms of their relationship to Marxism.

## Russia since 2000: the spectre of Marx

The first such group coalesced around the end of the nineteenth century. It consists of right-wing liberal critics of Marxism who regard it, predictably enough, not as a science but as an ideology, and an exceptionally harmful one aimed, *inter alia*, at smothering democracy and freedom, subjecting the individual to totalitarian suppression, and overthrowing the efficient market system in favour of a utopian and reactionary model of universal collectivism. In its pure form, this current is now rarely found in the scholarly milieu.

A second group consists of a 'cultured' version of the first. It recognises the right of Marxism to exist, at least as an area in intellectual history and even as useful in the study of some social processes. This current consists mainly of economists who reject the fundamental economic ideas of Marx (such as the labour theory of value or surplus value), along with virtually all the politico-ideological conclusions derived from them, but are open to using some Marxist theses from the field of social philosophy. It associates Marxist theory rigidly with the USSR as its practical application. Needless to say, this current displays an openly negative attitude to the Soviet system and takes a positive view of the capitalist West.

Somewhat greater sympathy for Marxism characterises a very diffuse current that might be termed 'reformist' or 'social democratic', so long as these labels are taken to denote not political ideology but scholarship involving a fundamental revision of the basic positions of Marxism. Writings in this vein include those of Vladilen Afanasyev, Alexander Veber, Alexander Galkin, Yuri Krasin, Vadim Medvedev, Roy Medvedev, Boris Orlov, Yuri Pletnikov, Valentin Tolstykh, and Georgy Tsagolov. Theodore Oyzerman's Marksizm i utopizm (Marxism and utopianism) (2003) is perhaps the most prominent work here. In it, the former ideologue of Marxism-Leninism repeats right-wing European social democracy's criticisms of Marx. Russian philosophical circles received this work positively for the most part. Because the left-radical criticism of it remained as old-fashioned as the theses of Oyzerman himself (i.e. in the style of social democracy of the mid-twentieth century), it did little to advance Marxist discussions.

Most representatives of this current are like their Western counterparts. They confine the validity of certain Marxist positions to the nineteenth century, and support Marxist ideas of progress towards greater social justice and the humanising of existing society. However, they either deny Marx's fundamental conclusions concerning the 'end of prehistory' and humanity's advance to the 'realm of freedom', are silent on them, or interpret them very differently as, for instance, referring to post-industrial society. The political scientists and social philosophers who mainly make up this current seek a "positive convergence" between Marxism and liberalism in the field of theory, and between capitalism and socialism in that of practice. A characteristic feature of this current in the twenty-first century, distinguishing it from the 'revisionism"'of a hundred years earlier, is its emphasis on the idea of post-industrial society.

Articles by Leonid Grebnev and Oleg Ananyin and a book by Alexander Sorokin, *Teoria obshchestvennogo bogatstva* [The theory of social wealth, 2009), are among the main works in this current. The articles propose that Marxist theory has not vanished from post-Soviet economic science, while the book argues that it is not so much Marx's economic and political theses concerning the fate of classical capitalism that are relevant, so much as his vision of a future world based on generalised creative labour, a world now described as the knowledge society or post-industrial society. Sorokin's book is one of the most comprehensive attempts to construct this argument on the basis of the original positions of Marx's labour theory of value.

The next group is an extremely variegated group of left intellectuals, who are Marxists to a certain degree and clearly pro-socialist. They also share a materialist understanding of history and seek a path to a future world that is qualitatively different from the present social system. The most salient among its philosophers are a number of relatively young intellectuals of the group 'What Is To Be Done?', including A. Penzin. Influenced by postmodernism, they concentrate on commenting on and developing the works of their European gurus. There are also isolated older critical Marxist philosophers of the Soviet epoch – Vadim Mezhuev is the best known – whose focus has been on differentiating Marx as a critic of political economy from those orthodox Soviet interpreters of Marx who emphasised the 'three sources and three component elements of Marxism' (philosophy, political economy, and scientific socialism). Mezhuev has also been concerned with examining Marx's thesis on the society of the future as being primarily non-economic and located in the realm of culture. Another such philosopher, the late Karl Kantor, operated in the familiar tradition of a religious-humanist interpretation of Marx.

One numerous group of left-wing historians includes writers who are closer to anarchism than to Marxism. Vadim Damye has written a number of works on the history of anarchism; Aleksandr Shubin's works critically but constructively analyse the experiencing of the USSR and examine the potential for a future society based on relations of self-organisation, horizontal network interactions, and grassroots democracy; while Yaroslav Leontyev is a harsh critic of Stalinism.

Political scientists figure prominently among these independent left intellectuals. Of these, Boris Kagarlitsky is closest to Marxism. Most of his works are historical accounts or political interventions. When he specifically examines Marxism, his views correlate theoretically with those of the mid-twentieth-century political current of Eurocommunism. There are also other writers working in the genre of left political journalism and political analysis, but their works as a rule do not touch strongly on questions of theory or method.

Among economists, there is, firstly, the relatively broad circle of economists who do not emphasise the Marxist paradigm, but are attracted to left-wing ideas (Georgy Gloveli, Sergey Gubanov, Mikhail Pavlov, Yuri Pavlenko, Eduard Sobolev, and others). Among them, a number of economic theorists of the Soviet school of critical Marxism show a bent for seeking to integrate Marxism with neoclassicism (Oleg Ananyin, Leonid Grebnev, Evgenija Krasnikova, Alexander Sorokin, Kaisyn Khubiev, and others); and with institutionalism (Alexander Moskovsky). Unlike these authors, the post-Soviet school of critical Marxism believes that an organic combination of Marxism and neoclassicism is impossible, although the critical use of the achievements of various currents of modern economic theory, including the neoclassical, serves as an important impetus for enriching the theory of our school. The theoretical conclusions of some economists who call themselves Marxists are strongly influenced by the ideology of Slavophilism – a theoretical direction that emphasises the determining influence of civilisational features on economic development, in particular, civilisational specificities of Russia on its economy (Victor Volkonsky, Victor Kulkov, and others). These themes, however, lie at a certain distance from the main topics examined in the present text, and we shall not characterise the works of these authors in more detail here.

Another group of economists, while remaining primarily within the framework of classical Marxism, attempts to revise it in line with the realities of the new epoch. These works do not pretend to any serious criticism of the works of Marx. They review familiar Marxist positions from various angles and in various contexts, and suggest additions, often connected with the specific nature of Soviet and post-Soviet society. This group is inclined to left social democracy and seeks ways to integrate the positive achievements of the Soviet system with their vision of social democracy, and some, such as Vladimir Shevchenko, Boris Kurashvili, and Vladislav Kelle, also stress the positive aspects of the Chinese model, often tending to idealise it. V.S. Semenov is, arguably, the most radical writer in this group.

Two groups of philosophers, extremely heterogeneous but on the whole very close to Marxism, deserve special mention. The first consists of students of the great Soviet philosopher Evald Ilyenkov including Vladimir Lazutkin, Gennady Lobastov, Sergey Mareev, Elena Mareeva, and Andrey Sorokin, while Lev Naumenko is a distinctive figure whose views are closer to those of the post-Soviet school of critical Marxism. Finally, it should be noted that orthodox Marxism persists in Russia; it has a number of representatives who come near to Stalin and Zhdanov in their grotesqueness, but others (chiefly Richard Kosolapov and David Dzhokhadze) who approach the status of classics. In most cases orthodox Marxism in Russia reproduces the main positions of the standard Soviet works of the mid-twentieth century, with minimal innovations and more or less pronounced Stalinist tendencies.

These currents form the context from which the post-Soviet school of critical Marxism, to which the authors of this text belong, has emerged and against which its distinctiveness must be assessed. We declare ourselves to be Marxists, with a strongly critical attitude to social-democratic reformism, but at the same time we emphasise not just the re-actualising of classical Marxism, but also its positive negation, criticism, and dialectical development. Our school has coalesced around three projects: the journal Al'ternativy (Alternatives), which has appeared regularly since 1991; professorial seminars, which have now been held for more than ten years in consultation with the Committee on Education of the State Duma; and the Centre for Modern Marxist Studies at the Faculty of Philosophy of Lomonosov Moscow State University, founded in 2017. It is time to describe this school more fully.

## The post-Soviet school of critical Marxism: an introduction

Our current is most closely associated with a series of sixty-seven books published since the early 2000s and written mostly by members of the post-Soviet school of critical Marxism, 'The library of the journal *Al'ternativy*'. The series includes works not only by economists, sociologists, and historians, but also by more than twenty well-known Russian philosophers representing the Institute of Philosophy of the Russian Academy of Sciences, Moscow State University, and many other centres of learning. Our current is far from homogeneous, and not all the authors of the above-mentioned books (above all, the text *Socializm-21* (Socialism-21) (Buzgalin, Mironov, and Arslanov 2009) can be considered to belong to the post-Soviet school of critical Marxism. Some of us (above all, Professors Victor Arslanov, Grigory Vodolazov, Vadim Mezhuev, and others) stress the uniqueness of their positions, prefer not to attach labels to themselves, or do not regard themselves as part of any particular tendency, current, or school. But they too are close to our school, since to a greater or lesser degree their works keep to the theoretical boundaries which in principle are characteristic of us all. (It is difficult to state *unequivocally* whether certain person is a part of our school or not. Many of them prefer not to identify themselves with a definite current.)

We share a formative heritage whose most important figure is Karl Marx, on whose works we were all raised. Unlike Soviet (and not only Soviet) dogmatic 'Marxism', post-Soviet critical Marxists seek to examine our Marxist heritage sceptically and fearlessly, to criticise, develop, enrich, and transform it in line with changing reality. While we vary far more in our attitude to the main followers of Marx – leaning variously towards Karl Kautsky, Vladimir Ulyanov, Nikolay Bukharin, or Lev Trotsky – none of us accepts on faith, as dogma, the works of any of the 'post-Marx' Marxist pleiade.

There is much twentieth-century scholarship that has enormous significance for us, including the work of György Lukács, Mikhail Lifshitz, Evald Ilyenkov, Jean-Paul Sartre, Erich Fromm, and other creative, humanist Marxist and Marxisant writers. Although almost all of us keep a distance from analytical Marxism and are somewhat closer to the Praxis school, we are inclined to dialogue critically and selectively with left-wing postmodernism. While we take a similar attitude to the theoreticians of Western social democracy, we are far closer to the theoreticians of new social movements, ecosocialism, left-wing theories of post-industrialism, and contemporary Trotskyist and Eurocommunist tendencies. In addition, our approach has something in common with the formulations of the American extra-party Marxism of the period from the 1950s to the 1970s, and with some ideas of the Frankfurt school. Our general approach to all these thinkers and tendencies is to take everything that is the result of the research into new facts and new problems (and new contradictions); and to reject everything that deviates from the dialectical and materialistic nature of Marx's method.

The boundaries traced above appear, inevitably perhaps, amorphous. After all, our school is defined more by an ongoing endeavour than by settled beliefs. Our members search in different ways, proceeding from the traditions and heritages of different teachings and tendencies, and we have not yet acquired any definitive, generally accepted formulas. However, there are some parameters that have acquired greater definition. Firstly, most of us proceed from the position that capitalism is a historically limited system. While it has brought humanity many gains, it has completed its progressive historical mission, and today any gains it offers are increasingly offset by losses, putting capitalism on an increasingly dangerous and ultimately doomed trajectory. Having said that, we do not idealise 'actually existing socialism' (e.g. as it existed in the USSR) as many orthodox currents do. We differ in our concrete assessments of 'actually existing socialism', while remaining united in our view that it represented the first large-scale attempt to advance towards a non-capitalist society. It has many social and cultural achievements to its credit, not only in Russia. However, the experience was profoundly tragic. Its basic forms and practices fell far short of even the initial stage of the 'realm of freedom', a fundamental principle and aspiration of a socialist theory which conceives socialism as a system that is more socially efficient, democratic, and humane than capitalism.

Secondly, we consider it possible and natural for humanity, and in particular Russia, to develop along a socialist trajectory that emancipates society from the power of alienated social forces. We look forward to freeing human beings from both economic and non-economic coercion, to their liberation from the power of both capital and of political authority that is not under their control. Within our school, the socialist trajectory of development is perceived as the transcending capitalism and the 'realm of necessity' in general. For the authors of the present text, this process is defined more exactly as the genesis of communist society, while other writers in our school understand it in less rigid fashion as the progress of a real humanism, of socialism as the world of culture.

We would like to stress two more points here. Firstly, we speak not of the destruction of earlier systems but of their transcendence, of their negation which yet hands on their achievements, including their cultural – that is to say, technological and educational as well as artistic – achievements and their principles of 'negative freedom', of freedom 'from' personal dependency, political dictates, and so forth. Secondly we speak of transcending not only capitalism, but all preceding relationships founded in social alienation. These include the market and commodity fetishism, the state, and other forms of political alienation which retain the forms of personal dependency, along with freshly developing imperial tendencies, religious fundamentalism, and many other phenomena which have, as it were, taken wing during the past century.

Finally, it is clear to us that a social order which definitively transcends capitalism will be based on and will develop first and foremost within the sphere of collective creative activity. One of our colleagues, Vadim Mezhuev, who has his origins among the Marxists of the 1960s, states forthrightly that socialism is the sphere of culture. Developing the argument of Karl Liebknecht that 'communism equals culture', Lyudmila Bulavka speaks in this connection of a new communist society (Bulavka 2011; Bulavka-Buzgalina 2017). For Mikhail Voeikov, Boris Slavin, Oleg Smolin, and others, the question is one of socialism as a new social system. For the authors of this book, Marx's concept of the 'realm of freedom' is closer. In sum, we are animated by a vision of progress towards a world in which capitalism has been done away with and humanity's horizons have widened far beyond the narrow horizons of the industrial system: a 'post-industrial socialism', if you will. At the same time, we do not identify such a socialism with contemporary post-industrial tendencies in the countries of the 'golden billion'. The overriding task of the socialism will, we imagine, be to alter the trajectory of development of new technologies, relationships, and institutions qualitatively.

For us, socialism is more than the development of individual qualities and the elimination of social alienation (above all, but not exclusively, exploitation). It also involves establishing such preconditions for these goals as a grassroots, participatory democracy giving power to civil society; and the unconditional observance of social and civil rights as the beginning of progress towards a new all-round self-government of open voluntary associations whose details are not, and cannot be, clear as yet. We understand that the 'building' of socialism 'from above' through coercion is a dead end. Many decades ago Vladimir Ulyanov stressed that socialism is not only the result of creative activity, but also the process, carried out by people themselves.

Furthermore, the experience of the twentieth century showed us that movement along a socialist trajectory is a lengthy process and one which is far from straightforward. It involves victories and defeats, successes and retreats. It is also a global process, all of whose links are closely interconnected. The task for the immediate future is to summon forth and nurture the first manifestations of this new world within the earlier system. Wherever elements exist that are transitional to socialism within various enclaves of world society (not only countries and regions, but also networks and the world of culture), these must be developed. This must occur wherever the tasks of socialist development are being posed, and where a struggle is being waged for a different world, one whose orientation is social, humanist, environmental, and prospectively socialist.

While sharing all these premises, our school also encompasses substantial differences on numerous questions. To start with methodology, some of us, especially the authors of this text, place a clear stress on dialectics. Others are mindful of a certain positive contribution by postmodernism. Still others do not make an issue of their methodological predilections. We also differ in the degree of radicalism of our critique of the existing capitalist system. Some scholars who are close to us do not put any stress on the question of doing away with capitalism, preferring to speak of the future in terms of a 'real humanism' (Vodolazov 2015). To others, socialism represents the development of the 'cultural space' to the point where it becomes the dominant sphere of humanity's social existence, while present-day economic and political systems are reformed while their basic elements – the market and parliamentary democracy – are retained (Mezhuev 2009). But for the central members of the school (Boris Slavin, Lyudmila Bulavka, David Epshtein, Mikhail Voeikov) and particularly for the authors, socialism is a qualitatively new world, the road to which lies through social revolution. There are many such differences, but the important thing for us is nevertheless the common ground, whose boundaries we have set out above, that unites us.

In summing up, we would like to offer the following reflection. Russia has witnessed the rise of an intellectual current which stresses the need to understand the modern period (broadly, since the twentieth century began) as an epoch of global qualitative change in the very bases of humanity's collective life. These changes are creating the preconditions not only for a post-capitalist society, but also for a post-industrial, post-economic society (the 'realm of freedom'). In this sense, we can describe our current as 'Marxism of the post-industrial epoch'. This approach allows us to view modern social and economic life in integrated systemic and dialectic fashion, within the context of its historical development. The crucial basis for such work is a new dialectical method, reconfigured in light of the transformations that have taken place in the past century.

This account of our school is simplified out of necessity. Therefore, in the next two chapters, we will show how this methodological and theoretical approach 'works' in the social sciences, using two questions as examples. The first of these concerns the re-actualising of dialectics as crucial to understanding the zigzags of the modern epoch and of 'postmodernity', while the second re-examines the social creativity of free association as the principal key to understanding the motive forces of social and human emancipation.

## Note

1  The analysis in this chapter is based on a general summary of more than 100 major works published by Russian-speaking Marxists over the past twenty-five years.

# 3

# Obsolete postmodernism: the dialectics of non-linear, multi-scenario social transformations

It is impossible to study social transformations without the dialectical method: only this can show a system in its development.[1] Although postmodernism is no longer fashionable, dialectics has not returned to popularity. On the contrary, the idea persists that dialectics is dangerous because it can reveal real contradictions in social development and realistic ways of resolving them.

Not only is the dialectical method necessary, but it needs to be developed further. Nineteenth- and twentieth-century advances in dialectics need to be supplemented by study of the dialectics of the genesis and the decline of social systems. It is necessary to show the regularities of the processes involved in the simultaneous emergence of new social qualities and the decomposition of the old.

The old social system is forced, at a certain level of its contradictory development, to include qualitatively new elements for self-preservation even though they may be alien to the old system and may undermine it from within. The preconditions for a qualitative leap from the old social system to the new are always created in such ways.

The thesis that postmodernist methodology is obsolete, though passé in Westen Europe and the US, has only just begun to penetrate the Russian intellectual milieu. This does not imply that our critical social thought is merely behind the times. Not being part of world's theoretical trends has its advantages. It allows us to present a substantial hypothesis: among constructively critical intellectuals, postmodernism will be replaced not by a deconstruction that is even more resolute than that practised during the last century by Derrida (1981, 1994) and Foucault (1980, 2000, 2005), but by a new dialectics capable of studying fundamentally non-linear social transformations that proceed in varying ways, via various detours and dead ends, across the *social* expanse of the modern world as it experiences global changes.

Such a new dialectics will face a number of problems. There is, firstly, the problem of the discrepancy between the logical study of the structure of production relations of a certain mode of production and the historical path of its formation and development. This was raised by Karl Marx and Friedrich Engels and became the subject of methodological discussions among both Soviet (Tronev 1972, 1975; Shkredov 1975; Khessin 1975b) and Western Marxists (Arthur 1997, 2002). Another problem concerns the possibility that the course of historical development may deviate from the basic logic of development of methods of production and the revolutionary transition from one mode of production to another.

The reasons for such 'zigzags' of history may vary: they may be, for instance, consequences of the influence of non-economic factors (social, political, ideological, natural, etc.) on the development of the economic relations. They may be results of the impact of global economic conditions on the development of a particular national economy. The need to take this impact into account led to the formation of the school of 'world-system' analysis.

Social transformations can also face blockages or can be premature. On the one hand, where the necessary preconditions do not obtain, qualitative leaps can be blocked by a combination of different circumstances. The result may be a a dead-end model of society which cannot escape its acute contradictions and can at best only weaken them by various methods, thus prolonging stagnation and decay (take, for example, the last years of the Roman Empire or the period of 'stagnation' in the USSR).

On the other hand, again as a result of some special conditions, the sharpness of the contradictions can reach a climax even before the conditions for a qualitative transition to a new method of production are quite in place. As a result, revolutionary changes may begin on an insufficient socio-economic basis, and more progressive modes of production cannot follow from it organically, leading to a 'backward' historical movement and a full or partial return to the old method of production (examples include the USSR and China).

What are the kinds of conditions that slow down the overdue resolution of contradictions? What kinds of conditions lead to a premature revolutionary leap? They are the same conditions that lead to deviations from the basic logic of development of the mode of production: social, political, ideological factors, as well as the influence of the world economic and political conditions. After the Spanish conquest in the sixteenth century, the further evolution of Central American societies was no longer primarily determined by the internal logic of their social and economic development hitherto. The circumstances hindering the resolution of the overdue contradictions can, for their part, serve as a catalyst for a premature revolutionary leap. Thus, in the Russian Empire at the turn of the nineteenth century, the delay in resolving the contradictions of the feudal remnants in the agricultural sector caused a lag in the development of agriculture and the consolidation of archaic, inefficient forms of management in it for more than seventy years, hindering the economic development of Russia as a whole and combining with the emerging contradictions of its capitalist development. This was what caused the bourgeois and socialist revolutions to become intertwined and mutually reinforcing. Neither could occur in isolation in Russia, and their combination led to a revolutionary explosion.

Why do non-economic circumstances lead in some cases to stagnation and decay, and even to partial involution (reverse evolution) of the mode of production (for instance, the rise of neoliberalism in developed capitalist countries after the 1970s), and in other cases, on the contrary, to premature revolutionary explosion? On the one hand, this is determined by the dialectics of the interaction of objective and determining conditions of socio-economic development, and on the other, by the projection of these objective conditions onto the formation and the behaviour of the subjects of historical action.

The subject of historical action is limited by objective conditions, but its activity is not predetermined completely by them: historical events are not inevitable. They occur as the result of many subjective wills, the direction of which depends on:

(1) the degree of the knowledge of the laws of historical process, of the objective logic of socio-economic development;
(2) the ability to organise social and creative actions in accordance with these laws;
(3) the ability to find adequate forms of resolution of the overdue socio-economic contradictions.

The impact of various social, political, and ideological conditions on the subjects of historical action determines what kind of deviations may be made from these three factors. However, the presence of these conditions and circumstances does not eliminate the responsibility of the subject of historical action for the consequences of its actions on historical development, on whether and to what extent its actions lead to progress or to regression. We believe that the criterion of historical progress exists and that it implicates the degree of human development and even the elimination of social alienation. Thus history does not always move in a consistent linear development. It often deviates from linear schemes, dodging to one side here, jumping over steps there, and even displaying retrograde motion.

These deviations from the linear course are subjective. They are rooted in a peculiar combination of the complex of contradictions determined by economic, social, political, ideological, world-economic, and other developmental conditions that affect the results of the subject's historical action and the willingness of the historical subject to respond to the historical challenge. This Summary of the above practices of historical development helps to explain why progress goes with regression, and why the attempts to move to the 'realm of freedom' often take bizarre forms.

Humanity is looking for, and perhaps groping towards (this latter imposes a great responsibility on theorists), a way out of contemporary contradictions towards the future. Along this path one can see many different 'socialisms', dictatorships of both the right and the 'left', perpetuating the backward model of 'peripheral capitalism' (Prebisch 1976, 1981) and the spurts of catching up with the development of new industrial countries, fluctuations in developed countries between Nazism and the 'welfare state'.

All problems, such as that of historical development, raise the question of how these circumstances should be reflected in the dialectical method so that it is developed beyond linear schematic conceptions of development: exacerbation, resolution, and removal of contradictions. Some of these social transformations include:

- The advent of qualitatively new technologies that change the content of work by making creative activity dominant. This development is comparable in importance not just to the industrial revolution, but to the Neolithic revolution.
- The rise and development, since the twentieth century, of large-scale non-capitalist social systems ranging from particular countries to the 'world socialist system' and global social networks which, at their height, encompassed more than a third of the earth's population.
- The growing acuity of global problems that are not just threats to all humanity, but also point to the increasing exhaustion of the model of development which Marxism described more than a century and a half ago as prehistory.

These have been either ignored and filed away or depicted in formal models that ignore qualitative leaps and sliced, diced, and 'deconstructed' into rows of incoherent texts lined up in voluntary order. Few have recognised that these problems exceed the potential of the currently dominant positivism and postmodernism and require a dialectical approach, the only approach that can reveal the full depth and power of the challenges posed by the current transformations. While it is understandable that intellectuals shrink from dialectics, it is not forgivable. Postmodernism, as a paradoxical synthesis of disillusion with the liberal paradigm of development and ultra-liberal philosophical individualism, is no match for the challenges of the present day. But what is? We cannot see any new influential philosophical currents. The philosophical landscape is still dominated by old currents – different sorts of positivism and post-positivism. We are forced to conclude that the new right-conservative wave rising in the world will be reflected in new philosophical concepts.

## On some of the reasons for 'forgetting' dialectics

If we examine writings in the field of methodology from the past two decades, a formative period for the present-day state of methodology, we find that most scholars have rejected the conscious or even unconscious use of the dialectical method, by which we understand the study of historical change as a dialectic between, on the one hand, the objective and material conditions and contradictions and, on the other hand, how the human subjects of history actually understand, assimilate, and act on them. Such historical change must be understood by using the method of the ascent from the abstract to the concrete. In the US and Western Europe the dialectical school of the 1960s had a few important adherents, such as K.B. Anderson (2007), R. Dunayevskaya (1973), I. Mészáros (1972, 1995), S. Michael-Matsas (2007), and B. Ollman (1993, 2003). There are also isolated followers of the dialectical method in China, India, and Japan. These exceptions inspire the hope that the line of succession will not be broken, and that the momentously creative development of the dialectical method by Soviet intellectuals will be passed on to future generations. This is important, as much from the point of view of preserving one of the schools of world philosophy as it is for an adequate comprehension of the qualitative changes that have been unfolding throughout the world for around a century.

To ensure this, it is important to understand why the dialectical method has been so widely abandoned. The abandonment of the method is the obverse of the coin represented by the spread of positivism and postmodernism. When practice 'renounces' the understanding of fundamental changes to the dominant system, its intellectuals must renounce the 'grand narratives' that once informed more radical forms of practice. They become superfluous. They are not required by such modest practice, and indeed it abhors them. There are several ontological reasons for this.

The first is simply that today even critical intellectuals are part of the dominant academic milieu. There they are objectively compelled to observe its rules, and these rules are generated by the dominance of corporate capital, which seeks to generalise market relations by turning everything into capital: human qualities and creative potential become, for instance, 'human capital' (Becker 1964), social ties and trust, 'social capital' (Fukuyama 1995), culture, 'cultural capital', and so on.

Accordingly, intellectuals in this system have an interest in urgent practical problems of great variety and are charged with resolving them into a single type. For them, all problems are ones of raising the efficiency and durability of the existing system by a never-ending search for profits and markets. This requires micro- and macro-economic research, but not in the vein of classical political economy with its dialectical method of stressing social contradictions and the historical limitations of any particular system. Corporate business needs research into how to manipulate buyers and defend the rights of property. This requires studies in the fields of marketing, public relations, and law, to be sure, but sociology, political studies, and other social sciences, too, are not exempt from its demands: they must produce the wider social understandings from which the marketing, political, or legal innovations must emerge.

The methodological needs of such studies are modest: they do not range beyond methods for solving the 'practical' problems noted earlier, which are identified by those with money and/or power. Philosophers in these circumstances either must issue a challenge to this 'imperialism of the pragmatic' or they must accept it and provide suitably wise-sounding justifications for this state of affairs. The overwhelming majority choose the second option.

Here, dialectical logic, with its integral and systemic reasoning, is too powerful and intricate a tool and one, moreover, not designed to perform large and complex critical tasks, but only for small and simple ones in keeping with existing rules. It would be like trying to use a space rocket capable of overcoming gravity and escaping the bounds of the earth for a trip to the local supermarket. Not only will it not work, but a rocket is dangerous to launch from anywhere except a cosmodrome and becomes monstrously destructive when used inexpertly. Dialectics is uniquely suited to investigating the genesis, development, and downfall of social systems, the problems of escaping from their bounds, and the tasks faced in surmounting them. But this means that dialectics is unsuitable for solving the problem of how to maximise the profits of a particular firm, or for deciding the public relations strategies of a party during an election campaign. Moreover, it can be destructive (in terms of the outcome of such analysis) for a firm or party: it can all too easily demonstrate that its actions are not conducive in any way to social progress. From this stems the 'superfluity' of dialectics to narrow pragmatic studies, and it is this which provides the first basis for rejecting dialectics.

As corporate society has demanded a narrow professional model of the intellectual worker, so the abandonment of dialectics has only grown. That is why the new society that is taking shape is described not only as the post-industrial or information society, but also as the 'society of professionals': 'Bell's vision was a coming society of professionals and technicians, one where "situs" rather than class conflict would reign' (Esping-Andersen 1999: 95). Incorporated into the world of corporate capital and subject to it, the individual professional and her or his activity are governed by special rules. They include subordination to the rules of the corporation in which the professional works, subordination to the rules of the professional group (also a sort of corporation), and so forth. They may be creative agents (though this is not obligatory), but they are forced to subordinate their creative being to their social status as professionals, and as such, they live and act as non-subjects. Professionals constitute 'functions', qualitatively realising certain rules of activity which they have mastered and accepted, *and not creators* who continually destroy existing stereotypes while creating a new world (to do the latter is to destroy the existing rules, and hence to be 'unprofessional'). Consequently, the 'professional non-subject' is, by the very logic of her or his being, oriented towards 'positive' rather than critical-dialectic approaches. Here we have the second ontological basis for the rejection of dialectics.

The third and arguably most important ontological reason for the rejection of dialectics is linked to the rise of new forms of spiritual alienation that are characteristic of the epoch of corporate capital. Its mechanisms include the total subordination of the human individual to mass consumption and mass culture, and political and ideological manipulation. Mass conformism is the result. A social system of this type gives rise to a particular spiritual atmosphere marked by mutant forms of social consciousness, an atmosphere within which demands are raised for appropriate theoretical and methodological conclusions which characterise these 'perverse forms', this conformism and servitude, as norms in relation to manipulative structures. A variant here is the proclamation of the total deconstruction of everything as a revolt against this servitude. This bespeaks an inability or unwillingness to analyse the causes of this servitude of the spirit and personality and to propose ways of ending it. In this form, it becomes left postmodernism.[2] In this way, the preconditions are established for a social orientation towards rejecting 'grand narratives', towards playing games with 'simulacra', and towards deconstruction.[3] From this situation proceeds the rejection of everything that is performed 'seriously', by real agents, substantially and existentially, in the world of real, socially non-neutral, responsible people and social groups who are acting in what Marx and Engels termed the 'realm of necessity'.

Against the backdrop of this turn away from dialectics and towards a methodology and intellectual orientation towards the resolution of only limited and discrete problems and the emergence of new challenges, we propose a hypothesis: to the extent that we wish to investigate the laws that govern the birth, development, and decline of 'grand' systems, we are faced inevitably with the need to use the systematic dialectical method. To elaborate: we propose that the very corporate capitalism that has demanded and received this intellectual transformation has generated social problems of a scale and depth that are insurmountable in terms of the intellectual culture of narrow postmodernism and professionalism it has fostered. If humanity is to overcome these problems, and not succumb to them, it will be necessary to reinstate the very dialectical methodology that the corporate world so fears.

In so far as the problems noted above constitute the social reality of the twenty-first century, the classical dialectical method remains relevant. In this sense even 'classical' materialist dialectics, which is profoundly alien to dogmatic versions of Marxism (which proclaim the dialectic, but fears to implement it), can now serve as a major step forward in comparison to the methodological obscurantism which now prevails in philosophy and the social sciences, and which is barely concealed by postmodernist rhetoric.[4]

We now turn to the important and difficult task of developing the dialectical method. In the form that Hegel gave it and in which Marx applied it in *Capital*, as well as in the form it took with its development in the work of the Marxists of the twentieth century, the dialectical method was based on a linear understanding of development. However, the practice of social development shows us, as noted above, multiple examples of nonlinear movement in the historical process. Accordingly, we face a scientific problem: how to reflect this observed nonlinearity in the categories of the dialectical method. Probably (although we are not experts in the natural sciences) this kind of problem can addresssed from the perspective of other sciences, for instance, evolutionary theory in biology. Although progress here has been relatively small, it is possible to point to a number of propositions that are important for the methodology of the new century. The examples examined here will be limited to those we have developed ourselves.

### New answers to the challenges of new problems: the dialectics of the decline and genesis of social systems

The paradox of our time is not entirely new in history. The past century played itself out under the sign of a post-capitalist future; it culminated in a crisis of attempts at creating it. The tension of capitalism's contradictions at the beginning of the century was high enough for the system to explode. But historical development during the century showed, that at the same time, that the prerequisites for the formation of the new type of coherent and stable society had been absent.

The new century is thus *re*-actualising the question of investigating the decline of particular systems and the birth of others. It presents us with questions of reforms and counter-reforms, of revolutions and counter-revolutions, rendering especially significant the issues of involution and non-linearity, of the reversibility of social development. These are relatively, if not absolutely, new challenges, and our dialectical methodology of the new century has already begun to find some answers.

In particular, we have continued the development, begun by our teachers, of the dialectics of the decline of social systems. This decline can be summed up as a natural self-negation. It involves the negation of a system's own genetic bases (qualities) as a result of the development within it of the fresh shoots of a new system. The paradox here is obviously the fact that these shoots are summoned to life by the need of the previous system to preserve and develop itself; it is impossible for this earlier system to make progress beyond a certain qualitative point except in so far as it sends forth the shoots of new qualities and essences.

This point where it is impossible for the system to progress further without introducing new elements that are alien to the system also signifies the beginning of its decline. In relation to capitalism, the first steps in this process of decline were described by Lenin in his thesis on the undermining of commodity production and the genesis of elements of planning as evidence of a transition to the 'dying out' phase of the system:

> The development of capitalism has arrived at a stage when, although commodity production still 'reigns' and continues to be regarded as the basis of economic life, it has in reality been undermined and the bulk of the profits go to the 'geniuses' of financial manipulation. At the basis of these manipulations and swindles lies socialised production; but the immense progress of mankind, which achieved this socialisation, goes to benefit ... the speculators. (Lenin 1916/1964b: 206–7)

> Free competition is the basic feature of capitalism, and of commodity production generally; monopoly is the exact opposite of free competition, but we have seen the latter being transformed into monopoly before our eyes, creating large-scale industry and forcing out small industry, replacing large-scale by still larger-scale industry, and carrying concentration of production and capital to the point where out of it has grown and is growing monopoly: cartels, syndicates and trusts, and merging with them, the capital of a dozen or so banks, which manipulate thousands of millions. At the same time the monopolies, which have grown out of free competition, do not eliminate the latter, but exist above it and alongside it, and thereby give rise to a number of very acute, intense antagonisms, frictions and conflicts. Monopoly is the transition from capitalism to a higher system. (Lenin 1916/1964b: 265–6)

These concepts were developed further in the Soviet political economy, though in a somewhat apologetic form.[5] We propose to develop this neglected thesis order to show that the negation involved cannot be confined to the undermining of this or that single original quality of the system, but must extend throughout its entire structure, transforming all its fundamental elements and giving birth within it to a complex system of transitional relationships. Here, the 'renaissance' of right-liberal strategy in the capitalist countries, and the present tendency for these countries to evolve in the direction of a proto-empire, have served to confirm the thesis according to which this undermining proceeds in a non-linear fashion.

The triumph of the neoliberal model of late capitalism by the end of the twentieth century was largely based on the processes of capitalist globalisation, that is, the expansion of the transnational capital of the 'core' of capitalist system into countries on its periphery. Such expansion inevitably generated a response in a variety of forms (isolationism, terrorism, economic protectionism, illegal migration, etc.).

The answer to these processes is the desire of core capitalist countries to strengthen their dominance in the world economy, including through the use of pro-imperial policy in a wide array of actions: direct military intervention, abuse of monopoly positions in the scientific and technological sphere, financial pressure, and ideological manipulation. The use of these methods has expanded with the crisis of the neoliberal model of development, which clearly manifested itself in the economic shocks of 2008–9 and the continuing economic stagnation.

Since the dominant elites of developed countries do not want to follow the path of the socialisation of capitalism and cling to the neoliberal order, their only methods of holding their positions are imperial ones. On the other hand, a number of weak states of the periphery and semi-periphery are trying to solve their problems by subordinating to the imperial patronage of stronger powers.

Under neoliberalism, the progress of elements of the future system, such as advances in social welfare, tendencies for society and the state to develop elements of conscious regulation, tendencies to limit the operations of the market and of capital, and so forth, was replaced by movement in the opposite direction, with the bases of the old system strengthened and the regulatory role of society and the state reduced, and attacks made on many of the social and humanitarian gains of the past century. Thus social systems, when in a descending stage of their evolution, can be said to be undergoing a strengthening of the non-linear nature of their development. Meanwhile, constant switches between progressive and regressive forms of self-negation of the bases of the system can be attributed to natural laws that are most typical of the stage of decline. For example, most of the past century has seen fluctuations between social-reformist (or social-democratic) trends and right-conservative and right-liberal trends in developed capitalist countries.

The reasons for this are well known; while generating and developing elements of a new quality, the old system inevitably undermines its own foundations, and in the process reveals the limits of its further evolution.

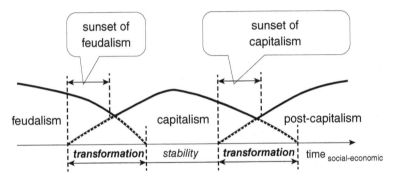

Figure 1 Transformations of socio-economic systems.

Correspondingly, the forces of self-preservation in this system begin the reverse process of trying to smother the growing manifestations of the new order. At a certain stage this retroactive process encounters the problem that ensuring the survival of the old is impossible without invoking elements of the new system. These latter grow in strength, lay bare the limits of the old, and so forth. This process of transformation of socio-economic systems is shown in a schematic form in Figure 1.

The strengthening of state regulation, social welfare, free education, health care, and so forth restricted the opportunities for capital accumulation, and capitalists then worked actively to roll back these popular advances. Struggles between supporters and opponents of the development of post-capitalist social relations within bourgeois society, which may favour now one side and now another, provide one of the simplest examples of how capitalism in the 'late' stage of its development evolves in a non-linear manner. The late twentieth century and the years since have been marked by increasing pressures for a return to market self-regulation, and for curtailing the social restrictions on capital. This situation has helped to bring about an unprecedented expansion of the most parasitic form of capitalist activity – speculative financial operations. The over-accumulation of capital and the world economic and financial crisis that began in 2008 spurred renewed demands for state intervention in the economy, this time on an unprecedented scale.

This crisis had been predicted by Marxist dialecticians some years earlier, as well as by fair-minded economists of different trends. To avoid referring to ourselves, we would point to Marxists who identified a housing bubble and the coming economic crisis from 2004 onwards, including the authors of a series of papers on the website of the International Committee of the Fourth International (Beams 2004a, 2004b, 2007; Uco 2005) and Michael Roberts, who forecast the crisis in 2006 based on the analysis of capitalist profit cycle (Roberts 2009: 74; see also Roberts 2016).

Meanwhile, when the social formation is in decline, its socio-econmic base ceases to be able to determine its evolution entirely, and as a result the role of the subjective factor increases. This makes the non-linear character of the process of decline still more pronounced.

The rise of a new system is characterised not only by *nonlinearity* in the emergence of the new quality, but also by the *multi-scenario* development of the new system as it undergoes its revolutionary genesis. In the process of social transformations, the old social and economic system is half-destroyed and becomes entirely unable to determine further development. At the same time, the emerging new social and economic system is not completed, and it too cannot determine future social development on its own. So in these circumstances, the subjects of historical actions are free to appropriate the various possibilities of this open-ended situation and to influence the path of development to a greater extent than in other historical epochs. The outcome of these subjects' struggles for the choice of path of development is not pre-determined. It is possible not only that different scenarios of development will be realised, but also that these scenarios will affect each other. This situation we call 'multi-scenario development'.

By definition, a qualitative leap involves the negation of one quality and the birth of another. As Hegel showed, the coming into being of a new quality involves processes both of emergence and of transience:

> Becoming is in this way doubly determined. In one determination, nothing is the immediate, that is, the determination begins with nothing and this refers to being; that is to say, it passes over into it. In the other determination, being is the immediate, that is, the determination begins with being and this passes over into nothing – *coming-to-be* and *ceasing-to-be*. Both are the same, becoming, and even as directions that are so different they interpenetrate and paralyze each other. The one is *ceasing-to-be*; being passes over into nothing, but nothing is just as much the opposite of itself, the passing-over into being, coming-to-be. This coming-to-be is the other direction; nothing goes over into being, but being equally sublates itself and is rather the passing-over into nothing; it is ceasing-to-be. They do not sublate themselves reciprocally – the one sublating the other externally – but each rather sublates itself in itself and is within it the opposite of itself. (Hegel 2010: 80–1)

And:

> From the qualitative side, therefore, the gradual, merely quantitative progression which has no limits in itself, is absolutely interrupted; and since in its merely quantitative connection the newly emerging quality is with respect to the vanishing one an indeterminate other, one which is indifferent to it, the transition is a *leap*; the two are posited as wholly external to each other. (Hegel 2010: 320)

Precisely because of this temporary 'mutual negation' of the qualities of the old and new systems at the moment of the revolutionary leap, fluctuations that are by no means solely dependent on the preceding objective development of the system take on particular importance.[6] Under revolutionary conditions, the 'old' objective determination of processes and phenomena, of the behaviour of individuals and of complex social subjects (social movements, parties, etc.), grows weaker or no longer operates. The new objective determination is only just emerging; it is not yet functioning, or at any rate is still weak. For a social revolution, this thesis is linked to the well-known phenomenon of the growing role of the subjective principle, but in our view this latter is only one of the manifestations of the more general law of dialectical revolutionary leaps.

On this basis we are critically rethinking the practice, in the past more or less accepted in Marxism, of interpreting any revolutionary birth of a new social system as a uniformly progressive phenomenon, leading to the appearance of a more efficient and humane new formation. In our view, such processes are characterised by the above-mentioned multi-scenario nature of development. Where, when, and why, and under what conditions, will a revolutionary transition render more probable either a genuinely progressive development of the new system, or else a contrary tendency for the revolution to degenerate into its opposite, a counter-revolutionary return to the earlier quality? Or will the birth of a new quality amid insufficient preconditions, followed by subsequent mutation of the progressive tendencies, lead to further crisis and counter-revolution as negative potential accumulates within the new formation,[7] making the revolutionary transition at best a stage in a longer transition?

This multi-scenario concept, of course, presents a challenge to dogmatic dialectics as presented in the main philosophical textbooks of the Soviet period, with its characteristic linear-determinist view of intrasystemic development. The dialectics of multiscenario evolution, of the decline, rise, and mutual transition of systems, still represents only a new field for our study. This field, however, is by no means empty. Several works on the dialectics of social revolutions and counter-revolutions, reforms and counter-reforms, and retroactive processes of historical evolution (see Plimak 1983; Vodolazov 1975; Volodin et al. 1976) have created a basis for general methodological conclusions on which many scholars are now working, including the authors of this text.

Correspondingly, another variant is also arising: the dialectics of the dead-end development of old and new systems, which may stagnate in this condition or undergo revolutionary (or counter-revolutionary) explosions. The dead-end state of a society is the consequence of the long-term failure to overcome social development contradictions which lead to standstill, stagnation, and decline. Such a social system is not capable of evolving into something more progressive.

It is possible to escape from the dead end through either a revolutionary transformation into a more progressive system or through regression, a return to the state which obtained at the beginning of the movement into a dead end, or the complete destruction of the society at the dead end. The first of these possibilities is illustrated by the series of Chinese revolutions during the first half of twentieth century, the second by the restoration of capitalism in Russia as a result of the period of 'stagnation', and the third by the death of the Western Roman Empire.

Analysis of retrogressive socio-historical trajectories has revealed certain features in the dialectics of regression, an area which previously lay outside the direct scope of Marxist studies. The experience of the past century has, however, provided a good deal of material for such analysis. The stage represented by the decline of the system may give rise to a paradoxical situation in which attempts are made to bring about the revolutionary destruction of an old qualitative state and to usher in a new one; while these attempts are objectively inevitable, they are at the same time just as objectively premature and lacking in the sufficient preconditions. This was the case not only with the revolution in the Russian Empire. The whole period of self-negation (decline) of a system is fraught with such, albeit thwarted, upheavals. All the attempts to bring about socialist revolutions during the twentieth century are clear examples of the decline of capitalism. These explosions become possible from the moment when the system enters this stage and can occur at any point during the ripening of the preconditions for the new qualitative state, including at points before these preconditions are sufficiently developed. This situation will give rise to regressive processes, characterised by resurgence of the old forms and by a reduced role for elements of the new within the context of the declining system.

All these components characterise the dialectics of the transition from one system to another. During the twentieth century, leading social dialecticians still maintained that this transition presupposed a relatively prolonged existence and nonlinear growth of the elements of the new system within the old, followed by a relatively lengthy and non-linear dying out of the elements of the old system within the new. These positions have now been thoroughly forgotten by the overwhelming majority of critics of dialectics, who fulminate at us about our exclusive devotion to revolutions.

In summing up these brief remarks on the dialectics of decline, we repeat that the processes of nonlinear decline of the capitalist system, and in particular the retroactive asocial processes leading to the destruction of earlier progressive achievements, have invariably given rise to the domination (especially among the progressive intelligentsia) of the methodology of postmodernism as a theory of deconstruction.

The apparent fiasco suffered by the dialectics of progress, the decline that has characterised the period in general and its retroactive stages in particular, and the broad spread of mutant forms have all served to enhance the preconditions for the development of postmodernism, creating an atmosphere of irrational thinking and vacuousness (we recall that mutant forms are forms which not only renounce their content, but also create the appearance of a different content and sense which in reality are non-existent). This objective domination of vacuousness could not fail to give rise to a philosophy of simulacra and similar postmodernist concepts.

Among conservative intellectuals who perceive the reversal of social progress in positive fashion, the most typical reaction to the changes noted above has been the philosophy of anti-modernism. In Russia this has been accompanied by a growth in the influence of conservatism and religious philosophy, by the romanticising of rural life, and by imperial fantasies.[8] In the West, and especially in the US, the trend has been towards the philosophy of liberal conservatism, extending also to apologies for a 'democratic empire'. These matters, however, do not fall within the scope of this text.

The new view of the dialectics of transformations (along with the old view, as it re-actualises itself) also allows us to pave the way for other novel aspects of dialectics. These include the potential of this methodology for studying the new realities which in recent times have increasingly been designated as 'the knowledge society', and which the authors of this text associate with a far more fundamental shift: the nonlinear progress of humanity's creative activity as the deep-seated basis for global transformations that were already under way in the last century. Here are to be found the origins of the question of the new dialectics – that is, of the dialectics of collective creativity and of multi-dimensional network interactions. This topic, however, extends beyond the framework of this necessarily brief summary of the authors' main works, which are detailed in the list of references.

Such are the first brief sketches which we have devoted to the problems of analysing some of the possible paths of development for the dialectical method under the conditions which accompany the rise of a new world – a world marked by the decline of old social systems, a world of the genesis of collective creativity and of network structures. These new processes, however, are only just beginning to operate, and it is the 'old' questions of social research which for the present remain dominant. The 'old' classical dialectical method, to whose tasks of re-actualising and development we referred earlier, remains relevant here as well.

These 'new' and 'old' dialectics provide us with the appropriate methodological key for analysing the fundamental challenge of the twentieth and twenty-first centuries: is it possible to take responsibility for declaring that social progress exists, and to claim to know how to speed it up through social creativity?

## Notes

1  The main sources that are subjected to critical analysis in this chapter include the works of Anderson (2007), Baudrillard (2005), Callinicos (1989), Derrida (1981, 1994), Grinberg and Rubinstein (2005), Hardt and Negri (2000, 2004), Jameson (1991), and Mészáros (1986, 1995).

2  There is a widespread view that postmodernism is a left-wing, oppositionist intellectual current. A certain basis exists for this; Baudrillard (2005), Jameson (1991), Derrida (1981, 1994) and Žižek (2009), and Hardt and Negri (2000, 2004) can all, despite substantial differences, be grouped with left-wing intellectuals. But to one degree or another all of them take a negative attitude to dialectics, above all because dialectics brings with it the potential for concrete, systemic, and most importantly positive negation, taking the form of the annulling-creation of the world by an active and associated subject. For postmodernism, the most important thing is asystemic (that is, constructed according to the principle of monads and based on deterrialisation and decentration) deconstruction and desubjectification. But more about this later.

3  Thus Jacques Derrida speaks directly of the need to 'deconstruct everything that connects the concepts and norms of science with ontotheology, with logocentrism, and with phonologism. This is a vast and interminable labour ... To deconstruct opposition means first at a certain moment to overturn a hierarchy ... As can be seen in the texts indicated and in the White Mythology by anyone who cares to read it, the most general heading for the whole question would be: castration and mimesis. Here I can only refer to these analyses and to their consistent nature. Essentially, the concept of castration is inseparable in this analysis from that of dissipation' (Derrida 1981: 35, 41, 84, 86).

4  We should note that in the USSR in the 1960s and 1970s a world-ranking school of critical Marxist dialecticians took shape, represented by such figures as Evald Ilyenkov, Victor Vazyulin, Genrih Batishchev, and others.

5  These arguments are posed, in particular, in Lenin's work *Imperialism: The Highest Stage of Capitalism* (1916/1964b, and in his notebooks on imperialism (Lenin 1939/1974). Soviet writers who have address this topic include Nikolai Tsagolov, Stepan Yanchenko, Vsevolod Kulikov, Anatoly Porokhovsky, and others from the so-call Tsagolov school, including the authors of this text.

6  These theses are developed in Part IV of Buzgalin and Kolganov 2004. The argument that revolutions constitute periods of social bifurcation is also explored in the works of Oleg Smolin. We did not, of course, formulate these positions on an empty field. Numerous well-known works on questions of the theory of revolution by Karl Marx, Friedrich Engels, Vladimir Lenin, Antonio Gramsci, Rosa Luxemburg, and various Soviet authors (especially Grigory Vodolazov,

who during the Soviet period defended the positions of revolutionary Marxism) contain ample groundwork for the conclusions set out here.

7  Here we can and should give postmodernism its due. Many of the representatives of its left wing are characterised not by a total rejection of any and all laws of evolution, but 'merely' by a stress on the existence of numerous variants of development, endlessly open and unrestricted and hence incapable of being known completely (or at all). In light of what has been said earlier, this stress is obviously no chance occurrence. In our view, it is precisely this aspect of postmodernism that is conditioned by the fact that at the present stage of 'decline' of the capitalist system the above-mentioned multi-variant (multi-scenario) nature of the processes of the decline and birth of systems and their mutual transition is becoming more the rule than the exception. This objective process also finds its somewhat mystified and absolutised reflection in postmodernism, especially in the writings of Michael Hardt and Antonio Negri (2000; 2004) and Jacques Derrida (1994).

8  As examples one might cite the numerous works by Yuri Osipov which examine this position in detail (e.g. Osipov and Zotova 2005).

# 4

# What drives the development of technology and the economy: production relations vs. productive forces, social creativity vs. activism

Most intellectuals who are remote from critical Marxism associate its social philosophy with the concepts of historical materialism and the idea of stages of history, not least because orthodox Marxism did consider them very important.[1] However, more than 150 years since the main works of Karl Marx appeared, modern Marxism has gone far beyond this orthodoxy and now consists of a multitude of schools, currents, and debates, often mutually conflicting. In this chapter, we discuss what we consider some of the most important additions and corrections that, in our view, must be included in the modern Marxist philosophy of history.

## Beyond the realm of economic necessity: the dialectics of progress and regression

Above all, it is now all but universally accepted that the Stalinist version of the stages of history had extreme limitations. The *pyatichlenka* – that is, the simplistic reduction of Marx's theory of social formation to five modes of production, from primitive communism to communism – applies a crude class approach to the analysis of any and all social developments, stressing the facts that the development of the productive forces leads to a change of socio-economic formations, the base determines the superstructure, and so forth. Such thinking is profoundly inadequate for the study of modern social dynamics. In any case, it has never been truly characteristic of Marxism, except for some dogmatic textbooks of the Stalinist era and the works of the most primitive anti-Marxists.

What is paradoxical, however, is the fact that most serious scholars who reject the ahistorical methodology of positivism and postmodernism and set about investigating qualitative changes in economic life generally borrow in one way or another from these simplistic approaches, usually when they discuss the defining influence of technological changes on the economy and social institutions. Among the most prominent examples are those who have studied the genesis of the postindustrial (information, knowledge-intensive) economy, starting with Daniel Bell (1973) if not earlier.

Our approach proposes a critical restoration of the classical view of the dialectical interaction between productive forces and production relations. This allows us to dispense with the orthodox formula that holds that the level of development of the productive forces determines the type of production relations in a fairly simple and direct fashion, and to give a more nuanced account of the more complex paths that this determination has taken in history, and where and how it is retroactive determination that prevails. Briefly, we regard determination of production relations by the level of productive forces as direct determination, and the converse, determination of the development of productive forces by certain production relations, as retroactive determination.

In particular, we wish to stress that it is not only productive forces that, as they develop, call forth new production relations. The development of productive forces within the context of one and the same formation also proceeds as a result of the often substantial changes to these relations that become necessary and occur as the contradictions of the system mount. Examples include the transition from simple cooperation and the manufacturing workshop to large-scale industry, from the formal to the real subordination of labour, as described in Capital.

While this may seem like a mere return to the classics, we also draw a number of less familiar conclusions. It is important to note that every historically concrete system of production relations (1) makes possible a greater or lesser stimulus to advances in labour productivity (this being one measure of its relative progressiveness), and (2) creates its own particular forms of progress in the productive forces. A well-known consequence flows from this: in the growth of material wealth and utilitarian consumption fostered by capitalism, nature, science, and art are treated by the market and capital not as universal heritage of humankind, but as means of enrichment that come free of charge, which therefore are subject to maximum exploitation. This same historically concrete system of production relations (3) sets the limits of the progress in the productive forces that is characteristic of a given mode of production. These, of course, are also no more than little-emphasised elements of classical Marxism.

In this problematic field, the key question of our times concerns the forms, potential, and boundaries of the progress of post-industrial technologies, and how global problems can be solved in the system of production relations of late (twenty-first-century) capitalism. Here we will show that productive forces of this new type (and the global problems associated with them) exhaust the potential for progress within the framework not just of capitalism, but of any social formation of the economic variety (of the 'realm of necessity', of prehistory), creating both the possibility of and the need for a transition to a new type of social development (the 'realm of freedom'). Contrary to the common approach to the 'economic', in which this word means anything related to the usage of resources for human needs and is therefore timeless, we reduce the meaning of this term to the sphere of human activity related to production, whose aim is increasing material wealth. That alone remains the overwhelming imperative for humankind as long as it remains in the 'realm of necessity'.

Our demonstration of this is probably the most complex and subtle element of the present work, and setting it forth concisely presents the greatest difficulties. There is, however, one thing that lightens our task considerably: to an important degree, modern theoretical work and even the practical slogans of new social movements have already been pushing at these boundaries. While they are not expressed in the terms of our critical Marxism, preferring political, moral, or abstract-philosophical imperatives, they are nevertheless useful to us in advancing our own formulations on the obstacles that our present system places in the way of evolution out of the 'realm of necessity' (and not only of late (twenty-first-century) capitalism).

The first such obstacle is that the existing corporate-capitalist and bureaucratic-state structures are inadequate to the tasks of ensuring free and generally accessible use of the main 'resources' for the development of society, intellectual and cultural resources, nature, knowledge, and human qualities. This inadequacy is countered by the slogan 'The world is not a commodity' and the demands for a transition to universal ownership (everyone's ownership of everything) – that is, to the possession by each individual of all cultural goods, including nature as a cultural value. The idea of universal property is based on Marx's theses on 'universal labour'. It 'depends partly on the co-operation of the living, and partly on the utilisation of the labours of those who have gone before' (Marx 1894/1998: 105). Research on universal labour by the representatives of post-Soviet school of critical Marxism has been summarised by Aleksandra Yakovleva (2014). This idea of Marx's was widely known in critical Soviet Marxism and is now being developed by the present authors (Buzgalin and Kolganov 1998), Vadim Mezhuev (2007), Vladislav Inozemtsev (1998a, 1998b), and others. In the West the idea has been expressed in recent decades in the work of Alvin and Heidi Toffler (2006), Michael Hardt and Antonio Negri (2000, 2004), and Slavoj Žižek and Costas Douzinas (2010). The core idea is familiar to most people in the common 'ownership' by everyone of all the treasures of a public library. This is not an abstract imperative: it is necessary if the contradiction between the new source of development (culture) and the private ownership of this resource by corporate capital is to be resolved.

The second obstacle that our current social organisation puts in the way of advancing the productive forces is the inadequacy of the forms of hired labour and of so-called 'human capital' to the tasks of developing the main productive force of the new world: the creatively active individual. Just as personal dependency restrained the progress of industry, the form of capital holds back creativity of the free association as the free dialogue of unalienated human beings. Our society is confined to seeking to resolve this contradiction through the forms of 'creative' (or 'adaptive') corporation based on intellectual labour (Toffler 1985; Drucker 1999), 'human' and 'social' capital, and so forth. 'Creative' or 'adaptive' corporations can, on the one hand, expand the limits of free creative activity of employees. On the other hand, however, they use this expansion only for profit. As for 'human' and 'social' capital, we see the same thing: the usage of human qualities to boost profits. They do permit some forms of advance, just as initial progress of the productive forces of capital occurred through the forms of serf factories, of farmed-out work, and of plantation slavery. However, these can be no more than transitional forms with historical and logical limitations.

The third obstacle is absolute environmental and resource limitations, which set the boundaries for utilitarian-oriented development. Arising out of the totality of the market, and after turning every imaginable material good into a commodity, this development proceeds to swallow up diverse forms of social activity (education, art, science, health care). In every country and across countries, powerful corporate capital seeks actively to overcome these boundaries through the simulated production of simulated goods for simulated consumption. The range of simulacra now includes not just the phenomenon of the 'branded' economy and other phenomena superbly described by Baudrillard and his colleagues (Baudrillard 1981, 1994, 1970/1998), but also the rapidly growing forms of fictitious financial capital, the accelerating production of armaments and weapons of mass destruction, the expansion of *faux*-glamorous 'culture', and much else. These sorts of production only accentuate the contradictions between wealth and poverty and between productivism and the environment. The ultimate contradiction, however, is that the development of the world of simulacra takes priority over that of the world of human qualities. It is the most obvious manifestation of the contradiction between the now-dominant system of relations of the power of corporate capital and the advance of human creative potential as the prime productive force. This, moreover, provides one of the most glaring testimonies to the fact that the advance of the productive forces of late (twenty-first-century) capitalism is following a trajectory that leads into a strategic dead end.

It is possible to resolve these contradictions to some extent and temporarily within the present system through the operation of the involution of systems during the stage of their decline – through the inclusion in the depths of the market and capital of elements of a new system of future relations, not only post-capitalist but also post-market and even post-economic. Such new elements make it possible for the capitalist system to survive, but at the same time they distort the integrity of the system, being alien to it. This inclusion is nonlinear and proceeds according to the familiar formula of 'one step forward, two steps back'. Such elements include socio-environmental norms, established and maintained by civil society with the help of the state; those forms of free, generally accessible education and health care that cannot be totally eradicated; the redistribution by the state and other institutions in many countries of anywhere from a third to half of Gross Domestic Product (GDP) according to non-market criteria; and other transitional forms. Half a century ago, such elements were on the increase, but today they are being driven back. This, however, is how the nonlinear process of evolution and involution of transitional forms must operate in the conditions of the decline of late (twenty-first-century) capitalism and of the 'realm of necessity'.

One important conclusion follows: whereas classical Marxism grew up on the basis of a study of the contradictions and limits of capitalism, and of the objectively possible ways in which capitalism might be done away with, the post-Soviet school of critical Marxism is growing up on the basis of a study of the contradictions and limits of the world of alienation (the 'realm of necessity'), and of the objectively possible ways in which this world might be done away with entirely. It should be noted that in the works of Karl Marx himself there are separate statements on this problem and that it is also found in the form of separate provisions or fragmentary theses in the works of the authors primarily of the 1960s. The post-Soviet school of critical Marxism has made these theses the subject of a special study, with a number of conclusions concerning the content of the transformation processes of the modern era (see for example Buzgalin, Mironov, and Arslanov 2009).

## The individual in history: the activism of agents of progress and regression

Our approach allows us to discern the fundamental contradiction of the historical process that is characteristic of the 'realm of necessity'. On one side of this antithesis is the dominance of the system of relations of alienation, transforming the human individual into a puppet of objective forces: of the division of labour, of personal dependency, of the market, of capital and the state. The other side is represented by creativity as an innate property of human beings. It is the creative activity of collective humanity in material production, culture, and social life that transforms the world in accordance with the laws of Truth, Good, and Beauty. Ensuring technical, scientific, and cultural progress, this creative activity makes possible the carrying through of social reforms and revolutions that overcome slavery and serfdom, colonialism, and the horrors of barbaric capitalism, and ultimately the capitalist system itself.

Here we are not only reinstating and asserting afresh the classical Marxist criterion of progress – the free and many-sided development of the personality – but also demonstrating its relevance. We insist that in the modern epoch this criterion is no longer just an abstract social and moral imperative tracing its lineageback to Aristotle and Kant, but also a practically applicable criterion for economic, social, and political action. In a society where creative activity is the main factor and resource (we *use this pragmatic economic terminology quite deliberately)* of development, creative activity plays a role analogous to that of land in pre-bourgeois systems and of the machine under capitalism. The transition to such a society automatically creates the need to enhance human creative potential as the overriding task of social development. The national and international power of capital, meanwhile, directs this tendency into the narrow corridor of the 'consumer society' and of the 'society of professionals', a corridor which leads, ultimately, into the impasse of global problems.

Postmodernism, by contrast, is indifferent to the question of progress. This indifference leads it to accept, nay celebrate, its global proto-empire, imposing its own criteria of 'progress' and 'civilised behaviour' through its methods of economic, political, ideological, and mass-cultural expansion. As specialists in political economy, we note that, for example, the methodology of neoclassical economic theory going back to the philosophy of positivism denies progress completely, while the policies it recommends take as their criterion of progress the degree to which economic systems approach the ideal of the free competitive market. The practical results were clear in post-Soviet Russia, where the achievement of this goal justified the imposition of massive regression in the area of 'human qualities'. In contrast to postmodernist passivity, the post-Soviet school of critical Marxism, developing the classical positions of the Marxist philosophy of history, stresses the active creative role of the human individual as the creator of social relations, capable of developing her or his social-creative powers in a period of progressive social reforms and revolutions, whether it is the American War of Independence or the Khrushchev 'thaw' in the USSR. But the post-Soviet school of critical Marxism, in contrast to dogmatic offshoots of Marxism, gives centre stage to the questions of the limits of human constructive-creative activism and of the responsibility borne by the passive, inactive conformism which makes stagnation and regression possible.

The experience of the twentieth century and the practical results of scientific and technical progress, along with the efforts of social reformers to improve the lot of humanity, showed how contradictory such 'activism' is. But it was merely that, and was not unwarranted or unjustified. It is now perfectly acceptable, as well as fully justified, to point to the victims of technical and social progress. At the same time, scientific and technical progress has yielded numerous absolutely indispensable benefits, including a radical reduction in childhood mortality and an increase in life expectancy world-wide by a third. Socially creative strivings of trade union activists, environmentalists, and adherents of left parties have allowed at least part of humanity to enjoy an eight-hour working day, free secondary education, and at least minimal social welfare. However, the artificial obstruction of reforms and revolutions in the neoliberal decades has led to cultural and creative losses, and hundreds of millions of people endure what the poet Alexandr Blok described as unmusical lives (Orlov 1980: 247).

Moreover, there is also the activism of the forces of reaction to consider. Twenty years ago these words would have seemed like a propagandist cliché, but in the new century, with its neocolonialism and asymmetric wars, activism of the forces of reaction is more significant than ever, enjoying the backing of corporate capital and its economic, political, and cultural influence, and aided by its alter egos, fundamentalism and terrorism.

While the postmodern ideologues of the proto-empire almost always proclaim their impartiality (to everything but their own incomes and security), in practice they do not neglect to impose their own simplistic notions of good and evil on the entire world. This situation has not only been typical of recent years; we recall the First and Second World Wars.

This is why post-Soviet Marxism is concerned with the philosophical problem of the limits of socially creative activism. On an extremely abstract level, one can say that the socially creative impact of the social subject on history is possible and necessary in so far as it conduces to ending alienation and furthering the progress of humanity. Determining this measure is always a concrete task, performed by painfully real social and cultural forces, but what is certain is that a strategy of 'impartiality' always involves conniving with reaction, whether this is the obscurantism of the Inquisition, Stalinist terror, or the stupefying propaganda of consumer society, with its mass culture and philosophical indifference to the individual.

This approach accords with modern Marxism's emphasis on the nonlinear nature of social development, on the possibility and typicality not only of progressive reforms and revolutions which help to develop human capacities and to raise the productivity of labour, but also of regressions, counter-revolutions, and counter-reforms. This concept, of a reversal of the flow of historical time, is especially apposite in periods when progressive activism goes too far (relative to the objective and subjective preconditions) in its attempts to advance to a new society, and when the backward swing of the pendulum of the historical process calls forth powerful regressive changes. Just such a 'backswing' has been particularly characteristic of the post-Soviet era and its transformations.

Moreover, and as noted earlier, modern Marxism, especially in Russia, has shown that in the development of social systems what is most significant and prolonged, and also most difficult to study, is not so much the mature, developed stages as the lengthy periods of the rise and dying away of historically specific systems. These periods are associated with the formation of a broad range of transitional relationships, with the contradictions of revolutionary and counter-revolutionary, reformist and counter-reformist processes. Meanwhile, these transitions are subject to certain specific laws: the nonlinear flow of social time; the mosaic-like fragmentation of the social space, which is greater than in stable systems; the role of non-economic determinants of the transition; the dominance of informal institutions; and many others.

The peculiarities of these transformational processes are revealed most fully in the socio-economic changes in the post-Soviet space. We believe that modern Marxist methodology is best suited to analysing these, thanks to objective features of the economies undergoing transition, and it is here that Russian post-Soviet critical Marxism has made the greatest progress (Buzgalin and Kolganov 2003, 2009a). Nor is it by chance that the most interesting results in the development of socio-economic theory (provided not only by pure Marxists) have been linked to research into late (twenty-first-century) capitalism, along with its specific features and contradictions at the stage of development of post-industrial trends and of globalisation. As we have set out to show, in this area the very foundations of the market and capital are undergoing self-negation: capitalist production's own contradictions lead to the inclusion of non-capitalist elements into the capitalist system. Moreover, and as in the epoch of imperialism from the late nineteenth century onwards, this self-negation is occurring within the framework of the previous system and is serving to strengthen it.

We will thus analyse this self-negation of capitalism on the stage of the contemporary 'late capitalism'.

## Note

1 The main sources on which this chapter rests, and in relation to which we propose qualitatively new ways of resolving the questions under examination, are works by Drucker (1993, 1996), Hardt and Negri (2000, 2004), Inozemtsev (1998a, 1998b), Mezhuev (2007), and Toffler (1985, 1990).

# II

The market, money, and capital in the
twenty-first century

# 5

# 'Late capitalism': stages of development

The term 'late capitalism' was used in the works of Mandel, Jameson, and other Marxist theoreticians (Mandel 1972; Habermas 1973; Jameson 1991).[1] We too use it, but give it an original meaning of our own. Our position is that at the end of the nineteenth century and the beginning of the twentieth century a special period in the development of capitalism begins. It is characterised by a partial evolutionary adaptation of capital to new conditions, generated both by the 'decline' of the social economic formation and by the evolution of capital itself. We witness the emergence of post-market relations in the depths of capitalism itself. These deny the quality and essence of capital, but at the same time give a new impetus to its development. This is what we call 'late capitalism', or the era of 'decline' of capitalism.

As mentioned already, much earlier, Lenin too had defined this stage of the development of capitalism, which for him was modern, as dying and decaying capitalism:

> Monopolies, oligarchy, the striving for domination and not for freedom, the exploitation of an increasing number of small or weak nations by a handful of the richest or most powerful nations – all these have given birth to those distinctive characteristics of imperialism which compel us to define it as parasitic or decaying capitalism. ... From all that has been said in this book on the economic essence of imperialism, it follows that we must define it as capitalism in transition, or, more precisely, as moribund capitalism. (Lenin 1916/1964b: 300, 302)

For us it is important to stress Lenin's understanding that this is the stage which self-denial begins, undermining all the basic systemic parameters of capitalism: its quality (with free competition being undermined and state regulation emerging as the beginning of the self-negation of commodity production), its essence (the transformation of accumulation and profit into the appropriation of monopoly super-profits and parasitism as financial capital transformed the relations of appropriation of surplus value), its forms, and so on.

While Lenin's terms 'decaying' and 'dying' are, then, oddly enough, correct, they are somewhat one-sided. They are correct because capitalism did indeed enter in that period – at the end of the nineteenth century and the beginning of the twentieth century – the era of self-denial and therefore dying. The terms are correct because the parasitism of capital at this stage had increased dramatically and continued to grow. They are one-sided, however, because in these characteristisations Lenin did not emphasise that this stage of self-denial can be (and proved to be) long, that it could lead (and did lead) not only to regress, but also to progress, as was especially noticeable in the conditions of victory in the second half of the twentieth century in a number of countries in capitalism's so-called 'centre' or 'core' (primarily Western Europe).

It should be noted that, firstly, this one-sidedness in the works that Lenin wrote a year before the October Revolution is quite understandable: the imperialism that gave rise to the First World War was genuinely monstrous and really proved to be the eve of the socialist revolution, and secondly, in others of his works Lenin repeatedly gave even more subtle characterisations of capitalism at the stage of 'decline'.[2] (By the way, Rosa Luxemburg characterised this stage similarly, but with an emphasis on the unity of imperialism and militarism (Luxemburg 1913/2003)).

As for Marxist works before and after Lenin, they basically gave similar characterisations of some features of imperialism (Bukharin, 1917/2003[3]) or else stressed one of its aspects (e.g. Hilferding's work on finance capital, 1910/1981). In works after Lenin, either the problem of separating the stage of self-denial, the 'decline' of capitalism as a fundamentally important scientific problem, is entirely ignored or, far more rarely, the capitalism of the twentieth century is given somewhat less definite characteristics, as in Mandel's concept of late capitalism.

The rest of left theory would divide capitalism into periods, as a rule, only in connection with an identification of the stages of the 'welfare state' and the subsequent neoliberal globalisation. We accept this division and will analyse it below, but it touches on another question: the question of the division of stages within the 'decline' stage of capitalism. Besides, this proposed division itself is reduced to a positivist characterisation of only one of the many transformations within the 'decline' stage we are investigating. Late capitalism, according to our view, passes through three stages, which will be discussed below.

First of all, we will analyse imperialism as the first stage of the development of late capitalism, and also as the stage that served as the basis for the present stage of late capitalism, which we call 'twenty-first-century imperialism'. Hegel's aphorism about history repeating itself, the first time as tragedy and the second time as farce, is well known. However, it does not always hold good: the First World War may have been a tragedy, but the Second was an even greater one. To take another instance, contemporary imperialism with its proto-empires is still gathering strength a century after the compelling critiques of imperialism by prominent Marxists (see Hilferding 1910/1981; Lenin 1916/1964b; Luxemburg 1913/2003; Bukharin 1917/2003) and is more than a match for the latter in terms of aggressive expansionism. If today's imperialism resembles farce in any way, it is only the Phariseeism of its attempts to present an attractive face (the defence of 'universal human values') while playing a dirty game (striving for world-wide domination).

What does this imply for our understanding of capitalism today and its relations to that of the early twentieth century? In our view, Lenin's modest pamphlet (as he described it) *Imperialism: The Highest Stage of Capitalism* (1916/1964b), which was written amid the heat of the First World War and the extreme heightening of the contradictions of world capital, deserves to be regarded as the foundation-stone of the analysis of the first stage in the self-negation of late capitalism. In this very clear and polemical but also theoretically profound text, Lenin provided a critical synthesis – based on a large amount of preparatory work recorded in his *Notebooks on Imperialism* (1939/1974) – of the conclusions of his colleagues in the study of imperialism; as Georges Labica has argued, most of Lenin's characterisations of imperialism remain relevant to the situation that arose in the first years of the present century (Labica 2007; see also Buzgalin, Bulavka, and Linke 2011).

Our appeal in our analysis of imperialism primarily to the legacy of Ulyanov-Lenin is due not only to the Soviet and post-Soviet traditions of close attention to the heritage of Lenin, but also to deeper reasons. The main one is that, unlike most authors of that era, Lenin pays very great attention to the systematic study of the productive forces and the production relations of capitalism at a new stage of its development. The emphasis that Ulyanov-Lenin place on the productive forces and production relations is a direct realisation of the method and theory of Marx's *Capital*, in which the logical and historical development of the two sides of the capitalist mode of production is analysed. The present volume also poses the task of continuing *Capital* and analysing the transformations of the productive forces and production relations of the twenty-first century. Therefore we have considered it possible and necessary to rely first and foremost, but not exclusively, on Lenin's analysis. At the same time, we are fully aware that the imperialism of the early twenty-first century is different from that of the early twentieth century, and these differences will be highlighted below. Let us recall the characteristics of imperialism from Lenin's definition, which was once familiar to every student but is now little known even to scholars:

> Imperialism emerged as the development and direct continuation of the fundamental characteristics of capitalism in general. But capitalism only became capitalist imperialism at a definite and very high stage of its development, when certain of its fundamental characteristics began to change into their opposites, when the features of the epoch of transition from capitalism to a higher social and economic system had taken shape and revealed themselves in all spheres. Economically, the main thing in this process is the displacement of capitalist free competition by capitalist monopoly ...
>
> If it were necessary to give the briefest possible definition of imperialism we should have to say that imperialism is the monopoly stage of capitalism. (Lenin 1916/1964b: 265–6)

Further, Lenin notes that this short definition, however, is not enough, and he expands on it, highlighting the five main features of imperialism, which later entered into Marxist as well as Soviet textbooks of political economy. Recall these basic features:

> (1) the concentration of production and capital has developed to such a high stage that it has created monopolies which play a decisive role in economic life; (2) the merging of bank capital with industrial capital, and the creation, on the basis of this 'finance capital', of a financial oligarchy; (3) the export of capital as distinguished from the export of commodities acquires exceptional importance; (4) the formation of international monopolist capitalist associations which share the world among themselves, and (5) the territorial division of the whole world among the biggest capitalist powers is completed. (Lenin 1916/1964b: 266)

Certainly, these characteristics cannot be applied directly to the realities of the present decade, but they are of fundamental importance to a 'genetically general' definition of imperialism as an attribute of late capitalism. Let us explain. The concept of the 'genetically general' is one of the most interesting of the methodological innovations made by E.V. Ilyenkov in the field of dialectical logic., yet is little known to theorists in the area of the social sciences.[4] 'Genetically general', in contrast to 'abstract general', describes the quality of a certain object on the basis of its simplest and earliest state from its very origin, which at the same time is the simplest element of the developed object and which remains invariable in quality from its genesis to its decline. It allows one to define the systemic quality of objects under study, and simultaneously the general form of their being. Just as great-great-grandfather Ivanov bestows a genetic commonality and generality of form (family) on the whole of the Ivanov family, so in the field of social development the origin *of a system bestows its systemic quality and general form*. For capitalism, as the opening words of Marx's *Capital* demonstrate, the genetically general category for capitalism is the commodity: 'The wealth of those societies in which the capitalist mode of production prevails, presents itself as "an immense accumulation of commodities", its unit being a single commodity' (Marx 1867/1996: 45).[5] This idea is further elaborated by our teacher Nikolay Khessin. 'The 'economic cell', Khessin writes,

> is an extremely simple economic form that contains in embryo all the main features and contradictions of a given mode of production. A whole diverse system of production relations develops from it. It plays the role (1) of the starting point for the development of a given mode of production; (2) of the basis out of which all the other, more complex types of relations develop, and on which they rest; (3) of the outcome, constantly being reproduced, and consequence of a given system of relations; and (4) of the general form of the relations between people in a particular society. (Khessin 1964b: 12)

For late capitalism, on the other hand, this general form is the 'undermining' (Lenin) of the relations of commodity production, and ultimately of capital, by large corporate capital and the state, by intervention into market relations, including labour–capital relations, if on a local and partial basis and not universally (from the points of view of scale and social basis of such intervention). One extremely prominent feature of this process, the undermining of free competition by monopoly, is at the same time also a characteristic of imperialism as the monopolist stage of the development of capitalism, the stage at which *late capitalism* (Mandel 1972, 1987; Jameson 1991) can be said to begin.

As quoted above (see Chapter 3), Lenin stressed the transformation of free competition to monopoly as a sign of transitional nature of monopoly capitalism. By employing Ilenkov's idea of the genetically general, we are proposing to return the study of capitalism from its contemporary tendency to pose questions regarding the mechanism of the functioning of this system, to the original inclination of classical political economy and Marx, which was to pose their questions in terms of the *historical* (from the point of view of the empirically observed development of an object) and *logical* (that is, theoretically established) stages in the development of a phenomenon, in our case, late capitalism. This approach makes it possible to hypothesise that the main features of particular stages will become the keys to understanding the concrete whole of modern capital (it should be recalled that '... the whole is the result together with the way the result comes to be'! (Hegel 2018: 5)).

We can now distinguish the historical stages of development of late capitalism. The first stage is the genesis of monopoly capital, which transformed the market),[6] which formed the economic basis for early twentieth-century-style imperialism and colonialism, and which ultimately spilled over into the nightmare of the First World War. We describe this stage with the phrase 'imperialism as a special (initial) form and first historical stage of late capitalism'.[7] Meanwhile we stress in particular that as the initial form of the 'twilight' of capitalism, imperialism is a genetically *general* component of the entire process, which means that all subsequent stages will *also* be characterised as imperialism, just as in Marx's *Capital* the commodity considered in the first chapter becomes the universal form of all subsequent categories, for according to Marx's theory money, capital, etc. are *also* commodities.

The second stage is the stage of searching, at the level of the state as a whole, for models to govern the deliberate regulation of the economy. In this period, gradually and not without conflict, a system of public regulation is formed that combines national regulation of general economic proportions (active industrial policy) and the regulation of socio-economic parameters (progressive income tax, limiting the power of capital in production) and the active expansion of public goods production (from public works up to free education and health). These processes occurred throughout the second half of the twentieth century nonlinearly in time and unevenly in space, finding their completed form only in the 1960s.

This period began after the First World War, and developed further following a number of socialist revolutions and other powerful anti-capitalist actions (general strikes, armed uprisings, and so forth) in Eastern and Central Europe: (the First Russian Revolution of 1905–7; the Romanian peasant revolt of 1907; the Xinhai Revolution of 1911–12 in China; the February and October revolutions of 1917 in Russia; the civil war of 1918 in Finland; the November 1918 revolution in Germany; the Bavarian soviet republic in Germany in 1919; the Hungarian Revolution of 1919; the Kemalist revolution in Turkey; the September uprising of 1923 in Bulgaria; the 1926 General Strike in Great Britain; the Civil War of 1927–36 in China; the March on Washington by jobless US war veterans in 1932; the Austrian uprising of February 1934; the Spanish Civil War of 1936–39, and a whole series of anticolonial revolts), as well as after the Great Depression and other world-scale tectonic shifts that took place in the 'social crust' of humanity and that showed the limitations of the old system. These searches for models to govern the deliberate regulation of the economy had their origins in extremely diverse socio-economic transformations. Among these transformations, those that were ultimately victorious were those that, for all their shortcomings, had a generally progressive character, including the 'New Deal' in the US and social-democratic models in a number of countries of Western Europe. One cannot, however, ignore the regressive models (fascism, National Socialism) that played a monstrous role in history and that even today retain certain roots that could permit their revival. Since it was the former, relatively progressive models that provided the main vector of transformation, we define this stage as 'the social-reformist model (stage) of late capitalism' (for simplicity, we use 'social reformism' to mean not a particular political current, but the type of late capitalism described above). The USSR, the Chinese revolution, the welfarist and developmentalist regimes of the 'first world' and 'third world' after 1945, and the further revolutions in the 'third world' are also included in the second phase of late capitalism's development.

The *third* period was signalled by the 'neoliberal revanche' that began in the early eighties of the twentieth century. As acknowledged by practically all the intellectual schools of the late twentieth century, this period has been distinguished (a) by a relative decline in the role of the state and by a sort of renaissance of the market, and also (b) by an accelerated development of financial capital, aided considerably by (c) the processes of globalisation. Accordingly, we use the phrase 'the neoliberal form (stage) of late capitalism' (or more briefly, neoliberalism) to designate this stage.

It is important to note that each of the subsequent stages represents the *sublation* of the preceding one; that is, it not only negates the features of the previous stage, but also inherits them. Meanwhile, the logic of the 'negation of the negation' causes the neoliberal stage, according to many parameters, to come to represent a 'restoration' of many traits of the first stage, imperialism.

We shall return to this latter topic later. For the present, it is enough to state that the above-noted stages of late capitalism – imperialism, social reformism, and neoliberalism – are very well recognised and may be considered to have a thorough empirical grounding.

Through the dialectical 'negation of the negation', the global capital of the early twenty-first century reproduces and sublates the features of the monopoly stage in the evolution of capitalism (imperialism). This capital is thus characterised by a range of features that represent the consequence of transforming neoliberal globalisation into a proto-imperial quantity. We may term the sum of these features 'twenty-first-century imperialism'. We shall set out these features briefly, referring the interested reader to a detailed study of the relevant phenomena in our previous works (Buzgalin, Kolganov, and Barashkova 2016, 2018), which in turn rest on a broad range of previous research (Amin 1997, 2004; Desai 2013; Harvey 2003, 2004; Mészáros 1995).

As noted, the 'new imperialism' of the early twenty-first century is characterised by the fact that global capital is acquiring a number of features that are inherited genetically, and that deepen and even in some ways negate the peculiarities of the monopolies of the early twentieth century.

First, this capital breaks out of the framework of state borders because of the overdevelopment of national capitalism and the chronic internal *over-accumulation* of capital. Second, it enters the world arena not as an everyday atomised producer, competing on an equal basis with other 'players', but as (1) capital on a hitherto unprecedented scale; and (2) capital that has the ability to continue the economic, political, and ideological manipulation of other actors in the world economy.

A single example will suffice to show the ability of transnational capital to manipulate other states against their own interests: ISDS (investor-state dispute settlement) practice. The conditions of ISDS in bilateral and multilateral treaties on investments are imposed by multinational corporations. These conditions make it possible to force 'third world' countries to either renege on their commitments on public health, environmental protection, and human rights, or pay the huge compensation of probable loses of multinationals. Research by the United Nations mentions the low level of accountability and transparency in the activity of arbitrators of investment tribunals (United Nations 2007: 92).

> Arbitrators who decide the cases are often drawn from the ranks of the same highly paid corporate lawyers who argue ISDS cases. These arbitrators have broad authority to interpret the rules however they want, without regard to precedent and with almost no public oversight. Their decisions carry extraordinary power. Often, countries are obligated to obey ISDS judgments as if they came from their own highest courts. And there is no meaningful appeal. (Hamby 2016; see also Business & Human Rights Resource Centre)

This capital becomes the subject of imperialist aggression, which to some degree (competition with other corporate capitals and national states is still present!) subjugates producers, consumers, and state institutions. It should be noted that the ability of capital to manipulate states and other actors depends on the extent of its monopoly power, defined as its share in the market and in capital assets, as well as its financial power and its access to non-economic instruments of manipulation in the countries of the periphery (here we are talking not about ministers and ministries, but about the 'rules of the game', on which more will be said later). The new 'capital-imperialist' of the present century is not simply a large corporation, but *the subject of aggressive manipulation*.

Third, these aggregations of capital, with help from subordinate states and international institutions, seek to establish the 'rules of the game' that are binding on all other actors in world economic and political processes. However, they can and do meet with opposition from single or groups of actors: examples of such opposition include the activities of the Organizaton of Petroleum-Exporting Countries, the Eurasian Economic Community, and other organisations of semi-peripheral countries. These rules (for example, the rules of the Word Trade Organization, or the rules the International Monetary Fund (IMF) imposes on creditor countries) have the appearance of 'universal, civilised' norms characteristic of a free market, but in reality they have the function of ensuring the dominance of vast transnational corporations, and of the states and supra-state bodies (such as the EU) that are their 'homes'. So-called freedom of trade and of the movement of capital provide only the appearance of equal rights when the movement of labour power is closed off, when openness to the privatisation of any and all assets is accompanied by an effective ban on active social or other regulation of the market, and while priority is given to international rules that guarantee the inviolability of private property in the face of the democratically expressed will of citizens. In essence, the largest economic and political actors have had their hands freed up for manipulating economies and peoples (see Zhdanovskaya 2015; Toussaint 2008; Toussaint and Millet 2010).

We shall not immerse ourselves in this area, but merely recall the point formulated above and supplement it with another that flows directly from it: capital, as it carries out its imperialist expansion, not only imposes its 'rules of the game', but also enforces obedience to these rules through economic, political, and also military means. Capital, in effect, becomes the '*world cop*'.

Fourth, twenty-first-century imperialism is something more than the export of capital. It is rather the export of productive capital, and in a form that creates technological dependence, while simultaneously subjecting countries to the control of the financial capital of the exporting country. *Ergo* the global capital of the twenty-first century, as it expands, not only exports assets, but *subordinates* the economies of other countries to its rule, imposing and maintaining control over the technical capacities, governments, and finances of these national systems.

Fifth, this capital, as one of the participants cooperating and competing within world financial capital, controls the world financial system. In particular, this control is exercised through the emission of and control over the circulation of freely convertible currency (world money, the 'gold of the twenty-first century'), and through the subordination to capital of the system of international accounts and of the institutions that regulate world financial processes (the IMF, the World Bank, and others).

Finally, but not least in terms of significance, this capital has, through the exercise of all its above-noted properties, the ability to appropriate a special, 'imperialist' rent (see, for example, Amin 2010c: 110–11, 127, 128, 134). Imperialist rent, like any rent generated by the non-economic restriction of access to resources, is rent associated with limited access to resources (see, for example, Amin 2010c: 2–3, 175). Imperialist rent is associated with external consolidation in peripheral countries of substantially lower wages (Amin 2010c), a higher degree of exploitation, and specific conditions for the accumulation of capital. Under the conditions of imperialism of the twenty-first century, the monopoly of high technologies, financial resources, and geopolitical control is the basis for this consolidation of the worst economic conditions in the countries of the periphery. To the extent that some peripheral countries manage to break these external constraints, they cease to be a source of imperialist rent and turn into geopolitical rivals of the countries of the 'centre' (a modern example is the confrontation between China and the US) or are integrated by global capital into the economic structure of the 'centre' (as it was in the case of Singapore) (Desai 2013 is the most consistent account of this process and its historical roots). It should be noted that according to Samir Amin the growth of the new middle classes at the centre of the system also is associated with imperialist rent (Amin 2010a: 175).

Amin notes the following similarity between imperialist rent and monopolistic rent, which is characteristic of the preceding stages of the development of capitalism:

> 'Monopoly rent' was defined by Marx as the difference between the price of production and market price where market price is set not by the average profit that results from equalisation of the rate of profits over time; instead the price is set by a few cartels or corporations. In the current imperialist epoch, a small number of oligopolies sets the world prices in various sectors of production (e.g. oil, medicines, biotechnology, agricultural inputs), and thus monopoly rent is often referred to as imperialist rent or rent of oligopolies. Where finance capital exercises the same control over prices, the term financialised monopoly rent is sometimes used. (Amin 2010a: 20)

But let us return to the question of the foreign economic, political, and ideological expansion of one or another national state. Under the present-day conditions described above for establishing proto-empires, we may conclude, it is only those states that possess their 'own' global capital that are able to implement their own imperialist policy and that come to exercise even the basic attributes of imperialism set out earlier. It should be noted that although capital from China, India, and Brazil is increasingly international, the US, European Union countries, Canada, and Japan are blocking almost all attempts of the capital of new industrial states to penetrate their own national economies. Hence this is true of the globalisation in the frameworks of the 'third world' only, or limited globalisation, if it is possible to say so.

To translate the above into socio-philosophical language, a modern proto-empire can be understood as an economic-political chronotope, a systemic quality of which is the presence in its defining capitals of the main attributes of imperialism. Simplifying this socio-philosophical and simultane-ously political and economic definition, we might say that the subject of modern imperialism – the proto-empire – is a social space (*topos* signifies a super-country, such as the US; a group of countries, such as the core of the European Union; or a global network of large-scale financial capitals), which at the present time (*chronos*) employs global actors (transnational corporations and so forth) as the institutional framework (in particular, possessing juridical, political, ideological, and military mechanisms) for manipulating and ultimately subordinating others. In particular, a national state is proto-imperial if it employs transnational corporations based within it as a mechanism for the political (and, in extreme cases, military) subordina-tion of foreign socio-economic systems. The latter in this case acts as the periphery of the world politico-economic space whose 'centre' is the proto-empires (we refer to the 'centre' and 'periphery' of the world political-economic space to distinguish between the countries that are the actors of global political-economic hegemony and those that are the objects of it).

In this case, the transnational corporations of the imperialist country acquire not only politico-military defence for their economic expansion, but also the opportunity to pursue this expansion according to rules that allow them to actively manipulate the economic players in peripheral countries. These rules include both economic institutions in the proper sense (those concerned with formal freedom of trade and investment, the openness of all assets to privatisation, a lack of serious social restrictions on capital), and also the other means required to enforce them: military (NATO); legal (the priority of the system of international law they have themselves devised, and of the international courts which they themselves, in the final reckoning, have set up); ideological (the priority of so-called 'European' values, which in their content are bourgeois politico-ideological institutions); cultural (the expansion of globalised mass culture and of so-called 'elite' culture); and educational (the 'Bologna system'). On this basis are created the foundations for the economic, political, and ideological subordination of peripheral countries (their economies, political systems, and even the world-views of their citizens), and as a result, for the systematic extraction of imperialist rent.

In so far as a country that is the object of imperialist pressure is able to withstand these economic, political, and other strictures, it acquires the status of part of the *semi-periphery*. Some of the semi-peripheral countries, and Russia in particular, try to make use of mechanisms analogous to imperialism to exert pressure on their weaker neighbours and/or to establish 'defensive alliances'.

Some have seen longer continuities in these tendencies. If we see the development of capitalism as being characterised, at the international level, as a dialectic of uneven and combined development (UCD), a paradigm not confined to Trotsky but also shared by Lenin and other Bolsheviks, we are today at a new stage of its unfolding (Desai 2013). This dialectic earlier led to the industrialisation of countries – such as the US, Germany, and Japan – that first challenged the British domination of world markets (and led to the competition for markets and colonies that culminated in the First World War and the Thirty Years' Crisis it inaugurated, encompassing the two World Wars, the Great Depression, and the economic dislocations they entailed). The collapse of the colonial system of Lenin's day thereafter, while it did not destroy imperialism, did lead to the strengthening of a number of new industrial countries, this time outside the core of world capitalism, and to thus a weakening of imperialism (Desai 2013). UCD was part of the intellectual universe from which Lenin's understanding emerged, and its relevance today may be formulated as follows:

> The classical theories of imperialism were embedded in a wider anti-imperialist understanding of capitalism's geopolitical economy, uneven and combined development. ... Postwar developments made UCD and the classical theories of imperialism more, not less, relevant. If capitalist competition did not lead to further world wars, this was substantially because the USSR became part of UCD's further unfolding. As a revolutionary state founded on UCD's understanding of the capitalist world order, it took opposition to imperialism beyond national (capitalist) opposition to imperialism to encompass working-class opposition as well. As such it represented the strongest form of combined development: rather than trying to hasten capitalist development it sought to skip capitalism entirely. That communist China did so too, and survived to rank as the strongest of the so-called BRIC contender countries in the early twenty-first century, is also telling. (Desai 2013: 51–3)

This explanation also demonstrates the role of 'premature' socialisms, whether that of the USSR (which is no more) or of China (which remains), in terms of the unfolding of world capitalism and its 'sunset'. It also enables us to appreciate that, despite the superficial similarities of various economic, political, and even military mechanisms employed in these cases with those of the 'new imperialism', these mechanisms as employed by semi-peripheral countries differ substantially from imperialist subordination in the proper sense. This does not, of course, in any way signify that the policies of semi-peripheral countries necessarily become more progressive as a result.

We shall here make just one additional remark, which despite coming at the end of this chapter is by no means the least important. The foreign influences exerted by actors of the 'central' countries do not always amount to impulses of imperialist aggression. In some instances, countries of the centre, or organisations based in them (socially oriented NGOs, movements, and so forth) may also exert a progressive influence on the outside milieu. In the case of states, this influence is something of an exception. Moreover, in most cases these positive practices of imperialist states are part and parcel of the states' expansion, and are subject ultimately to the basic goals of manipulating other societies and extracting imperialist rent.

In most cases, social movements and other counter-hegemonic, alterglobalist forces in these countries (see Abramson et al. 2011) exert a positive influence both on world politico-economic and socio-cultural processes.[8] Meanwhile, the countries of the periphery and semi-periphery can (and, to put it more bluntly, should) make use of the anti-imperialist potential of the internal opposition within the countries of the centre, working in harmony and dialogue with these forces. This is the thrust of the policies applied, for example, by Venezuela, Cuba, and a number of other countries of Latin America and Asia. We will next move on to a study of the shifts in the most fundamental production relations of capitalism: in the market and money.

# Notes

1 The main sources on which this chapter is based, and in relation to which we propose qualitatively new solutions, include works by Amin (1997, 2010a), Bell (1973), Galbraith (1973, 2004), Harvey (2003, 2004, 2014), Mandel (1987), Rifkin (1995, 2000), and Kagarlitsky (2010).

2 For more details please see our chapter Buzgalin, Bulavka, and Linke 2011: 425–42.

3 As Lenin mentioned in his preface, he had read Bukharin's work written in 1915, in draft, and he relied on Bukharin's book in his work.

4 For a more detailed treatment of the methodology involved in distinguishing genetically general qualities (Il'enkov) or "cells" (Khessin) in socio-economic studies, see Ilyenkov (1974) and (Khessin (1975b).

5 The dialectic of the development of the 'cell' into a system was revealed precisely and elegantly by our teacher Professor Nikolay Khessin in the early 1960s (see Khessin 1964a, 1964b).

6 This is acknowledged indirectly even by neoliberal doctrine when it singles out imperfect competition and anti-monopoly regulation as crucially important features of the modern market (Robinson 1969; Arrow 1985; Baumol et al. 1982).

7 This definition of 'imperialism' in political economy, which we share with V.I. Lenin, contradicts its other (primarily geopolitical) meaning, which denotes a characteristic of a world in which there are empires and, accordingly, colonies and metropolises, along with the oppression, as a rule, of the former by the latter. We should point out that, in our view, placing the emphasis on the geopolitical aspects of imperialism (this is characteristic, in particular, of Samir Amin (2004)) largely serves to mask the substantially different nature of the relations between colonies and metropolises at various stages in the development of empires that were themselves qualitatively different; this approach establishes only the external forms that these relations, taken in an abstract sense, have in common. In the

geo-economic and geopolitical respects, Amin is correct, but at the same time his critique of Lenin misses the mark. Lenin examined not so much the spatial aspects of imperialism as its essence. Rather than taking an expansive view of imperialism, he studied it in depth, and thus came to understand it as a special 'twilight' period in the development of capitalism. During this period, as a result of the transformation of the quality and essence of capital, both geo-economic *and* geopolitical transformations take place. For a more detailed account of the polemic surrounding this point, see Desai (2013) and Kagarlitsky (2014).

8　See also materials on the website of Aleksandr Surmava at www. bezrodnycosmopolit.com/ (accessed 20 November 2019).

# 6

# The totalitarian market: networks and simulacra

## The corporate market and the birth of a new type of commodity relations

Proceeding through a 'negation of the negation' evolutionary spiral, capital emerged from commodity production before developing into competitive industrial capitalism and then into the monopolity capital that Lenin classically analysed.[1] This form of monopoly capital was challenged and even substantially undermined during the period of social reformism in the mid-twentieth century before the neoliberal restoration of the power of the market as the dominant form for the coordinating and allocating of resources took place in the late twentieth and early twenty-first centuries. However, it was not mere a restoration: it placed capitalism on a new basis – that of information technologies, of the achievements of the preceding evolution of capital, of the crisis of 'real socialism', and of globalisation. The restoration thus has a new content, and the modern epoch is witnessing the restoration of the comprehensive dominance not of a generic sort of market but of a new variant of it.

Corporate capital in the epoch of globalisation is substantially altering all the basic features of commodity relations, setting in train the creation of a *total market*. On an empirical level, the total market was already clearly visible in the late twentieth century, when neoliberal ideology and practice were already pushing the boundaries of so-called market fundamentalism. Such fundamentalism was considered a threat to the 'open society' even by such an adept of the rule of capital as George Soros, who, after the financial crashes of the late 1990s, published a book with the neo-Stalinist title *The Crisis of Global Capitalism* (Soros 1998). The most important new quality of the total market was the completion of the transition, begun in the epoch of monopoly capital and described by dozens of scholars from Vladimir Lenin (1916/1964b) onwards, to a market dominated not by the consumer, but by a force which imposes a particular system of needs on the consumer – that is to say, by corporate capital. The latter consciously manipulates the other agents of the market, whether households or small producers.

In today's total market, the principal change in the social division of labour consists in the development of global communications and information technology. In place of a mobile, flexible atomic structure of individual producers and the ties between them, we find a viscous, amorphous structure that emerges from the superimposition and competition of different networks.

Networks become both 'actors' and the connections among actors. They can be compared to a system of webs, which are constantly being weaved, and moreover, being weaved by a certain 'spider'. These networks are flexible and amorphous and rapidly change their configurations while remaining under the strict control of the power centre that forms them (the 'spider'). We can understand this by analogy with the field of production of information products. Here the corporate centres that control this production constantly 'reweigh' the networks in light of changes in the product or production process. Or there is the field of financial speculation with its multi-level 'webs' of transactions controlled by 'rainmakers'. In the production of cars too, an assembly company in some 'third world' country is only one point in the complex supply chain, management relations, marketing, operations, public relations, and financial flows 'woven' together by a particular trans-national corporation under the specific conditions of assembly and, most importantly, sales in a given country (Castells 1996).

In this way, a sort of total market of networks ('spiders' webs') arises, in which the place of separate competing firms is taken by shapeless inter-penetrating webs. Importantly, in most cases, these webs operate either in fields outside material production or in borderline areas – that is, in various sorts of financial, information, energy, transport, mass-media, and similar systems. They are fundamentally different in their characteristics from the main agents of the market of the previous era – the industrial links in the social division of labour – because:

(1) they are related to the genesis of post-industrial technologies;
(2) they are mobile, amorphous, and weakly tied to a specific 'place' (from the point of view of the industry, territory, etc.);
(3) they are potentially, and in some cases really (e.g. in the case of the internet), global and open;
(4) they are infinite in size and constantly change their dimensions (i.e. they grow, then decrease, and vice versa).

The list could go on. The so-called 'network enterprise' comes closest in terms of technological nature to the corporate-network market. In such an enterprise, a single system of information and standards connects to a single 'just in time' production chain of thousands of links for a specific customer.

Perhaps the most complete and accurate analysis of the nature of the network society that we know of is given in the works of Manuel Castells (1996).

To employ several analogies, this market can be compared to an array of powerful webs or fields of attraction, whose centres of formation ('spiders', or generators of the fields) are large blocs of corporate capital, agents of globalisation (these will be discussed in more detail later), and, above all, transnational corporations. This is how the total corporate-network market, the market of webs, takes its form.

The transnational character of modern capital is expressed in the first instance in the dominant economic power of transnational corporations. These corporations account for more than two-thirds of foreign trade and about half of world industrial production. They control approximately 80 per cent of technological innovations and expertise. Their total cumulative volume of direct foreign investments exceeds \$4 trillion, and their sales amount to 24 per cent of the overall world figure; meanwhile, one-third of the output of the transnational corporations is produced by affiliated foreign structures. The volume of sales of these affiliates of transnational corporations now exceeds the entire sum of world exports.[2] Particular commodity markets are effectively controlled by the transnationals, which account for 90 per cent of world sales of wheat, coffee, maize, timber, tobacco, and iron ore, 85 per cent of the markets for copper and bauxite, 80 per cent of the markets for tea and tin, and 75 per cent of those for crude oil, natural rubber, and bananas.[3]

Modern transnational capital, however, is characterised not only by its significant economic share, but also by its high level of concentration of corporate power, whose networks enmesh virtually all large-scale capital throughout the world. Research by Swiss mathematicians has shown the extremely high level of concentration of this power within a small core group of the largest corporations. For these core firms, the network of dependency creates a real basis for the manipulation of production, the market, and demand.

> In principle, one could expect inequality of control to be comparable to inequality of income across households and firms, since shares of most corporations are publicly accessible in stock markets. In contrast, we find that only 737 top holders accumulate 80% of the control over the value of all TNCs. ... We find that, despite its small size, the core holds collectively a large fraction of the total network control. In detail, nearly 4/10 of the control over the economic value of TNCs in the world is held, via a complicated web of ownership relations, by a group of 147 TNCs in the core, which has almost full control over itself. The top holders within the core can thus be thought of as an economic 'super-entity' in the global network of corporations. ... they do not carry out their business in isolation but, on the contrary, they are tied together

in an extremely entangled web of control. This finding is extremely important since there was no prior economic theory or empirical evidence regarding whether and how top players are connected. (Vitali et al. 2011: 6, 32)

The socio-economic nature of the 'fields of dependency' generated by large blocs of corporate capital lies in the multiplication of the effect of 'local plan regulation'. This term emerges from Soviet political economy and refers to the ability of corporations to regulate some parameters of the economic life of other actors partially, causing them to depend on the regulatory centre. Such plan regulation is created by every monopoly capital and has been known since the late nineteenth and early twentieth centuries. It creates technological, financial, information, and other dependences. Soviet political economists term it 'local plan regulation' because under it planning spreads not to the entire national system, as in the Soviet-type economy, but to a certain part of it, a subspace, within which corporations do not face opposition to the regulatory impact of other corporations (or where the web area of the given spider does not collide with the webs of other spiders). The theory of local plan regulation was developed on the basis of Lenin's works on imperialism by a number of Lomonosov Moscow State University scientists (including Nikolai Tsagolov, Viktor Cherkovets, Vsevolod Kulikov, Anatoly Porokhovsky, and others), as well as by Stepan Yanchenko, a professor at the Belarusian State University.

The above-mentioned multiplication of the effect of local plan regulation is carried out on the basis, firstly, of the development of the socialisation of production to the point where a new, 'networked' system of the division and integration of labour takes shape on a global scale. This involves the dismantling of the achievements of social reformism and of the transformation of corporate networks into quasi-states, which extend their control and regulation ('partial planning') not only to the parameters of the market (prices, volumes of sales and purchases, etc.), but also to the socio-institutional parameters of economic life (what we would call the 'rules of the game'), which transform themselves alongside the state into sources for the formation and support of the institutional milieu. The multiplication also relies on the application of methods of socio-psychological pressure with the help of the mass media and so forth, with the aim of creating a social atmosphere in which the 'field' of their power can be expanded as easily and effectively as possible (the formation of norms of passive social behaviour on the part of consumers, clients, and 'professionals', for example), and, lastly, on the use of old methods of direct coercion in relation to third parties, to the extent of 'paving over' entire states. As Thomas Friedman points out, 'The hidden hand of the market will never work without a hidden fist – McDonald's cannot flourish without McDonnell Douglas, the builder of the F-15. And the hidden fist that keeps the world safe for Silicon Valley's technologies is called the United States Army, Air Force, Navy and Marine Corps' (Friedman 1999).

On the one hand, to the degree to which the total corporate-network market develops, the largest capitalist corporation-networks break free from their social restrictions. No longer subject to control by the state, by trade unions, or by other institutions of civil society, they breach the 'rules of the game', destroying the achievements of the social-reformist period. On the other hand, however, the contradiction within the total market comes to the surface. This market arises as the cumulative sum of the 'fields of dependency' that regulate the actions of the corporate structures. Meanwhile, when taken as a whole, the conflict between the corporate structures and their mutual interaction amounts to a spontaneous process that is not under any control, either from the corporations or from the state. The parameters of this process are set above all by the spontaneous development of the financial markets and by global processes.

This is the reality that, in the neoliberal era, lies behind the appearance of the restoration of markets and competition. Underneath this appearance, however, lies the quite different essence of the total market: of a market whose form is that of influence trading and whose content is that of the corporate networks. In this winner-takes-all system, the one who prevails in competition is not the one whose quality is higher and prices lower, but the one whose 'dependency field generator' is more powerful. It is only natural that amid the decline of the 'realm of economic necessity', the global problems created by this process, which we propose to call neomarketisation, grow increasingly acute and lead to fundamental contradictions. We understand neomarketisation to mean a new wave of commercialisation and the ever-wider spread of the corporate-controlled market to all spheres of social life, and not just to the economy. This new commercialisation emerged after the period of relatively wide market restrictions and active social regulation in the second half of the twentieth century. One of the widely used analogues of this term in post-Soviet Marxism is 'market fundamentalism', which as far as we know was, paradoxically, coined by George Soros (1998). The most important of the fundamental contradictions of such market fundamentalism catapults the antagonisms of the epoch of imperialism to a higher level. Its resolution requires the solution – both conscious and proceeding from the interests of the socium in general (meaning both nature and humanity as a generic essence) – of a complex of global problems that have grown substantially deeper since the beginning of the century. The second element of the contradiction is the fact that this system as a whole is able, at best, merely to stave off the problems for a time, while exacerbating them in the long term.

No less profound are the contradictions between the market on one hand and the emerging creatosphere on the other.

## The market of simulacra

The previous section of this chapter ended by concluding that the contemporary system of relations of commodity production, distribution, exchange, and consumption, along with the market that represents it at the level of surface phenomena, has changed substantially in comparison to the model described in the works of classical and neoclassical economic theoreticians of the nineteenth and twentieth centuries. These changes led to the development first of a market totalitarianism, and second of local manipulation of distinct segments of market space-time by large aggregations of corporate capital ('the spiders'), creating 'fields of dependency' ('spiders' webs').

These, however, are not the only changes the system of market relations has undergone. The commodity, which from the point of view of Marxist methodology is the initial category in the capitalist system of production relations, is simultaneously also the result of the reproduction of all the relations of capitalism, taken as a unified system. Under the conditions of late capitalism, commodity relations and the market that represents their forms are also products of the functioning of the system as a whole. As a result, the market under the conditions of late capitalism is:

- a form of the interaction of producers whose labour is increasingly of a creative nature;
- a form assumed by commodity relations in a world that includes not just material products and utilitarian services (services that satisfy material needs of the human individual and society), but also virtual phenomena;
- a product of manipulative influences exercised by the 'spiders', which artificially create demand for the various products, material and virtual, sold on the market;
- a socio-economic space that, as a result of financialisation, is fundamentally subject to the movement of financial capital of the twenty-first century, the specifics of which will be revealed in Chapter 7.

This market, however, has one more fundamentally significant characteristic that can be identified on the basis of a simple reference to the empirical evidence – the modern market for commodities and services. This analysis will show that the market is transforming itself (though this is not, and will never be, a completed process) not just into a total market, but into a *market of simulacra* (for a discussion of the socio-cultural aspects of the market of simulacra, and their economic bases, see Bulavka 2012a; 2012b). Here we focus chiefly on the economic aspects of the market of simulacra.

## Some preliminary remarks

Baudrillard pointed out long ago how:

> 'Commodity logic has become generalized and today governs not only labour processes and material products, but the whole of culture, sexuality, and human relations, including even fantasies and individual drives. Everything is taken over by that logic, not only in the sense that all functions and needs are objectivized and manipulated in terms of profit, but in the deeper sense in which everything is spectacularized or, in other words, evoked, provoked and orchestrated into images, signs, consumable models. (Baudrillard 1970/1998: 191)

It is clear in retrospect that he was expressing in his own fashion the idea of the birth of the totalitarian market of simulacra. Though written forty years ago, these words have become still more timely in the last few decades (these problems have not ceased to be important even now; see, for example, Hegarty 2004).

We emphasise that the term *'simulacrum'* is fundamental: it refers to the forms that the operation of capitalism creates when it operates in the space of artificially created forms, oriented from the very outset towards the simulation of reality, and not to its accurate depiction or (re)production. As noted by the evolutionary biologist Thomas S. Ray, for example, the simulacrum creates artificial life (AL), which is indistinguishable from life. Stuart notes how Ray:

> twists this paradoxical science still further, stating, at this new discipline's fourth international conference in 1994, that the life processes studied in AL are not themselves artificial but natural, the resultant life-forms merely 'live' in an artificial environment. Thus AL naturalizes the artificial, making simulacra of life indistinguishable from their real-life counterparts. (Stuart 2001: 74)

As Ray himself states:

> Whether we consider a system living because it exhibits some property that is unique to life amounts to a semantic issue. What is more important is that we recognize that it is possible to create disembodied but genuine instances of specific properties of life in artificial systems. This capability is a powerful research tool. By separating the property of life that we choose to study from the many other complexities of natural living systems, we make it easier to manipulate and observe the property of interest. The objective of the approach advocated in this paper is to capture genuine evolution in an artificial system. (Ray 1994: 181)

But let us take everything in due order. We shall begin with a typical example of a simulacrum commodity, a man's suit with a famous brand name on its label – in this case, a suit that is made of Chinese cloth in a Chinese or

Russian garment factory may have a cost price of $50 at most. But once the necessary label is sewn onto the lining and the suit goes on sale in a prestigious boutique, it acquires a price perhaps a hundred times greater – let us say, $5,000. For a suit 'by the fashion house NN' this is quite unremarkable. What is being sold in this case – a use value? Even if we assume that a suit from the house of NN is tailored with special care and that the cloth is especially good (which is also far from being invariably true), the real quality of the actual commodity bears no relation to the price of $5,000. A higher-quality suit might be worth two or three times as much as the cheap one, but not a hundred times as much. The reason why a customer buys such as suit for so elevated a price is not the quality of the stitching or the long-wearing nature of the cloth. Such a suit is purchased because ... because it is a *symbolic* good,[4] indicating that its owner is wealthy and successful (or, to use the jargon of Russian simulacra, *krut* ('steep'), that is, 'cool'.

As a real example, let us take two not-especially-cheap pure wool men's suits: the Black Signature Italian Wool Suit (price £199)[5] and one of the Paul Costelloe Wool Three Piece Suits (from £149).[6] By contrast, the Vanquish II Bespoke suit sells for $100,000. Crafted in France by the Dormeuil family, the Vanquish II suit is made from qivuik (Alaskan down feathers) and vicuña fibre from South American camelids.[7] Undoubtedly, the fabrics used are some of the most expensive in the world, and the buttons are set with diamonds. The Kiton K-50, made from fine sheep's wool, is designed by the famous Enzo D'Orsi and sells for $60,000.[8] On a more modest level, the Ermenegildo Zegna Bespoke has a price tag of $22,000–$28,000.[9] To be sure, the quality of these three expensive suits is very, very high. But who is prepared to insist that their quality is as high as their prices?

The same can be said of typical mass-produced automobiles and those of the prestige class. The attributes of two automobiles are compared in Table 1. The characteristics of the Rolls-Royce thus surpass those of the Volkswagen Polo at most by a factor of four or five (and in terms of fuel economy the Rolls-Royce is more than three times worse). Of course, the Rolls-Royce comes packed with all sorts of accessories, meant to ensure the highest level of comfort. However, one is more than seventy times the price of the other! An analogous difference can be seen in the price of a room in a three-star hotel – depending on the country and other circumstances it might vary approximately from $100 to $200 per night – and that of an exclusive suite, whose price per night might reach tens of thousands of dollars. One of the factors that cause this gap is the growth in income inequality over recent decades, as will be discussed in detail in subsequent chapters. Here we find the very same set of transformations that we described earlier using the language of postmodernist methodology. The first step

**Table 1** Comparison between prices and characteristics of the 2020 Volkswagen
Polo Origin and the Rolls-Royce Phantom VIII

| Characteristic | VW Polo Origin | Rolls-Royce Phantom VIII | Relationship (Polo = 100%) |
|---|---|---|---|
| Engine displacement (cc) | 1,598 | 6,750 | 422% |
| Maximum horsepower | 90 | 571 | 512% |
| Number of cylinders | 4 | 12 | 300% |
| Length (mm) | 4,483 | 5,982 | 133% |
| Width (mm) | 1,706 | 2,018 | 118% |
| Height (mm) | 1,484 | 1,656 | 114% |
| Volume of fuel tank (litres) | 55 | 100 | 182% |
| Time to 100 km/h (seconds) | 11.4 | 5.4 | 47,4% |
| Fuel consumption, mixed driving (litres/100 km) | 6.4 | 20,3 | 317% |
| Fuel consumption, highway (litres/100 km | 5.2 | 13,2 | 254% |
| Fuel consumption, city driving (litres/100 km) | 8.4 | 29,1 | 346% |
| Maximum speed (km/h) | 184 | 250 | 136% |
| **Price (rubles)** | 772,900 | 55,000,000 | 7,116% |

Sources: Rolls Royce Phantom VIII: https://rolls-royce-avilon.ru/availability/rolls-royce-phantom-viii-black/; Volkswagen Polo Origin: https://autospot.ru/brands/volkswagen/polo/liftback/spec/?utm_source=google&utm_medium=cpc&utm_campaign=aspot_arwm_ga_s_msk_dsa_all&utm_term=volkswagen&utm_content=astat:dsa-1252252259277|ret:dsa-1252252259277|cid:12571095599|gid:120074563352|aid:507413967037|pos:|st:|src:|d vc:|creg:9047022&gclid=CjwKCAjw7J6EBhBDEiwA5UUM2n28f9juNVSXqOBLpubau N9jNqmKYbMQE6AStO2Uclmio119RLS0WBoC44AQAvD_BwE

involves the use value of the material good (the suit) being deconstructed and transformed into a 'text'; from being an item of apparel, the suit turns into a *sign* of prosperity. This suit-as-text is then replaced by a 'context' – the label of a particular firm. In the third step, the label 'works' only within a certain discourse, involving its purchase in a boutique and use within the corresponding milieu.

In any case, the creation of a context (the 'brand') and of the related simulacra also requires enormous efforts. But the vital questions are: efforts of what kind? By whom are they exerted, and to what purpose? Here we find the sources of the political economy of the market of simulacra (s-market) in which simulacrum commodities (or s-commodities) are bought and sold

– or, as Jean Baudrillard termed it, of the political economy of the sign (Baudrillard 1981).

Another name for what Baudrillard designated the 'political economy of the sign' is the concept of post-classical political economy proposed by Mikhail Voeikov, who described the object of his study as follows:

> A new class of problems appears on the border of the market and the non-market (quasi-market), research and reflection of which can constitute a new problem field of the actual political economic research. This means that the problematic field of political economic research is changing. ... The selection and study of this range of problems, it seems, may be a new task of post-classical political economy. (Voeikov 2014: 124)

And further,

> Today there appears a new problem field of political economy on the border of the market and non-market. There are two lines. The first is that there are processes, relations, and benefits that by their nature do not have a market character, but because of the universality of the monetary economy, they receive a monetary equivalent and appear as a result of reification. That is, the non-market good begins to function as a market commodity. In other words, use value does not come through exchange, but directly becomes the subject of political economy (J. Baudrillard) or self-represented things become wealth (M. Foucault). The other line is the reverse. Many market products (commodities), due to social restrictions and other reasons, cease to be commodities and fall out of normal market functioning. For example, public goods, for which a 'quasi-market' is being created. All this is the subject of political economy, but different from the classical and better termed *post-classical* (Voeikov, 2014: 120)

Before proceeding to an initial systematisation of the world of s-commodities, we should note that almost any simulacrum in the world of the economy is to a certain degree *also* a real good, satisfying a genuine need. A designer suit is, as a rule, somewhat better than a suit bought in a cheap clothing store, while a Mercedes surpasses, in its reliability and driving qualities, most cars that lack such a high-powered brand name. In other words, when we speak of the s-market we should always bear in mind that it is no more (though also no less) than a particular modification of the 'normal' market. The whole question, however, is one of *degree*.

It is this empirically described degree (on the difference in content between s-commodities and 'ordinary' commodities, see below) that is fundamental to an initial, preliminary classification of the phenomena of the s-market. The type of commodity in the market of simulacra is the 'ordinary' commodity transformed into symbols and thus is assigned a price substantially greater than that of its analogues. An example is the designer suit that costs dozens of times more than one that has analogous qualities in terms of its use but that lacks the vital label. In this case, the price difference serves as an indirect quantitative indicator of the degree of simulativity of a certain commodity or of a whole segment of the market. This type of commodity does not just include 'brand-name' goods: any product that is accorded a higher price than its analogues through acquiring some simulative and/or 'sign' quality, all the phenomena in the field of so-called 'prestige consumption', from fashionable restaurants and clubs to particular lifestyles, is included in this type.

Markets of this type also give rise to the phenomenon of the 'person-brand'. This refers to the shaping of certain individuals as a simulacrum of a particular lifestyle and is the result of the objective working of the system of relations described above and the deliberate actions of the creators of brands. As a rule, it is one or another variety of the glamour through which the shaping of an image of various corporations is concealed behind a simulacrum of art, an individual artist. The result is the creation of a person-simulacrum (an s-person), who in turn creates an epidemic of simulative-imitative behaviour.

A second category of s-commodities consists of purely symbolic phenomena that lack 'ordinary' use value. The most typical examples are to be found in the stream of simulacra that issue from the mass media, and in other products of mass culture that are without real cultural value (that is, that do not help to elevate the qualities of human beings) but have a very high symbolic value, again created through specific methods (from 'everyday' advertising to the special mechanisms through which pop-stars are promoted). These symbolic s-commodities also include the numerous artificially created symbolic areas of leisure. While such commodities and services have a certain real use value (for example, an ability to divert people from mind-numbing everyday work and from the narrow bounds of a commonplace existence), on the s-market they acquire (or have imputed to them) a quite different symbolic, simulative value.

A third sub-category consists of virtual s-commodities. Especially typical examples are the commodities found in the markets that arise from modern-day trends in the evolution of fictitious capital and from the widening gap that separates it from the real world. Here, above all, are to be found the simulacra created by the process of financialisation occurring in the sphere of what we call virtual fictitious capital (the 'content' of artificially inflated financial bubbles, consisting of derivatives and other financial 'products'), which has become so important under the conditions of modern 'casino capitalism' (a more detailed treatment of this topic may be found in Chapters 7 and 9). A further example of virtual s-commodities is the whole range of goods and services of virtual consumption, from inane computer games to the habit of mindless, pointless web-surfing.

Here would also remind the reader of what Marx understood by fictitious capital, which had already developed in the capitalism of his day:

> In so far as the Bank issues notes which are not covered by the bullion reserve in its vaults, it creates symbols of value that constitute for it not only circulating medium, but also additional – even if fictitious – capital to the nominal amount of these unbacked notes. And this additional capital yields additional profit. (Marx 1894/1998: 538)

> The reserve funds of the banks, in countries with developed capitalist production, always express on the average the quantity of money existing in the form of a hoard, and a portion of this hoard in turn consists of paper, mere drafts upon gold, which have no value in themselves. The greater portion of banker's capital is, therefore, purely fictitious and consists of claims (bills of exchange), government securities (which represent spent capital), and stocks (drafts on future revenue). And it should not be forgotten that the money value of the capital represented by this paper in the safes of the banker is itself fictitious, in so far as the paper consists of drafts on guaranteed revenue (e.g., government securities), or titles of ownership to real capital (e.g., stocks), and that this value is regulated differently from that of the real capital, which the paper represents at least in part; or, when it represents mere claims on revenue and no capital, the claim on the same revenue is expressed in continually changing fictitious money capital. (Marx 1894/1998: 469)

As for fictitious capital, we will not dwell on this now, since this is the subject of the next chapter of the book.

### Markets of simulacra: their possibility and inevitability

A politico-economic study of the s-market requires, as a first step, an examination of the possibility of, and necessity for, its development on a mass scale. As we indicated earlier, the progress of technology and capital has brought about conditions in which the rise of just such a market has become possible and inevitable. We shall now turn these general positions into a system of arguments.

The *material preconditions* for the formation of markets for simulacra are provided by technological processes of two kinds. First, the development of technology, increases in productivity, and the growth of the creative component of labour have reached the point at which mass production of s–commodities, oriented towards broad layers of society, has become possible. It was only during the second half of the twentieth century that it became possible to mass-produce 'brand' commodities, aimed at both the so-called middle and upper-middle classes that had sharply increased their numbers, and broader layers in the form of phenomena of mass culture oriented towards youth in both 'first' and 'third' worlds, not excluding the post-Soviet space; and it was just a few decades ago that technological progress and growing productivity brought about a substantial increase in the number of people who were involved at least partially in creative activity and thus able to establish the preconditions for turning goods and services into simulacra. The appearance of tens of millions of workers in advertising and public relations agencies, of market analysts and image-makers, required material preconditions that humanity created relatively recently, and only for a certain (minority) proportion of the population.

Another component in this process has been the search for pseudo-alternatives to mass production in the areas of so-called 'individualised' or 'customised' production, oriented to the supposedly special, individual consumer. (More than a few researchers of post-industrial society have taken the bait of the unfolding process of individualisation that is supposedly replacing the epoch of mass production; in Russia, this thesis has been developed especially by Vladislav Inozemtsev (1999: 57).) This fundamentally rational trend also took on a simulative colouring when the field of s-individualised services began to develop again on a mass scale (here is a paradox!), and millions of beauticians and image-makers began mass-producing simulacra of individuality for millions of representatives of the upper middle class.

Secondly, the technological preconditions for the mass development of s-markets unquestionably include the development and universal spread of computer technologies and the internet. It was these that created the indispensable preconditions for the development of markets of virtual simulacra (s-markets of a third type), and it is these markets that are growing most rapidly of all in current conditions.

The creation of s-commodities for hundreds of millions (and in the case of mass culture, billions) of consumers thus required preconditions different from those created within the framework of capitalism of the first half of the twentieth century. These latter were based on mass industrial production, creating real use values for the consumer society that was formed at that time. The era of computers, the internet, etc., which came to replace them, created a global virtual space and preconditions for the formation of the market of s-commodities on the mass scale. The society of mass consumption of 'ordinary' goods, real use values on a mass scale, continued alongside.

The necessity for the genesis of markets of simulacra on such a massive scale is connected with the specific contradictions of the process of capital accumulation that have characterised the second half of the twentieth century and the early decades of the twenty-first. While our previous publications have gone into these contradictions in detail, we confine ourselves to saying here that the essence of the contradictions lies in the fact that the limits to the progress of capital accumulation in the real sector of the economy have been reached. These limits, which relate to the impossibility of endless investment in real production (that is, the production of goods and services essential for the advance of the productive forces and, above all, of human beings themselves), while maintaining the rate of profit without diminution, were reached for the first time by developed countries on the eve of the Great Depression. It was then that capital encountered the problem that the further progress of real production would bring about a lowering of the rate of profit, resulting in general stagnation for the first time on a grand scale. A way out was found through various means of altering the 'rules of the game'. The possible solutions to the problem that were tested ranged from neocolonialism and fascism on the one hand to the development of forms of social restriction and regulation of the capitalist system on the other. It is noteworthy that the policy of implementing these decisions has been reproduced in the twenty-first century. In the case of social-democratic reforms, the limits imposed by over-accumulation were surmounted by shifting a third to a half of the economy away from the power of the market and towards socialised consumption, to the advantage of society. This redistributed between a third and a half of the profits obtained by capital.

In switching to a fascist model (the threat of which persists to this day), late capitalism found a 'solution' in expanding and at the same time masking capitalist exploitation through total control by the ruling elite, exercised by subordinating the entire population to the apparatus of the corporate state. This unification saw the corporate state counterpose 'its' national population to all others, using the population as a tool of foreign expansion. (It should be said that in the first case too, state leaders did not scorn foreign expansion, as was confirmed during the middle decades of the twentieth century by the deaths of tens of millions of people in Africa and Indochina.)

However, both variants were eventually exhausted. From here on, the potential for a major expansion of the capital of the 'core' of the world capitalist system through 'globalisation' could not be realised without creating adequate global tools of socio-economic domination and subordination. Without them, the possibilities of resolving the problems of over-accumulation of capital within the real sector of the economy could not be realised. Capital then took the path of creating simulative commodities, for which the previous growth of labour productivity in the real sector had established sufficient preconditions. Also impelling capital along this path were the limits of the system of mass production, which, by the late twentieth century, had also exhausted its potential for progressive development. The limits to accumulation by global corporate capital thus created the need to produce simulative commodities, that is, offerings on markets of simulacra.

A similar impetus towards markets of simulacra also appeared on the demand side, where consumer society ran up against the limits to growth in the volume and variety of potential utilitarian goods and services in the real sector. Market agents belonging to various income groups are limited in their utilitarian consumption. A middle-class family will not buy three refrigerators and four economy-class cars, while the number of cheap dresses and suits needed by such a family is relatively limited, as is its need for real utilitarian goods in general. Meanwhile, the members of this class, in their overwhelming majority, cannot escape from the framework of their income group. Further, late capitalism as a result of its shift to a neoliberal model of evolution (a topic examined in Chapter 8 below) has created a tendency for the numbers of the middle class to contract. As noted, these limitations have been circumvented through the formation of a new class of needs: simulative or s-needs. These latter have appeared in extremely opportune fashion, since they have permitted the formation of new markets on the basis of goods whose costs of production are relatively low in comparison to the prices that can be charged for them. This has allowed the creation of a market for s–commodities, primarily virtual ones, for the mass consumer, including even the poor (Bodrunov, 2018).

S-needs have begun taking shape for the 'upper middle' class, for the bourgeoisie, and for the topmost strata of global capital, with systems of artificial signs denoting membership in one or another layer of the 'elite'. Most significant, from the economic point of view, has been the formation of a demand from capital for simulative means of development, above all for various simulacra of money and other investment resources. This has been a consequence of the increasingly severe limits on the expansion of capital that have resulted from over-accumulation.

Another group that has come into existence is a specific s-elite, for the most part formed semi-spontaneously by corporate capital and made up of the top layers of figures from mass culture and professional sport, together with professionals from finance, advertising, and similar businesses – that is, the peak groups from the fields in which simulacra of various types are created, advertised, and sold. This is accurately presented as a *faux* elite; it does not exercise real economic or political power, and largely represents a function of the operations of media, financial, and other corporations. Members of this elite are *obliged* to lead a demonstratively luxurious lifestyle, simulating their select status and parading their consumption above all of simulative goods, of conspicuously expensive brands and so forth.

We thus find the possibility and necessity of simulative production combined into a single process, satisfying simulative needs and hence also creating s-supply in response to the appearance of s-demand. The emergence of this new reality also conditions the most important features of the s-market.

### *The political economy of the simulacrum commodity*

While this sub-heading recalls Baudrillard, we present a theoretical hypothesis substantially different from that of the well-known French postmodernist.

Baudrillard was correct in his characterisation of the dawning epoch of postmodernism (a symbol of which in Western Europe was the defeat of the Parisian May and Prague Spring of 1968) as ushering in the further development of hyper-realism, leading to the replacement of real content and meaning by simulacra and signs. We, however, do not share Baudrillard's idea that the world of simulacra of his time grew out of the symbolic exchange found in pre-bourgeois societies, or his view that Marx was wrong in characterising capitalism as a sphere of the real material production of actual goods. In our view, Baudrillard and his left postmodernist comrades (Deleuze, Foucault) were the butt of a malicious joke in that they honestly considered the world of simulacra they inhabited to be, for practical purposes, the only *real* world. Baudrillard failed to note (or perhaps did not understand or know) the difference between perverse form and real content. (Recall that, as Marx so often noted, a perverse form arises when, in the realm of appearances as distinct from essences or realities, the surface of social life is covered with illusory phenomena that distort the actual content of real processes.) As a result, Baudrillard failed to convey the dialectic of the steadily advancing development of simulacra as perverse forms of the involution of material production under late capitalism.

Meanwhile, in conditions of late capitalism it appears that simulacra are coming to replace material production. This appearance is real, but it is the reality of a perverse form, not of content. Hence the stress on simulacra is proof not of errors on the part of Marx, but of the correctness of his methodology, which always maintained that Marxist theory needed to develop critically as practice changed. This is why it is only Marx's historico-dialectical view of capitalism that makes it possible to show how, why, and to what degree capitalism at a particular stage of its development, while basing itself on real material production, is transformed into a system for the production and consumption of simulacra that lie 'on the other side' of the real.

Let us examine these complex relationships in further detail. We proceed from the *hypothesis* that the s-commodity is a perverse form of the commodity as the initial and universal form of the capitalist world or of the so-called 'market economy'. The basis for this assertion is the nature of the simulacrum. In theoretical terms, the relationship should appear thus: if the s-commodity is a perverse form, it should present the appearance of a certain use and exchange value, but beneath this appearance should lie a different essence. If we succeed in substantially demonstrating these propositions, then our hypothesis will have been proved (to a lesser degree, within the framework of the Marxist paradigm).

The use value of an s-commodity should consist in the usefulness of the particular commodity to the consumer. In what exactly does this usefulness lie? In the satisfaction of some need that aids the development of production or of human qualities? No, in this case we would be dealing with an 'ordinary' commodity. The usefulness of an s-commodity lies in the satisfying of a simulative need – in this case artificially created and serving to dull the perceptions of the user. If, on the other hand, the need is 'natural', and not 'induced', then the good that satisfies it is an ordinary commodity, and not a simulacrum: such is the definition of a simulacrum under the original 'rules of the game'. The question therefore arises: how or by whom is this 'induced', artificial need created, and in what does its artificiality consist?

The answer to the last question has been provided earlier: the need is artificial to the degree to which it is not linked to the development of the human individual and to her or his productive strengths. The answer to the first question is more complex. Abstractly put, s-needs are created by the special conditions of life and/or by the conscious activity of certain subjects that created them. Let us consider further what conditions and what kind of activity are involved.

Let us begin at the end, since in this case the search for an answer is simpler and will help us to understand the beginning. Examples of the forming of artificial needs for simulative goods, or simulacra, are well known; for the most part they involve marketing activity and, above all, the advertising of goods and services that are largely useless (let us recall that we are not discussing advertising in general here, but the advertising of s-commodities, that is, of simulacra). When someone tries to persuade you to drink Coca-Cola so as to have things 'go better', you are being told to drink a weak solution of orthophosphoric acid, saturated with carbon dioxide and coloured with burnt sugar or a substitute for it; you are having imposed on you an artificial need for a drink that is, if not harmful, one that does you little good. This is an example of a conscious attempt to create an 'induced' need, and it is typical for such attempts to be associated with perverse forms.

In this case we are talking about simulacra of the first type – about a certain 'supplementing', using a simulative component, of a product that is useful in some way; ultimately, Coca-Cola is capable of satisfying thirst, though this is better done with the traditional Russian *kvas*, or simply with water. The same applies in the case of the sale, for a fabulously high price, of a suit with a prestige label; here, something that in principle is useful is given a simulative component.

In cases such as these, the use value of the s-commodity is not its ability to quench your thirst or cover your body, but the fact that you do this with the help of a commodity that bears a prestige brand. This prestige is created by the marketing and other activity of corporate capital, aimed at summoning up a 'field of dependency', and the examples we have cited above illustrate the use value of such s-commodities.

Properly speaking, simulacra in their purest form are produced when capital creates the need for a good or service that in itself has no use value (i.e. that does not satisfy any real need, being neither useful nor even harmful to the consumer). In such a case, the use value exists only in the imagination, as a sign, ideally of a symbolic nature. Here the use value of the s-commodity also consists in the ability to satisfy an s-need, artificially created through the deliberate activity of corporate capital in devising a field of dependency. In both cases the use value of Coca-Cola or of a pop-song as s-commodities is not created in the bottling plant that produces a surfeit of this drink or in the studio where video clips are scripted and filmed, but in the marketing and other activity of corporate capital that aims at the artificial formation of s-needs, so that people will want to drinkCoca-Cola rather than *kvas*, mineral water, etc.

Once again, we shall add a qualification: from the point of view of neoclassical economic theory and postmodernist philosophy, nothing of what we have said above makes any sense, since within the frameworks of their 'discourses', the criterion determining the usefulness of a private good is whether or not people pay money for it in the market-place. In the 'grand narrative' known as Marxist political economy, however, such a distinction is indeed made, and this distinction is important for everyone who thinks it is time that production began to develop the human qualities and productive forces of society, and not just anything whatsoever that brings in a profit. Within the framework of our theory, therefore, it is possible to distinguish the specific use value of the simulacrum, a value that at the surface level consists in the ability of phenomena to satisfy simulative needs. However, this, we repeat, is a perverse form. Rather than beginning to analyse its content, we should stress that s-needs are formed under the conditions of modern-day late capitalism not only through the purposeful activity of some particular bloc of corporate capital, but also through the objectively established way of life, which is created by the totality of the market (the ideological reflection of which is market fundamentalism). Market fundamentalism becomes an ineluctable rule of life with everything created by corporate capital, penetrating all the pores of human life including personal values and interpersonal relations as well as the fields of culture and morals. In this way, the system of the objective formation of s-needs is established not just as the product of deliberate activity by specific subjects (particular corporations), but also as part of a way of life objectively formed and reproduced by the total hegemony of capital.

Unlike that of the perverse forms described earlier, the content of the use value of s-commodities, a content shaped by the imposition on society of the s-needs and the general objective atmosphere corresponding to this imposition, is not directed towards satisfying people's needs, pointless and artificial though these might be. The real usefulness of the s-commodities produced by corporate capital, the content of their use value, lies in the fact that these commodities make it possible to remove the limits imposed by over-accumulation in the real sector of capital, and to receive average and even above-average profit rates under conditions in which the objective boundaries of the real sector no longer permit such an outcome. A less striking but no less significant example has been the production of simulative demand for the endlessly renewed repertoire of useless mass-culture phenomena and virtual 'games'.

As we have indicated, the special content possessed by the use value of s-commodities (that is, their ability to (partly) remove the limits to the over-accumulation of capital) is fundamentally different from the perverse form of their use value (their ability to satisfy artificially created needs). Indirect proof of this thesis is provided by modelling the situation in which society rejects modern capitalist organisation: in this situation, the products and services that allow human qualities and productive forces to develop are subject to no less demand than in the world of capitalism, while s-commodities lose their use value.

The exchange value of s-commodities – that is, the proportion in which they are exchanged for money or other commodities – is no less mysterious. If exchange occurs for money (and an s-commodity may in some cases itself be (quasi-)money), then we are faced with a problem which, at first glance, does not present difficulties with the price of the simulacrum. From the point of view of neoclassical theory there are not, indeed, any special features that distinguish s-commodities from others.

From the point of view of classical political economy, however, various subtleties come into play here. In the case of s-commodities, a more general problem which comes to the fore is the ability of large blocs of corporate capital, within certain limits (which are set by the power of the 'field of dependency' generated by a particular corporation, and by the presence of analogous fields of a certain potency generated by competitors), to exercise a deliberate local influence on the parameters of the market, and in particular on prices. The price of an s-commodity in most cases is not simply the price on an oligopolised market, but the price set by corporate capital, as a rule consciously. We shall note in passing that the indirect (market) quantitative assessment of the power of the 'field of dependency' generated by corporate capital is provided by what neoclassical economics terms the 'value of non-material assets'. The only problems here result from the 'nuance' represented by capitalisation of the intellectual rent appropriated by the given capital. We will discuss this fully in Chapter 8. Here we will confine ourselves to saying that notionally, this should be deducted from the value of the non-material assets, in order to take at least indirect account of the impact of local corporate influence on the market. As noted earlier, however, this property of prices is not only characteristic of simulacra: it is common to all commodities produced and sold by corporate capital in the modern market of 'spiders' and 'spiders' webs'. The point is simply that it manifests itself most clearly of all in the case of s-commodities.

A far greater complication is presented by a purely Marxist question: if the price of an s-commodity, like that of anything else, is the (monetary) form of value, then what does its value represent? And is the price of an s-commodity not a perverse form? Since, according to Marxist theory, the substance of a commodity's value is the abstract social labour embodied in it, the question presents itself: what labour is embodied in the value of an s-commodity if it has value at all?

On the basis of the characteristics of the s-commodity noted above, we may surmise that the substance of its value *cannot* be the labour expended in producing its 'material bearer'. Thus in the case of Coca-Cola the high price of this commodity is not determined by the costs of producing the solution of orthophosphoric acid, but by the presence of a particular brand. In the case of a forgettable pop-song, the effort invested in composing it creates no value whatever, since the song in itself, without promotion, is not a useful good. No one will either sing it or listen to it.

It may be supposed that the sum of all the activities involved in creating a simulacrum represents work underlying the value of an s-commodity. In the case of a brand, this is the work expended on conceiving, registering, and promoting it and so forth. It excludes the labour that genuinely produced the 'material bearer', which is devoted to bringing an 'ordinary' commodity, the 'bearer' of a brand, to practical fruition, and includes categories such as artwork. To distinguish this object of our analysis from 'normal' labour, we shall describe this 'non-normal' labour as the activity involved in creating a *simulative envelope*, or s-envelope.

Although we have assigned it a name, the problem is by no means solved. And on the way to solving it, more than a few difficulties lie in wait for us. From the point of view of Marxist theory, the labour expended on creating an s-envelope is unproductive, and thus cannot create *value*. Indeed, it constitutes a cost. Meanwhile, the costs of creating this envelope do not by any means always lead to the creation of an expensive brand. Unlike the case with a normal commodity, the question of the additional revenue received from an s-envelope is decided less on the basis of expenditures and quality than by the strength of corporate pressure on the market. So if the 'field of dependency' generated by the corporation by means of marketing, public relations campaigns, and other actions (as already mentioned, this is called 'market power' in neoclassical economics, and 'negotiating power' in institutionalism) is sufficiently powerful, then the corporation will succeed in imposing this product on the consumer at a price significantly higher than the total production costs and the average profit of a given quality product, and realise it on a scale far exceeding the real needs. Moreover, it can be argued that the difference in price and volume of sales of s-commodities in comparison with conventional commodities of this quality can serve as one of the indirect quantitative market indicators of this power.

Consequently, unlike the labour devoted to creating the 'material body' of an s-commodity, which creates value, the work that goes into devising its s-envelope does not create value. This conclusion corresponds to the previous thesis outlined above concerning the perverse form of the use value of an s-commodity. The form in this case gives the impression that we are dealing with a good that satisfies an actually existing (even if artificially created) need of a market agent who is exercising demand. Further, this need seems to conceal, in the quality of its content, an actual usefulness of the s-commodity, consisting in its (partial) ability to do away with the limitations imposed by the over-accumulation of capital. As explained in a commentary by Gerry Coulter, Baudrillard points out that:

> Marx was focused on 'classical' value – the more natural stage of use-value and the commodity stage of exchange value. Today value has passed through a structural stage (sign value), and is entering a fractal stage – a point of no reference at all 'where value radiates in all directions'. As he told Philippe Petit: 'we lost use-value, then good old exchange value, obliterated by speculation, and we are currently losing even sign value for an indefinite signaletics'. Baudrillard also pointed out (against Marx's expectations), that 'capital has not lurched from one crisis to another. (Coulter 2017: 23)

Interwoven here, as can be seen, are:

(1) a correct understanding by Baudrillard of the fact that a simulacrum has no value;
(2) an absolutely dogmatic interpretation of Marxism (according to Baudrillard, to be a Marxist means to repeat uncritically, 150 later, what Marx wrote; Marx would turn in his grave at such an interpretation);
(3) an obvious exaggeration of 'the effacing and loss even of sign value, which is being replaced by an indefinite signaletics' (even forty years later, the market of simulacra remains merely a superstructure above the market of things, while the effacing of signs by 'indefinite signaletics' is a clear exaggeration); and
(4) the idea, now obviously mistaken but extremely widespread in the last third of the twentieth century, that capitalism has saved itself forever from crises.

Where the price of an s-commodity is concerned, we have done our best to validate the conclusion that this is a perverse form which creates the appearance of a high value for a given phenomenon. However, it also conceals the actual content – that is, the deliberate formation of a special simulative environment, carried out through non-market methods of conscious influence on people, society, and the economy. According to the criteria of market production, this process of formation is artificial. The substance of the price of an s-commodity is *not value* – that is, the reified abstract social labour of a distinct producer – but manipulative influence on the producer and consumer, consciously devised by the subject of this influence and taking shape objectively under the conditions of market totalitarianism. Here we again are talking about the 'field of dependency' created by a corporation. This field, like a magnetic field, acts on the content, structure, and volume of the requirements of those who consume the products of a particular corporation; on the technologies employed by the corporation's suppliers (and again, by its customers); on the production programmes of those who cooperate with the corporation; on the strategies of development of formations that come under its influence; on the dynamics, volumes, and structures of purchases and sales; and so forth. This amounts to a sort of 'social hypnosis' that forces people and/or firms to expend more and more effort in earning money for the ever-greater satisfaction of ever-new needs for things that are unnecessary to them, in order to aid the (private) removal of the limitations on over-accumulation that afflict modern corporate capital.

We may sum up our position by stating that markets of simulacra are characterised by substantially non-productive and non-commodity relations that involve the conscious formation of the bases for the prices of s-commodities. The first element in this situation – a situation that is untypical of capitalism – is fully reflected both in neoclassical economic theory and in postmodernism. Neoclassical economics, seemingly at least, can celebrate a victory in this case: the most modern markets have taken leave of the labour substance of values and prices. Postmodernism can also rejoice: after forty years, Marxist politico-economic analysis has confirmed the conclusions of Baudrillard, who in his day (especially in his book *The Mirror of Production*, 1975) stressed the fundamentally non-productive substance of s-commodity, drawing the conclusion that virtually all of political economy was incorrect. Not by chance, Baudrillard tied markets of simulacra to the questions of symbolic exchange. Here almost the last remaining bastion of reality is death, on the fear of which the whole of the economy and politics is constructed.

We would repeat that the stress we have placed here on the non-productive nature of the simulative market world is completely justified. Meanwhile, both neoclassicists and the majority of postmodernists, remaining captive to the market-centric world,[10] fail to 'notice' that in the case of s-commodities, satisfying simulative needs, the market itself becomes a simulation of commodity relations.[11] In this market, simulacra are bought and sold whose use value and exchange value (price) are perverse forms of a non-commodity content. Moreover, in s-markets social and economic relationships themselves, the ways in which they function and their institutions (the 'rules of the game') have only the appearance of more or less free competitive market interaction. In reality they are basied on competitive interactions of the manipulative influences of corporate capital, creating a mind-dulling fog of artificial needs, satisfied by simulative goods.

In the next chapter, we will present our understanding of the other major new feature of late capitalism, the emergence of virtual fictitious capital in capitalist money relations.

## Notes

1 The main sources on which this chapter is based, and in relation to which we propose qualitatively new solutions, include works by Baudrillard (1981, 1994, 1970/1998), Bulavka (2012a, 2012b), Castells (1996), Deleuze (1994), Inozemtsev (1999). Klein (1999), and Mulgan (1991).

2 Data provided by 'Korporatsii, kotorye pravyat mirom' [Corporations that rule the world], 15 August 2011, https://rb.ru/article/korporatsii-kotorye-pravyat-mirom/6756067.html (accessed 20 November 2019).

3 Ibid.

4 Baudrillard has a wonderful passage on this topic: 'It is important to grasp that … this pursuit of status and social standing, are all based on signs. That is to say, they are based not on objects or goods as such, but on differences.' He goes on to show that in its form such a sign may be a deliberately, simulatively 'simple' commodity: 'Ladies, come to X for the most windswept look you can find!' (Baudrillard 1970/1998: 90–1).

5 www.next.co.uk/shop/gender-men-productaffiliation-suits/designfeature-signature#1_0 (accessed 30 April 2021).

6 https://milled.com/austin-reed-us/paul-costelloe-suits-now-from-149-premium-wool-three-piece-suits-y2pVqfLISSy_Qx4P (accessed 30 April 2021).

7 www.luxhabitat.ae/the-journal/top-10-most-expensive-suits-in-the-world/; https://moneyinc.com/most-expensive-ermenegildo-zegna-suits/ (both accessed 27 April 2021).

8 Ibid.

9 https://moneyinc.com/most-expensive-ermenegildo-zegna-suits/ (accessed 27 April 2021).

10 For our analysis and critique of the 'market-centricity' of modern mainstream economic theory see the Postscript of this book.

11 This needs explanations and illustrations showing what this market looks like and how it differs from other types of market, but we will leave this task for our future research.

# 7

# Money in the twenty-first century: financialisation as a product of virtual fictitious financial capital

Shifts in productive forces have imparted a qualitatively new character to the capitalist economy in the twenty-first century.[1] The changes in the nature of commodities and the market have been discussed above; in this chapter, we will focus on the changes in the monetary and financial spheres. We will discuss the problem of transformation of the money under capitalism, from the form of credit money, serving the circulation of commodity capital, to money reflecting the prevalence of virtual capital. At the surface level, this transformation has revealed itself as financialisation. Financial capital, the result of the fusion of banking and industrial monopolies, used the financial market both as an instrument of its reign and, at the same time, as a mode of solving of the problem of over-accumulation of industrial capital. The bubble-like growth of the financial market reflects the need of financial capital to appropriate profit on a global scale through financial instruments. This hegemony of financial capital (which became transnational) is developing in spite of severe international competition and conflicts. As a result, while financial capital cannot control the world as whole, different groups of transnational financial capital can penetrate and dominate almost any section of world economy. Let us examine these processes in more detail.

## The phenomenology of modern money: financialisation and other things

As modern corporate capital develops the total corporate-network market as the general form necessary for its hegemony, it also creates the mechanisms required for this purpose. Money and finance have evolved both alongside and on the basis of the evolution of the qualities of commodities and of the market. This evolution, it will be recalled, has passed through various historico-logical stages as follows.

At the start of its evolution, money, became differentiated from the world of commodities and became embodied in the natural form of gold and precious metals generally, as opposed to all other 'simple' commodities. In essence, however, its purpose was to present human relations as relations between things:

> But a particular commodity cannot become the universal equivalent except by a social act. The social action therefore of all other commodities, sets apart the particular commodity in which they all represent their values. Thereby the bodily form of this commodity becomes the form of the socially recognised universal equivalent. To be the universal equivalent, becomes, by this social process, the specific function of the commodity thus excluded by the rest. Thus it becomes – money. (Marx 1867/1996: 97)

Within the framework of the theoretical analysis of capitalism, this level of analysis corresponds to the abstraction represented by simple commodity production.

On the next level of historical development, and hence of its theoretical description, in spite of being the ideal representation of value of commodities, money began to represent the value of capital circulated and to serve this circulation. The development of various functional forms of capital, and above all of loan capital (banks, credit), resulted in a new transformation of money. From this point, money functioned as credit money, initially in parallel with the retention of the gold standard. The origins of paper money are to be found in credit: this form of money arose initially out of private promissory notes that served as instruments of commodity credit, later evolving into the promissory notes of banks and, later, of state treasuries and state banks. In this way, treasury bills and banknotes appeared: continuously circulating notes that at first could be exchanged for gold coins until this provision was abolished.

Under the conditions of imperialism as the first stage in the evolution of late capitalism in the late nineteenth and early twentieth centuries, monopolies came to exert a growing influence on market parameters and on the levels of prices, though changes in the properties of money were not yet apparent. These shifts started with the formation of finance capital. Our interpretation of financial capital is closer to Lenin's than to Hilferding's, and we use the term 'financial capital' to denote something distinct from Hilferding's concept of finance capital;[2] we respect its importance but consider Lenin's approach more accurate. Lenin characterised financial capital as an integration of productive and banking capital, which leads to the formation of a new quality, which we call, after Lenin, financial capital. A century after Lenin, the content of the category 'financial capital' can be defined as a merger of capital in finance with capital in production, leading to the dominance of financial capital over production capital and the dominance of financial goals over production.

This definition permits us, then, to launch our concept of virtual fictitious financial capital, the form that financial capital has taken in the twenty-first century. We will analyse this in more detail below, but here we will briefly note that virtual fictitious financial capital is the stage of development of financial capital at which fictitious capital, as the main form of financial capital, acquires a virtual character. The term 'virtual' in this case means an increased degree of separation of the movement of fictitious capital from the underlying real capital, in which the market valuation of a significant part of fictitious capital is more dependent on the manipulations of the largest capitals and states than on the movement of real capital.

For us the key question is not the question of whether finance or industry prevails. In spite of the interrelations between them, only industrial capital produces profit. Money capital can only claim a share of it. Finance capital, for us, is the new historical reality. Under it, the concentration of interest-bearing capital in banks has resulted in the formation of banking monopolies, and the concentration of industrial capital has resulted in the formation of industrial monopolies as well. The fusion of these monopolies – banking and industrial – gave them a new opportunity for control over the market and for the appropriation of profit. And – yes – the main instruments of this control and appropriation are the operations on the financial market, and, in this sense, financial capital prevails. Initially banking capital used control over the industry to promote industrial development and the corresponding growth of profit-making. Later, in the last third of the twentieth century, the financial market itself became the main field of profit-hunting as a dialectical unity of profit appropriation and profit redistribution.

The domination of financial capital made it possible to use the control over the financial market to increase financial instruments, thereby increasing the expansion of capital. This situation, however, was increasingly at odds with the narrow confines of a monetary system based on the gold standard, and in 1914 a period of fluctuations and degeneracy in the gold standard began, continuing for many decades.

The subsequent evolution of money is usually associated with the repudiation of the gold standard, but we would highlight a different parameter as the principal cause. With the transition to active regulation of the economy by society and the state in the developed countries since the mid-twentieth century, there has been an *undermining* of the objective bases of money as a commodity-universal equivalent. It is rooted in the limiting of the space for market competition and in the development of various norms and forms of association of workers and citizens as alternatives to the power of money. Ultimately, these led to the rejection of the gold standard and a definitive shift to a system in which the money supply is consciously regulated by the state, and reserve currencies, above all the dollar, became substitutes for money as the objective universal equivalent.

Throughout the period when the gold standard existed, the buying power of hard currency was tied closely to its gold content or, if we invert this relationship, to the 'price of gold'.[3] During this period, which lasted approximately from the seventeenth to nineteenth centuries, the 'price of gold' changed only slowly, fluctuating during these changes within a relatively narrow range.

As soon as the nexus between paper money and gold was broken, gold became an ordinary commodity (though a highly liquid one), and its price became subject to approximately the same laws as the prices of other goods. With the fall of the gold standard, the price of the metal began to grow by leaps and bounds. Since the 1970s, the dynamic of gold prices has approximately followed the general index of wholesale prices, while the buying power of gold has diverged sharply from the price of gold and from the dynamic of wholesale prices in general.

The shift to the 'dollar' standard (the Bretton Woods system) created still more powerful illusions to the effect that the whole 'secret' of money lay in its quantity. The quantitative theory of money had triumphed once more. Since that time, the attention of economists has been devoted largely to problems related to the quantity of money in circulation and to the resulting questions of inflation, currency issue, budget deficits, debts, exchange rates, the norms applying to reserves, and so forth.

Here, paradoxically, the triumph of monetarism during the last third of the twentieth century was a consequence of the undermining of the quality of money as a commodity-universal equivalent, and of its transformation into a product of conscious state regulation. In reality, the creation and circulation of money were always the subjects of state regulation to provide the balance between money and commodities in the national market. The new stage of money development was characterised by the transformation of this regulation into the one of instruments of coherent macro-economic regulation as the conscious impact on the overall process of reproduction of capital. The growth in the significance of the latter as the decisive factor in the stability of the market economy was also the main cause of the hyper-fixation of economists' attention on questions of monetary circulation.

This objective and subjective 'financial fetishism' was greatly strengthened by the growing might of financial capital, and its expansion in economic theory became a reflection of the dominance of financial processes in economic practice. The preconditions for financialisation had been established, but it was kept within bearable limits by still-powerful state regulation.

Paper money, having the nature of credit, thus ceased to be a real commodity-equivalent, distinguished from everything else in the commodity world. For that reason, it also ceased to be a representative of this *real* commodity-equivalent (the gold commodity). However, it did remain representative of an *ideal* commodity-equivalent, since the laws of monetary circulation, based on the movement of the commodity as a universal equivalent, also continued to apply in relation to paper money, which had no real connection with such a commodity. The ideal connection that is expressed in the law of circulation of money thus remained. Nevertheless, the development of fictitious capital and of the modern financial market, which was giving rise to virtual capital, was beginning to erode this connection as well. This, in brief, is the prehistory of modern money.

Today's situation, on which we will expand below, is marked by the formation of the power of financial capital, mostly in the form of fictitious capital, which is, moreover, largely transformed into virtual fictitious capital. The rise of virtual capital, and of the virtual money that services it, is the most recent stage in the evolution of the forms in which capital exists. The starting point for the formation of virtual capital is to be found in the differentiation of money capital as one of the functional forms of industrial capital, as it explained by Marx in volume III of *Capital*:

> The relations of capital assume their most external and most fetish-like form in interest-bearing capital. We have here M – M', money creating more money, self expanding value, without the process that mediates these two extremes. In merchant's capital, M – C – M', there is at least the general form of the capitalistic movement, although it confines itself solely to the sphere of circulation, so that profit appears merely as profit derived from alienation; but it is at least seen to be the product of a social relation, not the product of a mere thing. The form of merchant's capital at least presents a process, a unity of opposing phases, a movement that breaks up into two opposite actions — the purchase and the sale of commodities. This is obliterated in M – M', the form of interest-bearing capital. (Marx 1894/1998: 388–9)

As Marx explained, money capital became a commodity, interest-bearing capital (or loan capital), whose institutional envelope became the credit system (banks, investment companies, pension and insurance funds, and so forth):

> In this way, aside from its use value as money, it acquires an additional use value, namely that of serving as capital. Its use value then consists precisely in the profit it produces when converted into capital. In this capacity of potential capital, of a means of producing profit, it becomes a commodity, but a commodity *sui generis*. Or, what amounts to the same, capital as capital becomes a commodity. (Marx 1894/1998: 336–7)

The development of credit operations made possible the rise of fictitious capital, carrying out the circulation of titles of property in investment capital (we will return to Marx's characterisation of fictitious capital at the end of this section). Here, not only is capital-as-property distinguished from capital-as-function, but the right to property is also distinguished from the object of property. Acting as the institutional setting for fictitious capital is the stock market, where diverse property titles circulate. These include shares, bill of exchange, bonds, warrants, dock and warehouse receipts, futures contracts, mortgage deeds, and so forth, as well as derivative securities formed on their basis. These two groups of institutions, the credit system and the stock market (with the associated insurance and hard-currency markets), make up the financial market.

Both loan capital and fictitious capital, as well as the credit system that organised their functioning and the stock market, performed the functions of servicing the movement of productive capital as a whole, mobilising and redistributing temporarily free monetary funds. In the process, the opportunities for expanding capital came to exceed the capacity of the individual capitalist to accumulate. These opportunities, however, were still circumscribed by the overall potential for mobilising temporarily free monetary funds on the scale of social capital as a whole.

The valuation of fictitious capital circulating in the financial market ceased to have any relationship to the amount of real capital represented by securities – initially, simply by virtue of the relative independence of the stock market. And this property of stock markets became essentially important in the 1970s, when the bubble of fictitious capital became the instrument for temporarily overcoming of the limits of the expansion of real capital (see Figure 2).

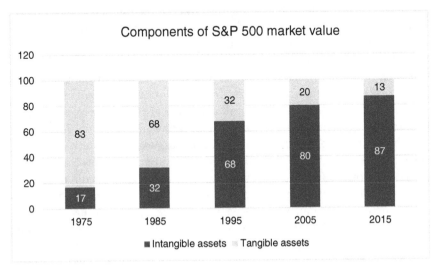

**Figure 2** Components of S&P market value, 1975–2015.

In present-day economic theory and statistics, it is customary to explain the excess stock market capitalisation of companies, the excess over the actual value of their assets, with the idea that the difference is accounted for by the corporations' possession of intellectual assets. Critics have pointed out the conjectural character of this explanation. Any analysis of financial markets based on the accounting of assets (both tangible and intangible) in the present day are, in any case, notional because of the influence of financial bubbles. These assets should rather be defined as elusive or impalpable, in line with the literal sense of the term 'intangible assets'. It cannot be said that the capitalisation of these assets bears any relationship to real intellectual assets set down in bookkeepers' ledgers, only that it results from speculative fever based on calculations of probable future profits. The market, however, is indifferent to what might stand behind the inflated capitalisation of assets; the main thing is that this capitalisation should be capable of realisation: investments must bear profits, not losses. When there was a slowdown in the accumulation of real capital, financial investments became more attractive. 'Money making' became the main channel for the appropriation of profit, giving the temporary illusion of making profit without the participation of real capital.

As this situation arose, opportunities opened up for purely speculative operations based on the great uncertainty surrounding estimates of the value of securities. It also led to the real possibility that money capital could be drawn from the stock market in quantities substantially exceeding the dimensions of genuine capital.

The opportunities described here expanded not only in the stock market but also in the market for loan capital, since securitised credit operations were becoming widespread (at the same time as the valuation of these securities distanced itself from the value of the assets backing them). Ensuring the emission of credits that were no longer based on the value of real capital, this situation not only made it possible to expand capital beyond the bounds of the real mobilisation of temporarily free money capital (and at the same time to increase consumer credit, allowing the growth of demand beyond the limits of real incomes). It also brought about a substantial increase in risk, linked to the growing attempts to appropriate profit through financial operations rather than real production. This situation resulted in a break in the relationship between the value of real and fictitious capital.

It was on this basis that fictitious capital came to be transformed into virtual fictitious capital. Whereas Marx used the term 'fictitious capital' to refer to capitalised streams of income, we use the term 'virtual fictitious capital' to refer to fictitious capital whose market estimation is decisively skewed by manipulation from the biggest capitals and the most powerful states and so deviates substantially both from value of real assets and capitalisation of stream of expected income. This manipulation is possible because information technology's 'virtual' processes, which increasingly dominate financial markets, enable states and corporations to control market estimation. Not only is the valuation of such capital indeterminate; so too is its location, thanks to the frequency of deals and the many stages through which they pass. Its owners are also, for the same reasons, obscure and elusive. The uncertainty of the valuation leads to a situation in which it is impossible at times to say whether a particular capital is worth anything at all, that is, whether it even exists.

For a certain period of history, between the 1970s and the 1990s, virtual fictitious capital served as an effective tool for overcoming the contradictions of capitalism associated with the over-accumulation of productive capital. The overflowing of relatively excessive capital into financial markets provided a safety-valve that saved the productive sector from a surfeit of capital, while also aiding in the creation of additional demand, whose fictitious (or, more precisely, virtual) character was not at first recognised.

This situation helped to moderate the fluctuations of the capitalist industrial cycle. However, there was no way to eliminate the fundamental connection between fictitious capital, even if it had taken on virtual characteristics, and real capital. Capital that had been over-accumulated in the area of production might find an effective use temporarily on the financial markets, and might even help to expand demand in the productive sector. Nevertheless, this situation could not banish the reality that genuine capital had been over-accumulated. All it could do was to put off the day when this reality would make itself felt in economic terms.

Economic growth that relies on a fictitious (virtual) expansion of demand rests ultimately on a real shortage of genuine money capital or income. When it is discovered that real monetary demand does not correspond to the version presented by virtual financial tools, the market is forced to limit the expansion of genuine capital (as occurred, for example, with the construction industry in the US and elsewhere following the collapse of the mortgage market in 2008). The transformation of fictitious capital into virtual capital thus also creates the danger of a significant sharpening of cyclical crises.

The dramatic growth in the importance of the financial market for all sectors of the economy requires very close attention, as does the increased reverse influence of finances on the area of production – a phenomenon that for more than a decade now has been labelled 'financialisation'.[4] As Samir Amin notes, financialisation occurs when

an ever-greater proportion of surplus value is unable to be invested in expanding and improving productive systems, and hence the sole opportunity for continuing accumulation under the conditions of monopoly control becomes the 'financial investment' of this excess surplus value. As a result of financialisation the main functions of control over the reproduction of the system of accumulation have passed primarily to the thirty largest banks (the 'triads'). The euphemistically named 'markets' are no more than the expanses on which the strategies of these subjects that dominate the economic arena are played out. This financialisation, which in turn is the reason behind the increasing inequality in the distribution of incomes and wealth, gives rise to the growing mass of assets on which it feeds. (Amin 2014: 9)

The financialisation phenomenon has many specific features, of which the most important include first, the qualitative and quantitative shift in favour of the financial sector, with a rapid acceleration in the volume of purely financial transactions, higher rates of profit in the financial sector, a flow of human and other resources into this field, the formation of new institutions, and so forth. Second is the all-but-decisive influence exerted by this sector on the entire system for the allocation of resources and coordination of their use, such that the directing of investment flows, the taking of decisions, the structure of prices, and so forth in the *whole* economy are now determined largely by the conjuncture in the financial sector. Further, the prioritised development of financial capital has caused a wave of deregulation; financial speculations have become the new 'regulator', a substitute for state action on the economy. Third, property relations and the distribution of income have become vastly more unequal (the system of rights to the ownership of constantly 'migrating' fictitious capital is a separate topic). Finally, the whole system of social reproduction has acquired many specific features, among which are the sharply increased dependence of this process on the risky nature and instability of the economic system, short-termism, and other traits that provide strong grounds for describing this system as 'casino capitalism'.

One result of this process has been the appearance of a special type of human behaviour oriented towards financial transactions as the principal mode of activity and model of conduct. As financialisation develops, 'homo finansus' (a category put into circulation among scholars by Iren Levina (2006)) is now close to becoming the dominant personality type. It is characteristic not just of entrepreneurs, but also of consumers.

This summary of the main features of the process of financialisation, albeit brief and incomplete, reveals a number of qualitative changes in the nature of capital. Before formulating these changes we should note that our characterisation of the phenomenon corresponds in some details with the broadly familiar list of features of the modern financial system that is accepted all but universally by scholars both in Russia and abroad.[5] In the present case, these characteristics will be treated as subordinate, on the basis of the logic of the process that sees money and its functions as phenomena of the nationally regulated and socially oriented economy of late capitalism, acquiring the properties of a virtual product of the fictitious financial capital at the neoliberal stage of the global hegemony of capital.

The abnormally inflated virtual capital requires an adequate technological basis for its large-scale circulation and very rapid transactions. This basis has been created by the development of information technologies, which has provided for the formation of electronic money. In order to enable the circulation of rapidly growing virtual capital, there has also been a corresponding growth in the quantity of money in circulation. This segment of money, the quantity of which fluctuates with the fluctuating value of virtual fictitious capital, has become 'virtual money'.

Accordingly, the function of the measure of value is performed primarily not by money in the narrow sense of the word, but by a new economic phenomenon – 'virtual money', a synthesis of money as conventionally measured with various forms of *virtual fictitious capital* that inhabit financial information systems. Here and subsequently, we use the concept of fictitious capital in Marx's sense, as set out in volume III of *Capital*. Marx understood it as follows:

> The formation of a fictitious capital is called capitalisation. Every regularly repeated income is capitalised by calculating it on the basis of the average rate of interest, as an income which would be yielded by a capital loaned at this rate of interest. … All connection with the actual expansion process of capital is thus completely lost, and the conception of capital as something with automatic self-expansion properties is thereby strengthened.
>
> Even when the promissory note – the security – does not represent a purely fictitious capital, as it does in the case of state debts, the capital value of such paper is nevertheless wholly illusory. We have previously seen in what manner the credit system creates associated capital. The paper serves as title of ownership, which represents this capital. The stocks of railways, mines, navigation companies, and the like, represent actual capital, namely, the capital invested and functioning in such enterprises, or the amount of money advanced by the stockholders for the purpose of being used as capital in such enterprises. This does not preclude the possibility that these may represent pure swindle. But this capital does not exist twice, once as the capital value of titles of ownership (stocks) and the other time as the actual capital invested, or to be invested, in those enterprises. It exists only in the latter form, and a share of stock is merely a title of ownership to a certain portion of the surplus value to be realised by it. (Marx 1894/1998: 464–7)

The main spontaneous regulator of the movement of this type of money is the financial market (and in this case more precisely fictitious capital), where virtual money also 'exists'. Because of the needs of the expansion in big transnational capital (which can also be described as financial capital), the financial market increasingly has a worldwide character. And under the pressure of this capital, the mode of national regulation of the movement of money in the narrow sense of the word has changed substantially to provide more space for capital circulation and risky financial operations, the burden of which very often are shifted onto the shoulders of taxpayers. The processes of emission (especially credit emission) and other national financial regulators depend to a considerable degree on the conjuncture in the financial market (and this market, we stress once again, has become global). Consequently, the movement of money, along with its functions as a means of circulation and payment, is increasingly determined by fictitious capital as a concrete-universal phenomenon. Further, within these functions it is also easy to identify empirically the birth of a new aspect of the movement of capital: the bulk of the transactions that service money are not connected with the movement of commodities and services, but with that monetary aggregates and surrogates. We can compare the world trade turnover with the turnovers of different financial instruments. In 2016 the value of annual world exports was $17.88 trillion,[6] and that of world imports was $18.133 trillion.[7] In the same year the turnover of the stock market was about $79.53 trillion.[8] At the same time $5.067 trillion was traded *every day* in foreign exchange markets in April 2016.[9] In the same year the *daily* turnover of futures was $5.152 trillion, and the *daily* turnover of options was $1.502 trillion.[10]

The role of *world money* is played by a complex organised system involving various national currencies and their aggregates (as the euro is). This system is more closed and non-transparent than national currency systems: the interests of states in issuing reserve currencies (and the big capital behind their backs) dictate this closeness in order to reap more benefits from it. In this system, savings, in the forms of deposits in the largest banks and other financial institutions, become the 'raw material' for virtual fictitious capital. Their role is defined by the latter in the sense that their movement depends on investments by the banks in securities, on quotations for securities emitted by the banks themselves, and ultimately on the conjuncture in the world financial markets.

On the basis of these facts, we may conclude that, on the whole and under present-day conditions, the functioning of money in the narrow sense of the word is determined qualitatively and quantitatively by global (whole-world) financial capital in its virtual fictitious form. The main connection is the high level of dependence of money circulation on the fluctuations of the virtual capital market, dominated by big transnational financial capital.

## Virtual fictitious capital: *differentiae specificae*

The term 'virtual fictitious capital' refers to the new form of fictitious capital dominating the financial world today. In this form, we see a new stage of transformation of interest-bearing capital, in which the connection with real capital almost disappears (and becomes visible only in a crisis). To reiterate, our understanding of financial capital is closer to Lenin's than to Hilferding's. Therefore for us the main point of evolution of financial capital is not the question of whether it is finance that subordinates industry or vice versa, but the evolution in the forms of the monopolistic control of the union of big industrial and banking corporations. The 'virtualisation' of fictitious capital is the modern form of appropriation of profit from the financial market, used by financial capital, which predominates over other participants in the financial market. This new quality arose from the development of (1) information technologies (the quality of 'technical virtualness'), and (2) the corporate-network market (the corporate-network structure of the financial market). Unlike the 'ordinary' fictitious capital of the nineteenth century, this capital is now itself' (3) infiltrating productive monopoly capital and to some extent 'financialising' it (as will be shown below, on the eve of the global financial-economic crisis even the corporations of the real sector were obtaining as much as half of their profits from financial speculation).

After passing through a stage of strict state regulation in the mid-twentieth century, financial capital became virtual, and on the one hand it (4) 'sublated' this stage as a result of the growing influence of transnational financial (and other) corporations on the politics of national states and international financial institutions. On the other hand (5), modern financial capital, using the influence of big powers and international financial institutions, has to some extent suppressed national and state regulation in order to create new fields of global financial speculation.

Under these conditions, as noted earlier, virtual fictitious capital turnover (controlled by financial capital) also determinates the circulation of money (viewed on the profound, elemental level of real determinants, not of perverse forms). Virtual fictitious capital, as we have seen, is meanwhile a repeatedly mediated perverse form, divorced from material production, of capital as the basis of the capitalist mode of production.

As a result, money reflects the virtual form of capital both in its technological nature and in its social form.

In the case of the former, this is a result of the development of information technologies that create (1) the appearance of a special, virtual reality that substitutes other symbols of value, and (2) the possibility of unlimited transference and transformation of forms within information networks and financial systems. The properties of money that since ancient times have been demanded of it as a universal equivalent, and that previously were embodied adequately in the material properties of gold (such as that it can be divided, stored, and so forth), have now found a still more satisfactory embodiment in electronic bearers. The latter permit sums of any magnitude to be expressed in an infinitesimally small bearer. The sums can be transferred almost instantly, without personal contact, from any point (if there is access to the internet), and can be stored for any length of time without significant cost.

All this leads to a conclusion that is both elementary and generally understood, but nevertheless important. The electronic form of money did not itself create global virtual fictitious capital (or today's world financial markets as one of its forms), but without this technology such a capital would have faced many barriers to its operation. Transactions of two or three trillion dollars per day (the volume of operations on world financial markets during the past decade) could not be carried out without computers and the internet. Paradoxically, the financial instruments that were created in order to reduce the risks of the operations of virtual fictitious capital – that is, derivatives – turned out to be the main source of financial bubbles, and hence of instability.

Derivatives (regardless of different definitions) have the following attributes: they are securities (securitised contracts) assuming operations with underlying assets, and their price is independent of the fluctuations of the price of underlying assets (e.g. securities, including also derivatives, some sorts of commodities, economic indexes and events). Another essential attribute of derivatives is the independence of their value from the value of underlying assets, making possible a separation between the accounts of derivatives and underlying assets, and a much more significant separation between the accounts of derivatives and real assets. Big financial capital, with instruments of manipulation of the financial market (hand in glove with the state), reaps the main benefits of the derivatives turnover. The derivatives market (mainly operating outside organised trade on the stock exchanges) has reached colossal proportions, tens of times greater than world GDP (see Table 2).

The financial and economic crisis of 2007–9 did not lead to an immediate crash in the derivatives market, though it is now in a depressed situation. The crisis showed clearly the risks that an excessive enthusiasm for derivatives carries. Figure 3 confirms the extremely close ties between markets for derivatives and for loan capital. The majority of deals involving derivatives occur in operations aimed at hedging loan interest rates. Operations associated with foreign exchange, equities, and commodities occupy a far more modest place.

In addition, money is now virtual in another, socio-economic sense: even the connection of money with the ideal (perceived) general equivalent has

**Table 2** Outstanding notional value of derivatives markets, 2009–13 (US$, billions)

| | Dec. 2009 | June 2010 | Dec. 2010 | June 2011 | Dec. 2011 | June 2012 | Dec. 2012 | June 2013 | Dec. 2013 |
|---|---|---|---|---|---|---|---|---|---|
| Over-the-counter derivatives | | | | | | | | | |
| Total contracts | 603,900 | 582,685 | 601,046 | 706,884 | 647,811 | 639,395 | 632,582 | 692,924 | 710,182 |
| Exchange-traded derivatives | | | | | | | | | |
| All exchange-traded | 73,126 | 75,427 | 67,940 | 82,888 | 58,331 | 61,511 | 54,122 | 69,124 | 64,628 |

Source: CME Group, *Derivatives Market Landscape* (Spring 2014), p. 4, based on Bank of International Settlements release, May 2014, www.cmegroup.com/trading/otc/files/derivatives-market-landscape.pdf (accessed 20 May 2021).

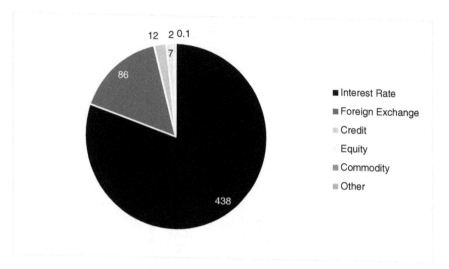

**Figure 3** Structure of the global derivatives markets: amounts outstanding (US$, trillions), 2015.

become blurred with the dependence of money on the fluctuations of virtual capital. Virtual money 'exists' only to the degree that virtual fictitious capital is preserved. As a product of the virtual capital that 'exists' in information networks, virtual money is totally dependent on this capital. The growth of instability of virtual fictitious capital simultaneously leads to the growth of instability of virtual money.

The virtual nature of money in this instance consists not only in its electronic form, but also in its casual, unstable form, being based on probability and not rooted in value created through abstract social labour. Money as a symbol of value has no value of its own. It has only ideal value, the image of value of commodity: it is, in short, a universal equivalent. And the connection of virtual money with real value is much more uncertain, more indeterminate than even this ideal connection. As a reflection of movement of virtual capital, virtual money to a significant extent has a 'ghost-like' nature': nobody can be sure of its real value. It is not the result of production but of the redistribution of value. From its initial existence as an 'absolute' universal equivalent (the product of abstract labour), intermingled with a durable natural form (gold or silver), money has finally been transformed into an amorphous totality of products of the activity of virtual capital. Meanwhile, this totality is qualitatively heterogeneous, and only in terms of probability (that is, virtually) does it fulfil the role of a measure of value, of a means of exchange, and furthermore of a means of accumulation. Paper money's property of being solely an intermediary in circulation, without value of its own, reaches its apogee in the case of virtual money, since virtual money does not have even the national and state guarantees that paper money possesses. As a product of world fictitious capital, virtual money lacks these guarantees entirely. Despite the fact that the movements of virtual fictitious capital are regulated by the national state, the value of virtual money is less guaranteed than that of conventional credit money, since it depends on fluctuations in the virtual capital market. This virtual money (and it is global in nature) will fulfil one or another of its functions with one or another degree of probability tomorrow or the day after.[11] This affects national currencies and all other established aggregates like M3 and M4, and also bonds, stocks, mortgages, and other securities.

Before continuing our investigation, we should note that, in the twenty-first century, alongside virtual money, a certain small quantity of real money survives in the form of national and foreign currencies, in the form of notes, and especially in the form of bank deposits. This real money can also have an electronic form, but socially it is not virtual to the degree to which it is based on the *real* economic wealth (value) of one or another country or (in the case of the euro) group of countries, and does not strongly depend on the conjuncture of world financial markets.

Now let us return to virtual money. The combination of an electronic bearer and a virtual social form transforms virtual money into a special (financial) super-network, a 'web of webs' (which also, naturally, has its 'spiders'). Virtual fictitious capital as a 'super-network' (which in this case is the 'universal equivalent') thus takes on a special role: that of a universal (semi-)spontaneous regulator of the 'network market', of company networks, and indirectly of all commodities.

Meanwhile, the transformation of this money from a virtual to a real state, along with the degree to which it fulfils its functions (in particular, as a measure of liquidity), is attended by a trio of problems. First, it is associated with a huge degree of risk, which is an inevitable consequence of the virtual socio-economic form of this money, the reflection of virtual fictitious capital. Here we find the cause of the great attention paid to this quasi-commodity under present-day conditions. The virtual nature of money for this very reason expands, on an unprecedented scale, the system of diverse types of economic activity dealing with risk. The speculative, probability-based nature of most of the transactions on financial markets transforms these markets into a special field where the production of commodities (the creation of value by social labour) is replaced by gambling with possible gains and losses, and by insurance measures aimed at guaranteeing the gains and preventing the losses. We thus see the emergence of a sphere of capital movement ('business') that has a completely virtual nature, and that is not only speculative in the strict sense of the word, and unrelated to the production of real goods, but also based on the large-scale and, in principle, indefinite gap between instruments of the financial market and the value of underlying assets. Virtual capital is inflated enormously and transformed into the main channel of appropriation of profit by the control of big transnational financial capital over the financial market. Its objectives, 'means of production' (probability-based models of random processes), and results are all virtual. It should be noted that in the period leading up to the global financial crisis, insurance in all its forms was the fastest-growing area of business.

Second, virtual money as such (and also, therefore, the 'network market', of which virtual money is the measure and means of development) is creating a higher level of instability, since it depends on the spontaneous development of the conjuncture of world virtual capital. The above-mentioned dual 'virtualness' of money (based on its bearer and its social form) that arises out of this speculative nature, instability, and indefiniteness of the financial sphere imposes high transaction costs (whether for insurance, property rights protection, or the defence of information against hackers).

Third, such money is genuinely dependent on the functioning of particular institutions of global capital. This situation needs special comment.

Hardly for the first time during the centuries-long evolution of capital, a restricted circle of the largest corporate structures (financial corporations, the central banks of a number of states, the IMF, the World Bank, and some other interlocked systems)[12] are acquiring economic (and to a degree political) power that previously was concentrated solely in the faceless objective phenomenon of world money. Meanwhile, as a result of privatisation, these structures, first, are falling increasingly into the hands of 'new private property-owners'. We repeat: this may affect even institutions that formally retain a state or supra-state character; what the new owners privatise is not only assets, but the real right of property, that is, *power*.[13]

Second, these structures are meanwhile less and less subject to the control of social forces of any kind, as a result both of globalisation, which reduces control by the national state, and of the general decay of the social state and of real democracy. This decay leads to the reduced role for associations of workers and citizens that is characteristic of the period of neoliberalism.

Third, these institutions operate in an increasingly favourable milieu created by the total network market. We repeat that such structures, representing global virtual capital, are becoming (as 'sublated' money) the universal measure and principal means of vital activity of the global economy and society.

Hence, the new quality of virtual money, unlike the quality of money in the epochs of classical and even early monopoly capitalism, consists in the fact that on the one hand the new electronic 'bearer' substantially simplifies and expedites the system of transactions, potentially allowing these transactions to be calculated, controlled, and regulated on any scale desired. It is significant that the more dependent the world monetary system becomes on the largest financial institutions, the greater this possibility is. The scale and role of these institutions are turning them into actors potentially capable of carrying out this regulation. At the same time, the split of world monetary systems in different blocks (dollar, euro, China-centred financial union, and so on) has introduced an additional factor of instability due to financial rivalry between them.

On the other hand, however, the social 'virtualness' of money that results from its nature as a product of global virtual capital – that is, of the special *supra*-network, the 'web of webs' that comes into being as a result of the spontaneous interaction of private financial capital with the private financial institutions that represent it – turns this supra-network into a 'black box'. This situation renders virtual money more and more unstable; the performance of its functions is turned into an uncontrolled, speculative, risky process. Because it possesses this character, virtual money capital can bring about a situation in which financial transactions are transformed into a special area of the economy, divorced from production and spreading at an accelerated rate (as a result both of the opportunities for absorbing speculative outlays, and of the growth of transaction costs). Meanwhile, virtual fictitious capital provides a suitable mechanism and form for the expansion of this area.

To use the words of Shakespeare, one might say that money as the *sole* universal 'genie' of the market world is able to turn everything that is black, white.[14] Now the 'genie' has ended up in a new 'bottle'. Initially, the 'bottle' was gold. Later, its role came to be played by treasury bills and other forms of paper emitted by the national states issuing key currencies. The states issued substitutes for gold only provisionally, and represented the interests of a broad range of differentiated capitals in their conflicts with the rest of society. Meanwhile, in *Capital* Marx wrote that world money exists in the form of gold. Now, however, the role of money (on a world scale, it should be noted) is migrating to electronic phenomena, produced by a limited range of mostly *private* transnational corporate structures.

Another analogy, even closer to the mark, might be that before our eyes, this 'bottle' is ever more rapidly dissolving in the computer systems of world financial institutions. As the 'bottle' (that is, money 'sublated' into virtual capital) dissolves before us, control over it lies in the hands of a relatively narrow range of increasingly privatised structures. But the 'bottle' does not slip from those hands, since the 'genie' keeps growing. Meanwhile, the most important thing is that these structures are in a state of active struggle with one another and, for their own purposes, are trying to determine the rules of the conflict.

In virtual money, corporate capital is thus acquiring a universal mechanism for imposing its hegemony. This is not a hegemony of any particular financial corporation but one of corporate capital as a whole, as a totality. Nevertheless, the 'genie' itself, world virtual money developed to its most powerful form to date, transforms money into a powerful mechanism of control. While money is supposed to be a spontaneous objective measure and a regulator of market processes, when financial structures assume power over virtual money, its character is transformed: these financial structures become sort of world-wide group *Gosplan* or State Planning Committee, whose various departments wage an irreconcilable struggle with one another. At the same time, this *Gosplan* attempts to regulate a process that of its nature is elemental and spontaneous. It should also be noted that no one controls the system as a whole. It consists of separate spaces governed or manipulated by the largest financial spiders.

The result is that financial corporations on the one hand appear as functions of the process of spontaneous movement (via computer networks and, more rarely, in real markets) of world capital, a process over which they have little power. On the other hand, they are the embodiment of this capital, and its private owners. This capital therefore comes to pose a hyper-realised threat of deregulation.

## The new mode of being of the universal formula of capital: virtual fictitious capital

In the second part of volume I of *Capital*, Karl Marx set out the general formula of capital, M – C – M′: money, used to purchase commodities that are then used for production of other commodities and sold, bringing in additional money. He also put forward the contradiction and antinomy of this formula. On the one hand, production creates additional value. On the other, it is just as certain that this additional value cannot appear if all that happens during circulation is an exchange of equivalents.

Equally well known is the fact that Marx resolved this antinomy by investigating the process of production, the famous 'hidden abode of production' where, as his theory explains, surplus value is created even though it appears to arise from circulation. In its outward form, late capitalism re-enacts this antinomy. Virtual fictitious capital, existing outside the sphere of production, appears to have the *miraculous* ability to create profit exclusively within the sphere of (its own) circulation. This semblance is not something fortuitous, and like most of the perverse forms that are characteristic of capitalism, it has an objective existence. It is thus all the more important to investigate the real content that lies behind this latest *volte-face,* this 'mutation' of capital.

## *Profit without production, or the illusory forms of the 'debt economy'*

This question was first discussed some decades ago and has become extremely topical since the crisis of 2008 (see, for example, Epstein and Jayadev 2005; Krippner 2005; Lapavitsas 2009; Orhangazi 2008; Stockhammer 2004; van Treeck 2009), so we shall begin by posing a question linked directly to practice: can the fluctuations on the financial market destroy the real economy? And if so, then why?

It is well known that effective demand in the modern world is not for the most part based on real money, but on debt obligations and on certificates claiming a right to future profits (that is, on credit and fictitious capital). But when demand rests on these two legs (or crutches?), it provides an extremely unstable basis for supply. Debt may expand without special problems for a relatively prolonged period – but only so long as provision is made for paying it back, or while interest receipts are able to cover the principal sum of the debt to a significant degree, even if there is no hope of this main sum being returned. In the case of claims on future profits, expressed in the financial instruments of fictitious capital, the situation is more complex. The market perceives these instruments as liquid resources (quasi-money), not only so long as (1) it counts on these future profits materialising, but also while (2) it counts on the market value of the particular fictitious capital increasing. The increase in market valuation creates the possibility for profitable operations with fictitious capital, regardless of whether the real capital of which the fictitious capital is a reflection brings in actual profits or not. This growth, however, also has its limits, and is not absolutely independent of real capital.

This situation is in some features similar to a Ponzi scheme. However, the financial market, in contrast to Ponzi schemes, does not need to attract more and more participants (it is desirable but not obligatory). The growth of virtual capital is based on the growing market evaluation of fictitious capital instruments, making hopes for future benefits from investments in such securities. And as demand increases and inflates the market price of these securities, they become more profitable. This is creates the illusion of a self-sustaining scheme. But the vulnerable point of this scheme is the existence, albeit not self-evident, of a final connection with real capital. When the overproduction in the US housing industry (provoked by the growth of mortgage credit) was finally confronted with the limits of demand, it led to the slowdown in mortgages market, and this was enough to crash it.

The most fundamental reason for the negative effects of financial market instability on the real economy is the loss of the connection between the movement of money capital and that of real (productive) capital, which manifests itself in the suppression of the 'legitimate', 'natural' functions of money capital (that is, those conditioned by its genesis as a means of servicing the movement of productive capital, its being-for-another), and the growth of its 'self-sufficient' functions (its 'being-for-itself'), based on the exploitation of speculative effects (see Mirgorodskaya 2007; Mityaev 2009). (In this case, 'money capital' should be taken as incorporating all its forms, both productive and perverse, including loan, fictitious, and virtual fictitious capital.)

Why is that, with the development of capitalism, not only grants of credit but also debt certificates themselves (credit agreements, promissory notes, and so forth) have ended up serving to expand demand? Why has fictitious capital in its turn become the basis for credit expansion (that is, come to be accepted as security for credits)? These are questions of fundamental importance for characterising the relationships between real and virtual capital.

Promissory notes and claims to future income are able to constitute real demand on the condition that they function as 'symbols of value', that is, as substitutes for money in its various functions, as means of circulation, and means of payment and of store of value. In essence, they create a *private* mass of money, which is not under the direct control of the state. However, they can create this for the totality of commodities only indirectly: (1) they form the basis for the credit, and (2) they provide capital gain income extracted from the financial market.

This is how the 'being-for-itself' of financial capital becomes socially necessary and contributes to strangling productive investment and increasing inequality. Further, it is as a result of this that non-financial corporations, too, have increasingly been drawn into operations aimed at extracting profits directly from the financial markets. Until 1997 non-financial corporations in the US made losses on their financial operations, and this was to be expected, since in relation to the credit system they acted as borrowers of funds, and the effectiveness of their operations on the stock market was low, since it consisted of moves forced upon them by their need to attract the capital they lacked. From that date onwards, however, their operations became profitable, to the point where in particular periods the share of their profits that non-financial corporations have gained from their financial operations has exceeded 50 per cent.

As shown by the calculations of Greta Krippner (2005: 185–7), the share of financial income (interest, dividends and capital, gains) in the total cash-flow

*Money in the twenty-first century*

Table 3 The ratio of portfolio income to cash flow of non-financial US corporations, 2005–13 (US$, billions)

| Year | Annual profit | Depreciation allowances | Total cash flow | Portfolio income (dividends, interest, capital gains) | Ratio portfolio income to cash flow |
|------|---------------|-------------------------|-----------------|-------------------------------------------------------|-------------------------------------|
| 2005 | 4,119,717 | 671,806 | 4,791,523 | 2,436,447 | 0.51 |
| 2006 | 4,765,268 | 720,518 | 5,485,786 | 2,736,544 | 0.50 |
| 2007 | 4,455,911 | 773,003 | 5,228,914 | 3,135,160 | 0.60 |
| 2008 | 3,578,144 | 942,303 | 4,520,174 | 2,517,937 | 0.56 |
| 2009 | 3,024,226 | 903,573 | 3,927,799 | 1,854,722 | 0.47 |
| 2010 | 4,169,627 | 920,248 | 5,089,875 | 1,766,950 | 0.35 |
| 2011 | 4,109,149 | 1,069,943 | 5,178,192 | 1,703,140 | 0.33 |
| 2012 | 5,073,479 | 910,719 | 5,984,198 | 1,698,269 | 0.28 |
| 2013 | 5,287,852 | 938,54 | 6,226,392 | 1,634,087 | 0.26 |

*Source*: Calculated by authors according to the data of National Income and Product Accounts (US) and Internal Revenue Service (US): US Bureau of Economic Analysis, 'Nonfinancial Corporate Business: Profits before Tax (without IVA and CCAdj) (A464RC-1Q027SBEA)', FRED, Federal Reserve Bank of St. Louis; https://fred.stlouisfed.org/series/A464RC1Q027SBEA (accessed 2 June 2021); Internal Revenue Service, 'Corporation Income Tax Returns: Balance Sheet, Income Statement, and Tax Items for Income Years, 1990–2013, Expanded', www.irs.gov/statistics/soi-tax-stats-historical-table-13 (accessed 2 June 2021).

(profit and depreciation allowances) of US non-financial corporations in the period 1981–2001 fluctuated between approximately 30 and 40 per cent. More recent data, which we have calculated by the same method (for comparability reasons), show that before the Great Financial Crisis the share of financial income of non-financial corporations was above 50 per cent, and after the crisis it diminished significantly to the level of the 1980s and 1990s (see Table 3).

Nor is this all. In relation to the credit system, non-financial corporations since 2003 have at certain times been transformed from net debtors to net creditors, with the interest they obtain from their own credit operations exceeding the interest they pay on loans. Through the use of credit and fictitious capital (as demonstrated in Marx's *Capital*), real capital thus manages an additional expansion, thrusting aside the framework, which is now too narrow for it, imposed by the conditions for the realisation of value and surplus value on the basis solely of monetary demand and ordinary sale and purchase. However, in the past half-century, financial capital has been forced into excessive use of high risky financial instruments and has formed the large field of implementation of virtual fictitious capital. This has come at the cost of strongly increased market instability, but without it capital cannot reproduce itself. This is the evidence of the transfer of capital from the stage of maturity to the stage of decrepitude and senility.

Debts, fictitious, capital and virtual fictitious capital can all serve the movement of real capital to the extent that the additional demand they create corresponds to the possibilities for the expansion of real capital, an expansion that is hemmed in by the narrow bounds of monetary, income-based demand. This additional demand allows capital to increase the real production of goods and services, drawing all available resources into the productive process and exploiting all possible improvements. However, this growth has an *internal* boundary: capital has to find a profitable application. Once this boundary is exceeded, part of capital can no longer be employed at a normal, average rate of profit, and the demand that earlier appeared to be present proves to be imaginary, that is, virtual. Or, to be more precise, to the extent that production has nevertheless carried on, this demand is not completely imaginary so much as inadequate for the profitable use of capital. The demand that operates is not excessive, as might be thought from observing various inflated 'financial bubbles', but insufficient (the nature of this 'insufficiency', which fraught with the danger of a 'seizure' or crisis, will be explored below). The main problem is thus the existence within real capital itself of an internal boundary, preventing its profitable application. This confirms Marx's idea that the main limit of capital expansion is the capital itself. The possibility of almost infinite capital expansion conflicts with the narrow frameworks of effective demand, sufficient for profitable usage of capital.

### Virtual fictitious financial capital: the hyper-realised dangers of crisis and deregulation

Up to what point, then, does the internal limit to the expansion of capital remain hidden? The answer is, in principle, well known: to the point where it is discovered that the production undertaken in expectation of future profits cannot be realised (this relates primarily to the real sector, though on the surface the problem might seem to be a sudden fall in the price quotations for securities), or that meeting the obligations it has involved neither is possible nor can be put off. The high-risk funds that are invested in the stock market, it should be noted, are mostly borrowed, and the expectation of rising prices draws in additional funds. The hitch is that when credits cannot be repaid, a panic ensues: the dumping of shares in an effort to make payments then causes a further deterioration in the situation, leading, *inter alia*, to higher interest rates to offset increased risks, increased demand for deposits on repurchase agreements, and calls for early repayment of loans.

Here we encounter the effects of two laws of the capitalist mode of production in general, and of late capitalism in particular. The first of these is the presence of a contradiction between the general striving of capital for unlimited expansion (aided by the growth of virtual financial bubbles creating the illusion that a limitless increase of demand is possible) and the urge to safeguard private interests, avoiding the risk that profits will be lost. Private capital cannot be content endlessly with the mere illusion of demand and the illusion of payment. It is prepared to take the risks involved in exploiting these illusions, but ultimately it wants to turn its goods and services into real money, to realise in actual practice the value and surplus value that have been created.

Second is the cyclical nature of the reproduction of capital. Properly speaking, this also forces the capitalists to include themselves in the chain reaction represented by the compelling need to ensure their private interests amid the inevitable decline of the business conjuncture. The slowdown in the real economy, and also in the financial market, can sound the alarm, forcing investors to convert their virtual capital to real money before it is transformed to zero. The result is that, while defending their private interests and seeking the actual realisation of the value and surplus value that have been created, and while trying to meet their obligations in real money, capitalists also discover the imaginary nature of the inflated demand they have created with the help of virtual capital. This imaginary nature, however, is not of course discovered during the phase of revival and recovery, but during the phase of decline, when the effectiveness of employing real capital is falling.

How, then, has capitalism in the developed countries managed, almost uninterruptedly and with only small hitches, to develop without serious crises in the twenty-four years (two business cycles) between 1983 and 2007? In 1975 and 1982 the world GDP annual rate of growth diminished to the less than 1 per cent (and in some national economies much less), but in 1983–2007 this rate fluctuated between 1.4, and 4.6 per cent.[15] This is the most complex question in this entire history.

The mechanism of financial expansion through rapid expansion of the market for virtual fictitious capital formed in 1970s for reasons that included the need, when a phase of decline sets in, to cut it short with the help of a virtual expansion of demand. The question of why this trick should have worked (that is, why the expansion of virtual capital was able to provide the additional demand in the real economy) not just once, but more or less systematically, we leave aside for the moment. The growth of virtual capital based on credit expansion, and vice versa, creating the basis for additional credit, resulted in the growth of indebtedness. However, the securitisation of debts could prolong the credit leverage for only as long as the market for these securities remained liquid, and ultimately the truth that indebtedness cannot be increased without any limits laid the basis for the crisis.

A whole range of additional factors is thought to have affected the growth of financial bubbles. The first of these is the state regulation of the market, both anti-cyclical regulation (involving stimulation of demand during slumps and cooling the conjuncture during upswings) and structural measures (i.e. an active industrial policy), all aimed at smoothing out the cyclical character of the renewal of capital.

The second is the creation of the so-called welfare state (the 'society of universal well-being'), which has allowed the expansion of demand through redistributive mechanisms. If millions of people have a certain quantity of money saved but are somewhat short of the price of a refrigerator, a car, or an apartment, and if the state supplies them with the shortfall through social transfers, then real additional demand is created, for whole sectors and extending far beyond the budget transfers involved. These transfers turn part of the deferred demand that exists in the form of private savings into real demand.

Third is the fact that the collapse of the colonial system and the shift to neocolonialism opened the way for the processes of globalisation. The political barriers to the flow of capital represented by the division of world into different colonial empires were eliminated. The transfer of production to countries of the 'third world' allowed a reduction of costs in the real sector, a cheapening of the elements of the value of labour power, and so forth, temporarily smoothing over the phenomena associated with the over-accumulation of capital. Politically, all these processes were stimulated by the factor of competition with the world system of socialism.

All these factors have now exhausted their effectiveness, and this conclusion is certainly reinforced by the slack economic dynamic after the financial crisis of 2008. They have not disappeared, since capitalism cannot renounce them, at least not entirely. However, there are no longer significant prospects of raising the effectiveness of capital through these means. Regulation remains, various forms of social compromise remain, and 'globalisation', continues, though with ever-greater hiccups. Nevertheless, the 'cream' from all these factors has already been skimmed.

Meanwhile, the computer, information, telecommunications, and similar revolutions, for all their importance (particularly in contributing to the victory over world socialism, due to its inability to implement them effectively), have not led to a qualitative technological renewal of capitalism. In technological terms, capitalism remains industrial, as before. Moreover, the possibilities for a substantial growth of efficiency through computerisation, confronting the limits of capitalist system, have already substantially been exhausted during the first years of the present century.

Now, it would seem, we can define exactly what virtual profit, drawn from the financial market, actually is. It is the payment that financial capitalists (agents of the financial market) derive by providing capital with the opportunity for seemingly unlimited expansion and for receiving income from the sale of goods and services that satisfy imaginary demand. Properly speaking, imaginary demand is also created by capital in the financial sector in order to appropriate virtual profits. The illusory character of both is determined by the fact that financial expansion extends far beyond the bounds set by the conditions for the balanced reproduction of capital.

In place of a single, integral universal equivalent in the form of money as a commodity that objectively is always needed by everyone (since it is the means to purchase the products of general socially necessary labour), we find the elemental world market of virtual money, subject to a mysterious conjuncture (while on the other hand dependent in each of its concrete links on the subjective forces represented by one or another financial corporation). As already noted, this market may be correlated directly with world financial markets that, moreover, are filled with gigantic 'bubbles'.[16] The place of gold as universal regulator and stabiliser of the market (anchor and safety valve simultaneously) has been taken by virtual money capital – an unstable and elemental super-network, privatised by an indeterminate range of corporations but controlled by no one.

This elemental, erratic character of the financial markets (which represent the core of the vital activity of the modern market) is in essential contradiction with production, which is thoroughly ordered and mutually interdependent (or, more precisely, highly socialised) on a world scale. For many years, production in technological terms has not operated spontaneously (e.g. restoring proportionality through constant disproportions, through crises of overproduction); rather, it has functioned on a basis of constantly supported proportionality, but has exploded from time to time in world-wide systemic crises which, although relatively rare, are exceedingly powerful, affecting the very foundations of the power of capital.

These systemic crises have arisen since the Great Depression and will continue to arise when virtual financial capital crosses a certain boundary of its expansion (over-accumulation). From the qualitative angle this boundary may be provisionally defined (this is no more than a hypothesis) as that degree of over-accumulation of virtual capital (a substitute for money) that no longer allows it to perform functions analogous to money in the modern market. The precondition for this is an excessive disconnection (again, the degree needs to be defined) of this capital from (1) real production, and (2) regulatory influences on the part of society, in particular state regulation of monetary circulation. The monetarist ideology misrepresents this danger as if in the distorting mirror image of the illusion that it is possible to ensure the smooth development of capitalism by means of a stable balance between the level of economic growth and amount of money.

With total marketisation also deepening the global problems of humanity, and with only virtual money as a means for securing the relative stabilisation and regulation of this system, the obvious conclusion is that the world financial-economic crisis that began in 2008 was a natural result of the causes set out above.[17] Further, the failure to do away with the central causes of this crisis (above all, the problem of the over-accumulation of capital in general and of virtual fictitious capital in particular still remains) makes a repetition of such phenomena more than likely unless essential corrective measures are taken, at a minimum on the institutional level and within the framework of economic policy. This topic will be addressed later, in Chapter 9 dealing with the problem of capital reproduction.

From the point of view of political economy, the more difficult task is not that of explaining why the world financial-economic crisis occurred, but why it was postponed for so long. These reasons, which were identified by the authors long before the crisis began, lie in the fact that the present-day economy also contains a whole series of powerful counter-tendencies.

Let us begin with the fact that, for the moment, the processes described earlier are merely unfolding, and have not yet reached their culmination. The basis of money remains to some extent in gold, though in steadily lesser measure. More important is the fact that, for the present, the largest states still control the movement of a significant part of the money aggregates within their countries and on the world market, employing these aggregates in the interests not only of corporate elites, but also of general stability. Meanwhile, the privatisation of state functions has not proceeded excessively far (here the qualitative-quantitative boundary – excess – is marked by state retention of the ability to ensure that monetary circulation is regulated). The power of private transnational corporations does not yet rival that of the largest states of the First World, and for the present, international financial bodies answer to the latter rather than to the former. But the situation is extremely shaky (as shown by the first tremors in the form of local financial crises, and still more by the world-wide shock of 2008), and the expansion of the total market, together with monetarist trends towards the curtailment of social-democratic control and regulation of market functions, could finally release the 'genie' of financial crisis from the 'bottle' (which in any case is dissolving) of control over world financial operations. *Ipse fecit.*[18] This scenario is determined by the reign of financial capital as the main economic and political force in the present-day capitalism. The probability of a turn towards stronger state regulation also cannot be excluded. However, this turn, apparently, will be possible only as a reaction to very deep economic crisis, forcing the implementation of extraordinary measures for capitalism to survive.

Under the present conditions in which neoliberalism is undermining the very foundations of capitalism, the birth of the total 'market of networks' and of virtual money opens the way for one of the most important developments in the weakening of these foundations. Extremely ambiguous and contradictory, this development is concealed behind a surface appearance of restoring the 'classical' features of capitalism. However, it amounts to the eroding of the very form of capital as a productive relationship, that is, of the general formula governing the circulation of capital.

To those familiar with Marx's *Capital*, it is no secret that the essential form of capital is expressed in the general formula $M - C - M + \Delta M$: money, bringing in increased money.[19] The contradiction inherent in this formula was expressed by Marx in the form of an antinomy: $\Delta M$ arises, and does not arise, in the course of circulation.[20] As noted earlier, today's capital has as its historical prototypes the primeval forms of capital, merchant and usurer capital acting in isolation from direct material production. Marx's theory shows that the contradiction present in the general formula of capital is resolved on the basis that in material production the commodity of labour power creates not only the equivalent of its own value, but surplus value as well.

The breaking of this nexus is now proceeding as if (this is an objective semblance) through a 'return' to the extraction of $\Delta M$ in isolation from material production and within the framework of circulation, where transactions (to use this fashionable term of the new institutionalism) and deals with commodities (C) and money (M) *seemingly* (again, the objective semblance) in and of themselves bring in additional money ($\Delta M$, or expressed in the language of conventional economics, profit).

The present stage, however, does not represent simply a return to the speculation carried on by trading and usurer capital during the epoch that saw the birth of capitalism. It is something more. Superimposing itself on the expansion of socialisation on a world scale (through cheap, highly efficient transport and telecommunications systems, and so forth) and, most important, on the rise of information technologies, on the 'market of networks', and on virtual money, capital creates, in the process of its self-negation, the sphere of transactions. This requires a certain amplification.[21] Virtual capital exists not just in the world of transactions, but also in the world of virtual speculation (including gambling on the stock market), spheres that proceed not only in space but also in time. In this sense, virtual capital multiplies still further its artificial, probability-based essence, but at the same time draws into its orbit the powerful creative potential of humanity, 'leading it away' from the creatosphere while, like a latter-day Pied Piper, playing on its magical pipe the melody of easy enrichment. The sphere of transactions is a new space and time characterised by the dominance of virtual capital. The present stage is above all the space and time of the activity of global virtual fictitious capital. This space and time may be correlated with the form of the financial market. Concentrated here today are the capital holdings of the modern world, hegemonic in terms of their role and gigantic in terms of their size, which exceeds the combined budgets of many states.

Of its very nature, this fictitious capital is divorced from material production, and only *in the final instance* (following on a complex system of mediations) does it owe its existence (1) to the capital that has accumulated over centuries of its dominance, and (2) to material production in the proper sense, in which hired workers create surplus value. (It is important to bear in mind that surplus value is produced by a class of hired workers who are now more numerous than ever before, and who are concentrated primarily in countries of the 'third world' in material production and in other sectors where value is created. This is the key to analysing one of the central contradictions of globalisation – the contradiction between world capital and world labour, which also has its own geopolitical economy – but this will be discussed further below.)

This fictitious capital makes use of the previous growth of labour productivity, which, in developed countries, led to a sharp curtailing of material production and to the birth of information technologies. As a result, fictitious capital occupies and subordinates to itself the most modern area of activity and of human intercourse: the information systems that created the necessary basis for the existence and expansion of corporate fictitious capital. Thus has arisen the special world of this virtual capital with its particular space, time, laws, and life values. It is this capital – corporate virtual capital – that is now the *main socio-economic force* within the total hegemony of capital as a whole.

As was observed earlier, the virtual form of this capital exerts a significant influence on its content. In the first place, virtual capital is becoming incomparably more mobile in time and place than capital in any other form. For capital, meanwhile, the velocity of circulation is of fundamental importance, as was shown in volume II of Capital. Where capital is virtual in character this velocity is qualitatively increased, allowing virtual capital to relocate itself to any point almost instantaneously and with minimal 'transport' (transactional) costs. In order to understand what this means, it is enough to compare virtual money capital with capital in the form of gold or securities.

(This thesis is easy to demonstrate empirically, and was deduced theoretically earlier in this section; it is important because it serves as one of the proofs of the theoretical construct advanced above.) The result is that virtual capital acquires a bearer and material embodiment that in itself is world-wide and eternal; information becomes obsolete only in a moral sense.

Second, virtual money-capital, through possessing these qualities, becomes linked to a specific subject (a physical or corporate person, with a specific position in social space-time) only in terms of the form of property involved, and can change its ownership as quickly and as often as may be desired (something that happens constantly on financial markets). If we add to this the fundamental complexity identified earlier (that is, the complexity represented by the fact that depicting all the connections within the system is no longer possible) and the diffuseness of the modern system of property rights, it becomes clear that virtual capital is capital that is not merely divorced from production, but has no firm place in the private property of any particular physical or juridical person. That means (here we return to the conclusion drawn above) that virtual capital is not the object of firm regulation or control on anyone's part, except the partial local influence of largest financial spiders on the financial market spaces they control.

Third, the contradiction between the properties of information and the properties of capital leads to a situation in which private ownership of virtual capital, along with its alienation and appropriation, become phenomena dependent above all on the formal and also virtual 'rules' that regulate its movement. In the casino-type financial market, material-productive and personal ties of all types (including those that connect owners of capital with workers, as well as the ties between owners and physical objects – factories, land, buildings, and so forth) are constantly disappearing, to be replaced by processes occurring within computer networks.

Further, virtual capital as a whole is becoming completely dependent on the quality of the institutions that ensure support for and development of the capitalist form of the information network as a whole (for example, private ownership of information, guarantees of commercial secrecy, and so forth). The information network, it should be remembered, is unified in time and space (it should be noted that the information network is both universal and divided into different networks, because they may be partially controlled within national and corporate frameworks). Humanity could thus, if not today then in the near future, end up dependent on hackers who not only might threaten to launch nuclear-armed missiles, but could also infect financial computer systems with viruses, and in this way precipitate a world financial crisis. Moreover, the situation is gradually arising in which a subject that dominates the world's information networks would also control the sole material bearer of all virtual capital, the material bearer of 'all the world's money' (but not of money *as such,* since money, even gold, is not a material bearer; it is a generally known fact that on an uninhabited island, gold is not money).

Consequently, the virtual nature of capital, the acquiring by capital-money of a new bearer, also signifies substantial changes in the social and economic content of capital.[22] This bearer in principle allows any capital to become in tendency world-wide, eternal, and supremely mobile. A capital that has such a bearer is linked only formally to a particular owner, and these ties are constantly changing, a characteristic attribute of capital of this type. Such capital depends in all its elements on the global information system, and is at the same time extremely powerful and extremely vulnerable.

Existing above all in virtual form, within computer networks, such capital nevertheless soaks up all the highest achievements of civilisation (from the best experts to the best offices), and constantly strengthens its dominance, sucking the juices from material production (which now is concentrated increasingly in the post-socialist world and 'third' world); from nature (indirectly swallowing a gigantic volume of resources); and from humanity (appropriating not just a large part of the surplus value created throughout the world, but also the achievements of human culture and the creative potential of humankind).[23]

To summarise and in part repeat what has been said here, we may conclude that unlike the fictitious capital of the nineteenth century, the virtual fictitious capital and its substratum, the virtual capital-money of the late twentieth and early twenty-first centuries:

- is a global, virtual network (these characteristics are essential; see the earlier remarks on the new qualities of capital created by its new 'bearer'), and not an atomised sum of monetary units, regulated by a national state or by a totality of distinct financial corporations. This network is globally distributed in all its elements (virtual capital moves instantly through its 'capillaries', reacting to changes in any of the 'nerve centres' of the network). As a result of its unity and global character it functions spontaneously as a matter of definition, and is thus only partly subject to control by national and supra-national state bodies;
- as a world-wide super-network, has been privatised by a limited number of individuals, but at the same time is not subject to their control; virtual capital is owned by a virtual (indeterminate, operating on the basis of probability), archaically unorganised, internally contradictory range of proprietors from the modern corporate-network market;
- plays the new role of a general 'regulator' and universal equivalent (measure of value, means of carrying out transactions, store of wealth, etc.) in the corporate-network market: the role of a sort of 'network of

networks' that renders the whole system of prices (for commodities, capital, labour power, etc.), transactions, savings, and so forth dependent on the state of this super-network. The prices system now depends on the 'network of networks' just as it once depended on gold (we may recall the 'prices revolution', the world-wide cataclysm that occurred in the sixteenth century as a result of the appearance of large quantities on imported gold);

- possesses, as a result of the properties listed above, the quality of virtual self-augmentation (accumulation of virtual, probability-based value, expressed, however, in 'ordinary' money – dollars, euros, etc., since these also become virtual), and connected only indirectly to the production (and accumulation) of surplus value; the limit of this virtual accumulation, like the threat of its collapse, has been described in the first section of this chapter.[24]

In concluding this section, we would like to note also that the present period, that of the undermining of the very bases of capital, is marked not only by the dominance of corporate capital, but also by the efforts of this capital to correct (to its own advantage, naturally) the mechanism of the formal and real subordination of labour. The essence of this correction lies in the development of transitional relations that create the possibility, on the one hand, of partially overcoming (within the context of the hegemony of capital) the alienation of labour from capital, and on the other, of exploiting not only the labour power of the individual worker, but also the creative, innovative capabilities of the integral human being. This, however, is already a new topic, and will be taken up in the next chapter.

## Notes

1 The main sources on which this chapter is based, and in relation to which we propose qualitatively new solutions, include works by Binswanger (1999), Lapavitsas and Levina (2010), Minsky (1986), Tobin (2003), Toussaint (1999), and Sweezy (1994).
2 Hilferding's concept applies to the form financial capital took in a certain historical period, around the beginning of the twentieth century, in Europe and the US. There banks invested in industry, controlled it, and was guaranteed to appropriate part of the profit. By 'industrial' Hilferding meant all non-financial sectors. Lenin saw the matter more broadly as the interweaving of banking (finance) and industrial capital, in which financial capital participated not only in the control of production, but also in property rights and enjoyed a preferential position in the appropriation of profit. (In his definition Lenin does not write about the dominance of financial capital over industrial capital, although in other places

he points to this.) This is not just a new stage in the participation of banks in financing industry, in which banks take a more active part in organising production in order to guarantee its profitability: it is *a new quality*, providing first a potential and then, later, a real transition to the predominance of the dominance of financial capital over production. It is to denote this quality that we refer to 'financial capital' instead of 'finance capital'.

3  The quotation marks here are essential, since 'price of gold' during the period when the gold standard existed was an irrational expression. Price is an expression of the value of a commodity in money, which during that period meant its value in gold. The 'price of gold' was merely an inverse designation of the gold content of a monetary unit.

4  The main characteristics of financialisation are set out by the authors here on the basis of Levina 2002 and Lapavitsas and Levina 2010. These works summarise a broad range of foreign research on this question, in particular such texts as Binswanger 1999 and Minsky 1986.

5  Among the sources for the conclusions advanced here are the substantial edited collection of Timberlake and Dowd (1998); a number of reports by Professor Michael Brie (Brie 2016; Brie and Schütrumpf 2021); and texts by Iren Levina that provide not only summaries of Western writings, but also the author's original views (see Levina 2006). Other important sources include Guttmann 2003; Osipov 2004; Porokhovsky 2002; and Tobin 2003.

6  World Bank, World Development Indicators, 2017, online tables, 4.4: 'Structure of Merchandise Imports', http://wdi.worldbank.org/table/4.4 (accessed 2 June 2021).

7  World Bank, World Development Indicators, 2017, online tables, 4.5: 'Structure of Merchandise Imports', http://wdi.worldbank.org/table/4.5 6-10.

8  World Bank, World Development Indicators, 2017, online tables, 5.4: 'Stock Markets', http://wdi.worldbank.org/table/5. (accessed 2 June 2021).

9  Bank of International Settlements, Triennial Survey, www.bis.org/statistics/d11_1.pdf (accessed 2 June 2021).

10  Bank of International Settlements, Statistics, Table D1, www.bis.org/statistics/d1.pdf (accessed 2 June 2021).

11  We reproduce here, in unchanged form, a note written in 2004, prior to the financial (and subsequently also economic) crisis that began in 2008. This crisis provided a direct confirmation of our theses: 'In the Russia of the epoch of "reforms" this virtual nature of money (including old-fashioned paper money) was demonstrated to us repeatedly and in the most obvious fashion. In our case we had mostly encountered "ordinary" inflation, familiar since the nineteenth century. But here were the "Asiatic" and other financial crises of the late 1990s, as well as the "hyper-realised" threat of a collapse of the dollar, about which hundreds of works have been written. These were more immediate examples of the "probabilitistic" essence of the universal equivalent. Now we cannot tell where, when, and to what degree this universal equivalent is a measure of value, or where, when, and to what degree this is no longer the case' (Buzgalin and Kolganov 2004: 225).

12 We stress that in their actions, the institutions that regulate the monetary system (national states, the IMF, etc.) now often respond to narrow corporate interests and not to those of the forces they formally represent (for example, the totality of citizens of the particular country).

13 This thesis was formulated by the authors at the very beginning of the twenty-first century, well before the world economic crisis. The course of the crisis and the problems of overcoming it have placed a certain brake on this tendency, but have not done away with it entirely.

14 In Capital, Marx quotes lines relating to gold from Shakespeare's tragedy *Timon of Athens*: 'Thus much of this will make black white; foul, fair; Wrong, right; base, noble; old, young; coward, valiant' (Marx 1867/1996: 97–8).

15 World Bank, 'GDP Growth (Annual %)', https://data.worldbank.org/indicator/NY.GDP.MKTP.KD.ZG?view=chart (accessed 2 June 2021).

16 As early as the beginning of the twentieth century, Vilfredo Pareto observed that the number of financial transactions grows more rapidly than the number of commodity transactions and that this leads to the formation (to use his terminology) of a multitude of financial 'bubbles'. By the late twentieth century this process had intensified many times over, as has been shown by numerous researchers in Russia and abroad.

17 This thesis was advanced by the authors for the first time *before the crisis began*, in the first (2004) Russian edition of *Global'nyy capital* (Global capital), where theauthors wrote: 'it is quite probable that in the near future a crisis of the world financial system could act as the detonator for a series of global cataclysms' (Buzgalin and Kolganov 2004: 228–9).

18 'Their own doing' (Latin).

19 We should note that it is through this form – investment, bringing in profit – that neoclassicism defines capital, where it defines it at all.

20 In Soviet political economy and philosophy, many debates surrounded this antinomy and its interpretation. These debates were especially intense during the 1960s and 1970s. The essence of these discussions is conveyed by the texts in the collection *Dialekticheskoe protivorechie* (1979), and especially in the article by F.F. Vyakkerev (1979).

21 This has been prompted by comments from our colleagues, especially V. Krasil'shchikov.

22 A more detailed account of changes in the 'bearers' of financial capital may be found in the numerous works on the theory of the information society. The most interesting, in our view, are the above-mentioned books by Castells (1996) and Etzioni (2001).

23 We are now seeing many attempts to introduce a 'common' criterion for evaluating works of art: they have to be sold, and their valuation in terms of money is the one that ultimately matters. Space exploration and fundamental scientific research meet with the same response: there are constant attempts to assess their value in terms of their ability to pay for themselves and yield a profit. This assessment itself, however, is extremely expensive, and thus falls into the hands of influential financial institutions. So it is that humanity's supreme achievements

depend on the benevolence of the owners of virtual money, since those who do not possess such sums cannot take part in decision-making.

24  We understand fully the limited nature of such a definition, and merely provide a list of interconnected features; in any case, we have attempted earlier to show the essence and contradictions of virtual capital. We should also stress once again that the world is now moving towards (but has not yet reached) the hegemony of corporate capital in general and of virtual capital in particular. Consequently, everything stated above is a description of only one of the dominant trajectories of development, a trajectory that is counterposed by relatively powerful counter-tendencies and forces.

# 8

# Capital of the twenty-first century

## Capital of the twenty-first century as a dialectical negation of the previous evolution of capitalism: relations of exploitation

Before reviewing the most modern forms of exploitation involving the subordination of creative activity to capital, we should stress that modern capitalism is a complex system involving all the basic 'layers' of interaction between labour and capital, in their modern spatial reality, that characterise the historical evolution of the capitalist mode of production.[1] To put it more simply, the modern 'geography' (socio-spatial being) of the world capitalist system is also simultaneously a living history of capitalism, from semi-feudal pre-industrial forms, through the 'classical' exploitation of industrial workers in industrial enterprises, to highly specific forms of subordination of the creative activity of programmers and teachers to capital. In other words, the structure of the principal layers of exploitation in modern capitalist society reproduces the main stages of development of this relationship in the history of capitalism, including its most recent stage.

In seeking to understand contemporary relations of exploitation, we can distinguish a number of features, easily identified empirically and theoretically, which will serve as the starting-point for our analysis. Firstly, the world still contains many hundreds of millions of people who are engaged primarily in manual pre-industrial or early industrial labour and who are the objects of semi-feudal, semi-capitalist exploitation in forms very close to those described by Karl Marx in the concluding chapters of the first volume of *Capital* (1887/1996) dealing with the history of capitalist accumulation, by Vladimir Lenin in 'The Development of Capitalism in Russia' (1908/1964), and by Samir Amin in *Global History* (2010b).

Secondly, since the late twentieth century, the stratum of classical hired industrial workers has become more massive than ever. In the world as a whole, their numbers amount to more than a billion people or, if we consider the economy of China to be mainly state-capitalist, more than 1.5 billion. The quantity of labour that creates surplus value in classic capitalist fashion is now immense; in the world as a whole the volume of hired industrial labour is now greater (even in per capita terms) than in any previous epoch, and so is its productivity.

Thirdly, substantial numbers of workers in the so-called services sector, now viewed as the post-industrial sphere, are engaged in productive labour. From the point of view of classical Marxist theory, their work creates value and, consequently, surplus value. These people include all those who are employed in areas that directly maintain the functioning and reproduction of the productive forces, including labour power. Accordingly, the areas in which value is created (from the point of view of classical Marxist theory) include not only that part of trade where the process of producing material goods in the broad sense is continued, but also that part of the services sector which is analogous to it in its nature and functional role.

Consequently, within the services sector, an area can be distinguished in which value is created and hired labour is performed – that is, an area in which surplus value is created. This is the part of the services sector that involves services that are essential links in the reproduction of labour power, including modern, highly qualified labour power. Clearly, a large proportion of trade in the means of production and in non-simulative consumer goods should be assigned to this area, along with much of the area of the services sector that creates non-simulative goods. In the latter case, this can and should include large numbers of enterprises in the food industry, everyday repairs and related services, recreation, and so forth.

Here we shall not try to estimate the number of people in the world economy who are employed in this way precisely, but it must be significant – of the order of half those working in the international services sector, that is, around 1.5 billion people. It should be stressed that most of them are engaged in the specific form of manual work, of early and late-industrial productive labour, creating value and surplus value. Hence no fewer than *half of the world's workers* are now employed in the traditional areas of productive labour, those that create surplus value in the classical fashion. Taking into account the capital value accumulated over centuries, this production creates the mass of wealth that not only allows modern reproduction to go ahead, but also provides certain foundations for the growth of a 'perverse' (or useless) sector that is parasitic on it, though not on it alone.

To sum up: modern-day capitalism is characterised by the retention of 'classic' relations of capitalist exploitation. Accordingly, we can conclude that the first 'layer' of the subsumption of labour to twenty-first-century capital consists of the classical relations of formal and real subsumption of labour to capital. (Of course, such subsumption is limited. Formal subsumption is limited by various regulations, such as those on the length of the working day, compulsory vacations, or working conditions. Real subsumption, for its part, is limited by the regulation of various forms of the 'humanisation of labour', and the extraction of absolute and relative surplus value is also correspondingly limited.) It will be recalled that nowadays, despite the contraction of industrial production and the more complex social structures that are characteristic of the developed countries, in the world as a whole, the scale of the exploitation of manual and industrial hired labour is greater than in any preceding period.

Nor should it be forgotten that the neoliberal stage of late capitalism is also characterised in most countries (including, in the developed world, for example the US (Gilbert 1998)) by a persistent tendency to restore a relative, and in certain periods also absolute, impoverishment of the proletariat. In the US, for instance, average real hourly wage rates declined between the mid-1970s and the early 1990s and then approximately stabilised with some fluctuations. The gap between high- and low-paid groups increased; the difference between the remuneration of top managers (who now receive a share of surplus value in addition to payment for their labour power) and that of the majority of hired workers almost doubled.

This inequality shows up particularly starkly in the US, and is clearly visible in the different pension benefits enjoyed by CEOs and ordinary workers:

> The 100 largest CEO retirement funds are worth a combined $4.9 billion. That's equal to the entire retirement account savings of 41 percent of American families (more than 50 million families and more than 116 million people). ... Nearly half of all working age Americans have no access to any retirement plan at work. The median balance in a 401(k) plan at the end of 2013 was $18,433, enough to generate a monthly retirement check of $104. Of workers aged 50–64, 29 percent have no defined benefit pension or retirement savings in a 401(k) or IRA. These workers will be wholly dependent on Social Security, which pays an average benefit of $1,223 per month. (Anderson and Klinger 2015: 1–2)

The present period is characterised by the partial desire of capitalism to return to its classical model, 'unburdened' by the compromise with hired workers that was forced on it in the past. Capital was pressured into accepting this compromise essentially by the danger that conflicts between labour and capital would be resolved in revolutionary fashion, and by the effects of the example presented by the existing socialist system. Since the dissolution of the USSR, the pressure on capital has weakened, and it clearly wants to take back the concessions it had made. Signs of this include both the reduction of social spending by the state (although this spending also made capitalist sense by, for instance, increasing productivity) and also the growing differentiation in the wealth and incomes of the population (see Figures 4 and 5). A massive gap has appeared between the average (mean) and median

**Figure 4** The income share of the top 0.01% of the US population, 1913–2019.

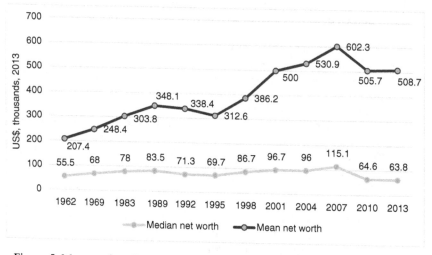

**Figure 5** Mean and median net worth in the US, 1962–2013 (US$, thousands), 2013.

wealth figures in the US, signifying that the great majority of US citizens have incomes nowhere near the average, and indeed, many times lower (see Figure 5).

How is this situation to be explained? It results from the extreme concentration of income in the hands of the ultra-rich who make up a tiny proportion of the US population. The figures for average income are thus

**Figure 6** Top 0.1% wealth share in the US, 1913–2019.

relatively high, but they have no real relation to the incomes of the majority. Figure 6 depicts the share of total household wealth held by the richest 1 per cent of families, as estimated by capitalising income tax returns. As noted by E. Saez and G. Zucman (2016: 519), in 2012 the top 1 per cent included about 160,000 families with net wealth above $20.6 million.

The second 'layer' in the subsumption of labour to capital is associated with the 'dialectical negation' (critical succession) that, under modern conditions, occurs in the relations between labour and capital – relations that are characteristic of the next historical stage (and at the same time the next logical level) in the evolution of late capitalism. Here we find new aspects of exploitation and of the subordination of labour to capital, aspects that also belong to the first stage of the undermining of the foundations of capitalism, the stage of monopolistic capitalism or imperialism. Among the elements preserved from this historic-logical stage are, in particular, a multi-level hierarchy for the redistribution of surplus value to the advantage (1) of developed countries; (2) of monopolistic corporations and cartels of these countries (as monopoly (super-)profits) involving a dual, triple, or greater burden of exploitation for hired workers in developing countries; and (3) of financial capital.

Preserved from the next historic-logical stage in the evolution of late capitalism – the stage of social reformism – we find in the developed countries (though in somewhat truncated form) a complex system of limits to exploitation in the narrow sense of the word. These limits range from restrictions on the length of the working day, week, and so forth to a progressive income tax and various forms of social security. Also present are 'corrections' to the mechanisms of formal and real subsumption of labour, from worker protection laws to workforce participation in ownership and management. This is the third 'layer' in contemporary relations of the subsumption of labour to capital. The neoliberal period, however, has not only cut back the gains made in the preceding stage, but has also undermined the mechanisms through which these gains were achieved. The roles played by various associations of workers have been weakened and reduced under the pressure of *neomarketisation*, and together with the privatisation of people's social existence, this is destroying the basis for resistance to the growth of exploitation.

At this point, the most interesting question from the point of view of the Marxist theory of exploitation is that of the apparent change in the nature of capital and of the so-called 'overcoming' of the exploitation of hired labour through the setting up of numerous pension funds and the like, which act as 'new' capitalists. These institutions combine the savings of hired workers and, it would seem, turn these workers into a collective capitalist. This achievement of the 'universal prosperity state' has now been substantially transformed, but its basic elements have not yet vanished into history and so need to be analysed. As noted earlier, the thesis of the diffusion of capital and the birth of 'post-capitalism' achieved wide currency in the second half of the last century. In our view, the conclusion that the world has undergone a transition to 'post-capitalism' (Drucker 1993), based on arguments about the disappearance of capital as accumulated surplus value and its transformation into the savings of citizens, is fundamentally untrue, at any rate from the point of view of the Marxist theory of surplus value. This is not because we deny the role of pension funds and other forms of savings used for capitalisation; their role is unquestionably great, though not decisive in terms of the global economy.

The point, however, lies elsewhere. Under a non-capitalist system of social appropriation, pension funds and similar institutions (medical insurance, savings funds for the education of children, and so forth) could accumulate primarily the surplus product of society, which at present is quite large and should be used to prolong people's healthy lives, to allow the rational use of free time, and to maintain those who cannot yet work or are no longer able to do so. Under capitalism, things are more complex. Classical capitalism, which featured child labour, short life spans, and the like, did not foresee including these costs in the necessary product of the worker. Technological progress during the last century created a need, at least in developed countries, to make a shift to workers of a different type. The provision of technical and higher education to a significant sector of workers became a condition for the accumulation of capital. In parallel with this, increasing the length and stability of people's lives was now necessary for ensuring the reproduction of the labour power of 'professionals'. Other factors too, such as organised struggles by workers and other popular layers, competition with the 'world system of socialism', and ultimately the shift to social reformism, propelled events in the same direction. The result was that, during the twentieth century, a part of these costs was incorporated in the price of labour power, while another part became a *deduction from surplus value* that was redistributed (under pressure from forces opposed to capital) to the advantage of working people.

In a number of countries, the crisis of social reformism and of the society of the two-thirds, involving the partial curtailment of social benefits, either has led to this spending as a whole being cut or has brought a change in the proportions, with a greater share of expenses being met out of workers' savings; in some countries, social spending has also declined in absolute terms. It has also led to these savings being concentrated in private funds; that is, it has brought about the privatisation by capital of part of the necessary product and of the social surplus product used for social and humanitarian ends. This privatisation has also become the real content of the process which assumes the guise of the diffusion of capitalism.

We must also bear in mind that to a significant extent, the savings involved are made by workers whose wages are paid out of surplus value (and more broadly, from the surplus product that takes the form of value) extracted from material production and the creatosphere. The hired workers in this category include all those in the 'perverse' sector and all higher managers in so far as their incomes are derived from surplus value (profits).

Let us explain. The concept of the perverse (useless) sector, which we introduced more than a decade and a half ago (Buzgalin and Kolganov 2004; see Chapter 6), refers to the sector that produces simulacrum commodities (s-commodities), that is, commodities which satisfy fictitious needs formed under the influence both of the unlimited desire of capital to increase sales by any means and of the development of fictitious forms of capital and their derivatives. These phenomena are useless for the development of the forces of production and for the progress of culture (and above all, of human qualities).

As already explained in Chapter, 6 s-commodities have certain key characteristics. Above all they comprise the huge range of s-commodities created in such areas as mass culture; the output of products and services for prestige consumption; brokerage services; marketing; public relations; and so forth. This phenomenon has become especially obvious in relation to the burgeoning of financial speculation and to the widening of the gulf between the financial sector and the real economy. We should stress that the products mentioned are useless exclusively from the point of view of progress as the development of humanity and culture in dialogue with nature. From the point of view of the capitalist criterion of usefulness – the extraction of profit – they are most useful.

Secondly, in the areas of finance and mass culture, the production of brands, and so forth, not all activity is simulative and useless, or not in full measure. In these areas, goods that are useful for the development of humanity can also be created, both directly and indirectly (as by-products). Moreover, late capitalist production cannot survive without a perverse sector. This does not mean, however, that truly useful production cannot proceed without it. Meanwhile, the volume of production of quasi-goods is now excessive even by the standards of 'late capitalism'. We shall return to the question of perverse sector later when analysing the specific nature of creative activity.

The resources of the perverse (useless) sector, just like profits from material production and wealth that is forged through the process of creative activity and has the form of value, are transformed directly and indirectly (through savings from 'salaries') into sources of the formation of new capital value. These processes show how the camouflaging of the process of exploitation occurs, and how an objective appearance is created that capital as such (the private property of a physical person who engages a hired worker) has disappeared; all that is present, in this version of things, is savings which have been derived from the incomes of workers, and which are used by 'professionals' for the expanded reproduction of the economy.

We can thus establish that in the modern global economy one of the main sources of income and of capital formation remains 'classical' surplus value, created by the productive labour of hired workers. We will see later that the universal wealth, in the form of value and arising out of intellectual labour, is similar to this classical form. These sources, however, are transformed into investments and into the personal consumption of the complex system of classes and intermediate layers of capitalist society, including the corporate hierarchy, 'professionals', and the like (more will be said later about the structure and social nature of these layers), that mediate the complex system of perverse forms. One of these forms is the camouflaged appropriation of profit (including in material production) that is disguised as the salaries and other income of higher managers and 'professionals'. Another form, scarcely less important, is the redistribution of part of the surplus value created in the world (including part of the 'salary payments' of higher staff and 'professionals') to the advantage of the perverse sector. This redistribution proceeds via two main channels: the investment of the accumulated funds of firms in the perverse sector (to cite just one example, before the world crisis, corporations in the non-financial sector in the US received as much as half of their profits from investments in financial speculation), and the directing into the same sector of personal savings derived from surplus value and intellectual rent.

In addition, late capitalism (especially in the period of neoliberalism) features the privatisation by corporate capital of the part of the necessary social product which is saved for the reproduction of highly qualified workers: the cost of labour power. This part is also used for the reproduction of capital, including for investments in the perverse sector.

Finally, a complex system of redistribution is characteristic of income that is obtained from such sources as intellectual rent; it will be recalled that this comprises the income of corporations that own intellectual capital, and part of the income of intellectual workers. Part of the savings from this income also becomes a source of the reproduction of capital, including that of the perverse (useless) sector.

The fourth 'layer' of the subordination of labour is that specific to the contemporary stage of capitalism. It includes the new relations of exploitation emerging from the exploitation of subjects of creative activity, and from the subjection of the person as an individual human being and not simply as labour power to corporate capital.

Modern-day capital produces not only classical industrial output but also that of creative activity, in which the 'creative class' is engaged. It is here that new forms of capitalist exploitation are arising since, as will be shown below, modern capital appropriates part of the wealth that comes into being through universal creative labour. (Creative labour is necessarily universal in that it relies on the universal intellectual heritage of humankind.) The areas of activity in which creative components play a significant role (we have termed these areas the creatosphere) now include a broad range of the sectors of social reproduction, including education and training in all their diversity, health care, technical and scientific creativity, the recreation of nature and society, the productive elements of managerial work, art, and so forth. In all these areas, labour is productive, but by general human criteria rather than essentially capitalist ones, since it serves the reproduction and development of the human species irrespective of the social system.

Universal creative labour, in contrast to abstract social labour, is not at the same time a private labour of a separate producer. And commodities are created only by such labour, which is both private and social, as Marx shows in chapter 1 of volume I of *Capital*; here he writes that in the exchange of $x$ of commodity A for $y$ of commodity B, not only does the use value of commodity B become a 'mirror' of the value of commodity A, but the concrete private labour becomes a 'mirror' of the abstract public labour. Marx adds: 'Only such products can become commodities with regard to each other, as result from different kinds of labour, each kind

being carried on independently and for the account of private individuals'
(Marx 1867/1996: 52).

In this case, we emphasise once again that our understanding of universal
creative labour is derived from Marx, who distinguishes universal labour
from ordinary cooperation: 'Universal labour is all scientific labour, all
discovery and all invention. This labour depends partly on the co-operation
of the living, and partly on the utilisation of the labours of those who have
gone before. Co-operative labour, on the other hand, is the direct co-operation
of individuals' (Marx 1894/1998: 106). Universal creative labour creates
cultural benefits that are directly public from the outset. Later in this chapter
we will clarify this further and give a detailed description of our understanding
of creative labour.

Creative labour gives rise to genuine (non-simulative) social wealth. In
in a totally market-dominated setting, it acquires a sort of 'envelope' of
value. For creative labour this value-form is perverse, but the social wealth
itself is real and productive, and lies at the basis of reproduction of the
material and cultural goods appropriated by modern capital. Moreover,
under the conditions of private ownership of the results of creative activity,
this wealth is acquired by capital, to a large degree free of charge, in the
form of so-called 'intellectual rent', which under late capitalism is the main
form of income from such activity.

As has been empirically established, a proportion of intellectual rent
consists of a sort of 'addition' (over and above the value of labour power)
which is hidden in the wages of the hired intellectual worker. Meanwhile,
a greater proportion of this rent is appropriated by the owner of the 'creative
corporation' that employs hired creative labour. A further part is appropriated
by self-employed creative workers, whose labour is not hired, but here too
a significant portion of this rental income is re-invested (mediated in the
form of savings) in capitalist reproduction. Alongside classical surplus value,
intellectual rent thus becomes a basic source of the profits of modern capital.

In conclusion, the modern system of exploitation presupposes a contra-
puntal, contradictory, and by no means always organic integration of four
historico-logical 'layers', or sub-systems of production relations, of the
exploitation of labour by capital, as follows:

(1) the 'classical' system of relations of production (by hired labour) and
    of appropriation (by capital) of 'normal' surplus value;
(2) the relations of production and appropriation of monopoly (super-)
    profits and financial profits;
(3) the relations, ended by neoliberalism and reproduced in curtailed and
    distorted form, of redistribution of a part of surplus value, and of the
    'diffusion' of capital;
(4) the relations of exploitation that pertain to creative activity and to the
    appropriation of intellectual rent.

Late capitalism is also, of course, framed by other components of the total hegemony of capital, and in particular of exploitation, that are specific to the current stage. As we continue our investigation, we shall build as before on the classical Marxist theory of capital and abstract from neoclassical interpretations of this phenomenon.

## The exploitation of the 'creative class': its specific nature, content, and forms

Within the classical Marxist category-field, and from the point of view of content, the appropriation of surplus value and the exploitation of hired workers ('exploitation' is used here in the classical sense, to refer solely to the relations that govern its appropriation) contradicts all the main parameters of the space and time of co-creation of the 'creatosphere' (Buzgalin and Kolganov 1998). The creatosphere, in our definition, has three components. The first is the *resources of creativity* – that is, all the phenomena of culture, information, and so on, including the results of scientific, educational, technical, artistic, and social activity that can be defined as new cultural value. Abstracting from the socio-economic form, in particular from private ownership of information, we can assert that, on a 'technical' level, these resources, by virtue of their nature as cultural phenomena, are unlimited. The creatosphere is thus a qualitatively different world from that which economists have traditionally analysed, the world of scarce or finite resources in which only wants are infinite. By contrast, in the creatosphere, not only are resources unlimited, but needs are limited (mostly by human abilities; not everyone has the desire to study calculus or to read the novels of Tolstoy and Hesse). However, once they are placed in concrete socio-economic relationhips – the market, capital, private property – the situation changes. The resources of the creatosphere, which are by nature limitless, become objects of private property, and this gives rise to a whole series of important consequences, which will be examined presently.

The second component of the creatosphere is the process of *creative labour*, which, like labour in general in Marx's terminology, represents 'universal' activity, and which includes unalienated cooperation by creators in unlimited social space and time. In Soviet critical Marxism (and not only there), these ideas were developed to a substantial degree (Bakhtin 1963; Bibler 1975; Batishchev 1984/1997), and in particular it was shown that creativity is always *co*-creativity, a dialogue of all creators. In this sense, the product of the activity of scientists, artists, and teachers is always simultaneously the result both of their individual activity and of their dialogue with all their teachers and colleagues; with the authors of all the books they have read and the composers of the music they have listened to; with nature, understood in this case as an aesthetic and cognitive value rather than as a source of raw materials; and so forth. Because of this, it is fundamentally impossible to define in collective terms a particular creative worker's share in the new creative product. To this important and consequential point, we would add that the subjects of creative activity in the modern world are not only members of the free professions, not only the financial and management 'elite', but all actors of 'ordinary', 'mass' creative activity: teachers, doctors, artists, scientists, gardeners, social workers, engineers, librarians, and so on.

Of course, any labour process includes elements of creativity, of intellectual effort, which are the basis for the distinction between human labour and the labour-like activity of animals. However, the capitalist system develops the division of labour to the point of an almost total separation of intellectual functions from the majority of workers, owing to the implementation of factory system. Marx explained this separation as follows:

> The separation of the intellectual powers of production from the manual labour, and the conversion of those powers into the might of capital over labour, is, as we have already shown, finally completed by modern industry erected on the foundation of machinery. The special skill of each individual insignificant factory operative vanishes as an infinitesimal quantity before the science, the gigantic physical forces, and the mass of labour that are embodied in the factory mechanism and, together with that mechanism, constitute the power of the 'master'. (Marx 1867/1996: 426)

It should be borne in mind that, by definition, the labour of a person is creative, because it is precisely a person's ability to create new phenomena in accordance with a pre-established goal that distinguishes her or him from animals; Marx remarked on this, rightly emphasising what differentiates the work of 'the worst architect from the best of bees'.[2] But here it is necessary to take into account at least two circumstances.

The first of these is the development of relations of alienation in the 'realm of necessity', the 'prehistory' of humankind,[3] that is, both pre-bourgeois and bourgeois societies. Such relations ensure that the creative function, in particular the goal-setting and pre-conception that are critical to creativity, is, to a greater or lesser extent, always alienated from the worker, whoever he or she is – a slave, serf, or employee – tightening the nuts on the conveyor belt.

Second, the isolation of creative labour, in contrast to reproductive labour, is a theoretical abstraction. Any creative labour, even the labour of a prima ballerina, contains a lot of routine actions, just as any routine labour contains some elements of goal-setting and decision-making. However, in the activity of the ballerina, the main thing that determines the content and specificity of her labour is creativity – the minutes of dance, and not the hours of rehearsals. Similarly, in the case of a worker on a conveyor belt, the content (in this case, rather, the emptiness) of the labour is determined by the fact that the worker acts as an appendage to a machine tool or another machine. As Marx wrote:

> In handicrafts and manufacture, the workman makes use of a tool, in the factory, the machine makes use of him. There the movements of the instrument of labour proceed from him, here it is the movements of the machine that he must follow. In manufacture the workmen are parts of a living mechanism. In the factory we have a lifeless mechanism independent of the workman, who becomes its mere living appendage. (Marx 1867/1996: 425)

To sum up the findings of our teachers and previous research (for more details, see Buzgalin 2015), we can identify the following main features of creative activity that qualitatively distinguish it from reproductive labour. So Creativity is not just about creating something new. It is an activity that combines:

- the dissemination of a cultural phenomenon (see Batishchev 1967) in which it is not consumed or used up (the physical consumption of its material bearer may be, at best, a prerequisite, but it is not the content of the disseminative creative activity), and its use as a cultural source (of information, meaning, inspiration);
- the creation a new cultural phenomenon which is ideal in the dialectical materialist sense (for more, see Buzgalin 2015; Buzgalin and Kolganov 2019c: 85–6, 93, 119–26).

The results of creative activity are unlimited and potentially generally accessible: since the costs of replicating and disseminating cultural goods tend to zero, they can be distributed without loss. The result of creativity, however, is multifaceted:

- it is a cultural phenomenon (a work of art, a scientific or design product, a person who has learned something or who has become healthier physically and morally);
- in the activity of creating a new creative result, people grow and enrich themselves;
- because of the latter qualities, creative activity is characterised by the property of self-motivation: creative work ceases to be a burden and becomes a need.

Thus creative activity is at the same time a special social relationship: a subject–subject dialogue between a creator and all other cultural figures in time and space (see Buzgalin and Kolganov 2019b: 102–4 for more details); both an artist and a scientist, both the engineer and the teacher, create new things only in dialogue with their full-time and part-time teachers and partners. Because of this, creativity is at the same time both a universal activity and a purely individual activity, and this contradiction is resolved and reproduced whenever the creator enters in-person and correspondence dialogue with all her or his predecessors and colleagues (e.g. reading a book, listening to music, arguing with friends, enjoying nature).

The universality of creative activity determines that it creates a phenomenon that

- is *a priori* a universal (cultural) value and therefore
- does not require social and economic mediation for its public recognition (purchase by a market agent or another).

Recognition of its value occurs exclusively in the process of distribution of this phenomenon in another creative activity (in the process of co-creation). The purely individual character of creative activity determines that it is unique, 'indispensable': it cannot be replaced by the functioning of a machine (see Freeman 2016).

The third component of the creatosphere consists of the *results of creativity*, which technically (if we abstract from socio-economic institutions such as intellectual property rights) can be objects of universal property – objects of the ownership by everybody of everything (Mezhuev 1977; Hardt and Negri 2009). Everyone potentially is an owner of Tolstoy's novels or of Newton's formulae; the inherent nature of cultural products does not create any boundaries to each of us being able to desobjectivise them, to make them 'our own', part of our thinking or feeling. Herein lies the fundamental difference between the ownership by each of everything (universal, generally accessible property) and private ownership (or even most other forms of ownership), which always restricts access in one way or another. Meanwhile, as noted earlier, it is by no means the case that everyone has the ability to perform this desobjectivisation (not to speak of the socio-economic limitations, starting with the ability to afford education and ending with the payments for information that are a typical feature of modern economies).[4] But this, we repeat, is a question of the social organisation of production, including cultural and creative production, not of the essence of creative activity. It is 'technically' unlimited. Only the socio-economic form (for example, private property) may introduce a limitation of this kind, giving rise to a contradiction between the 'technically' *unlimited* nature of the resources and products of creative activity on the one hand, and the socio-economic *limitations* on them (private ownership) on the other.

We can now move on to the question of the exploitation of subjects of creative activity. First, we should point out that we examine here only the relations of the exploitation by capital of hired creative labour. We leave aside the relations in which creators act as (self-employed) 'members of the free professions', as members of cooperatives, as workers in state (public) clinics, schools, and universities, or as employees of NGOs; had the status of slaves (as did, for example, the legendary Aesop) or of serfs (many eighteenth- and nineteenth-century Russian actors and artists were in this category); performed their creative labour in the USSR as genuine enthusiasts, working for trivial sums or completely without pay for *their* Soviet homeland; or created new technologies in Stalinist labour camps. The object of our analysis, we repeat, is all those subjects of creative activity who work for hire in capitalist enterprises.

Workers of this type first appeared centuries ago, but hired creative workers have become a substantial stratum only in recent decades, as the professions of programmers and researchers in private corporations, and of teachers in private schools and universities, have taken on sizeable dimensions. It is true that even today the greater part of the workforce still consists of hired industrial workers and non-creative workers of service sector, as explained earlier. A peculiarity of the present stage of late capitalism, however, is that hired creative workers are being transformed into a social layer whose activity is determining the face of modern technical (and also social) progress.

Second, since we are operating at a high level of abstraction, comparable to that of the first volume of *Capital*, we deliberately refrain from includng numerous details of the present-day relations of hiring and exploitation of creative workers of one type or another.

We can now put forward our initial thesis: the classical capitalist exploitation of hired labour, in the form in which Marx described it, presupposes (1) that what capital acquires is not labour, and not the worker, but only labour power. Under the conditions of classical capitalism, the human individual, with her or his 'immortal creative soul', is not sold; the characteristically human functions of labour, above all that of determining the goal to which it is directed, are carried out by the capitalist. Hence (2) it is the capitalist, as the owner of the means of production, who organises the process of production and who commands labour (ignoring for the moment managers and the like). The role of the worker is reduced to carrying out the orders of capital. Accordingly, (3) the result of this activity is the product of cooperation as set down by capital, and its qualities are determined by capital. If a worker cannot ensure this designated result, he or she is replaced by another. Finally, (4) the creative labour should produce commodities whose value exceeds the combined total of the cost of the labour power expended in making them, plus the value of the means of production transferred to these commodities. This excess constitutes surplus value, the result of the exploitation of the hired worker.

However, in the creatosphere, unlike in material production, the product is not a commodity sold on the market, but an active process and the self-development of the worker that occurs in this process, plus a cultural product or commodity. The process and the result of creative activity, defined above, are not alienable from the creator in its content; they are an attribute of the creator's personality. But alienated social relations (in any form – from slavery to wage labour, from direct violence to the market) can and do lead to the alienation of material carrier (e.g. a manuscript or picture) of the product from the creator. As the great Russian poet Aleksandr Pushkin put it long ago in 'Conversation of a Bookseller with a Poet' (1824): 'The inspiration is not for sale, / But one can sell the manuscript.' The most famous modern example in this case is private intellectual property. This phenomenon makes the impossible possible: the author can sell her or his 'I', for the author's theory, poem, or picture is nothing more than the alter ego of her or his personality. Moreover, the world of alienation creates relationships in which creators can alienate their inspiration by selling their divine soul to the golden devil.

Such illustrations and metaphors help us frame the contradiction between the inalienable content of the creative labour – which in this sense is not amenable to exploitation – and its alienated social form. Even so, the creative worker is still the object of exploitation in late capitalism. Although the income of creative workers may exceed that of even the highest-paid workers who are not owners and top managers, the profit obtained from the use of creative labour as hired labour in creative corporations brings the owners of these firms income which is, as a rule, substantially greater than that which they receive from the exploitation of industrial workers engaged in reproductive labour. (This reproductive labour consists of standard routine operations which are repeated from day to day and is characterised by the separation of the creative, intellectual side of working process from the workers.)

We thus face a contradiction: the content of creative activity makes it impossible to exploit, but the fact that exploitation occurs, and that it takes a capitalist form, is obvious. Morevoer, although the same practice shows that in many respects the hired creative worker is far less subject to capital than the 'usual' worker, the fact that corporations practise the exploitation of hired creative labour throws down a challenge to Marxist theory, which demonstrates that such exploitation is impossible.

We shall leave to one side the answers to this challenge yielded by standard neoclassical economics. According to this, everything is simple: the 'normal' capital which Bill Gates invests (we recall that he began by investing a few hundred thousand dollars in his business and is now the owner of more than a hundred billion) is several thousand times more efficient than the 'intellectual' capital of even the most talented programmer who 'invests' her or his creative abilities ('created' by spending a similar sum of hundreds of thousands of dollars on many years of education) in Gates's business, and who during a lifetime receives at most a few tens of millions.

Our method of proceeding from the abstract to the concrete, revealing the system of relations through which the owner of capital is able to appropriate the value that results from the labour of the creative worker, yields a very different answer. We shall begin with a relationship between creator and capital in which the form of hired labour is preserved. In direct terms, this process looks very much the same as if the labour power of the subject of reproductive work were being purchased. Nevertheless, the essence of this relationship is substantially altered. Here it is necessary to clarify the distinction between the concepts of 'labour power' and 'creative potential'. In the first case, we are talking about the commodity, a person's ability to work, which can be sold, or separated from the person. As is known, the relationship of wage labour and capital differs from that of slavery, in that the human personality is not for sale as it is in the case of slavery: only what is separable from the person is sold, i.e. the ability for such work, which does not require the involvement of personal qualities and can be carried out under the command of another person, in a mode that very accurately conveys the saying 'He is the boss, I am a fool.' Here, in particular, the potential possibility of the subordination of labour to capital is hidden. It becomes a reality when capital buys a person's labour power, which as a result becomes part of the functioning capital. However, the function of capital becomes not the personality of the worker (which is just not for sale; the employee, unlike the slave, remains personally free). At the same time, the hired worker is the carrier of the abstract ability to work, which any worker in the market possesses, and he or she sells it. This is an abstract locksmith, turner, driver, of which there are thousands and millions in the labour market. An 'ordinary' (non-creative) hired worker can therefore be dismissed at any time because he or she has an abstract, non-personified ability to work and can be replaced at any time by any other worker.

Creative potential is something qualitatively different. This is talent, which is an attribute of a person's personality. A human being does not exist outside her or his creative potential. The disappearance or collapse of the latter is the death of a person's personality. Conversely, creative potential is always purely personal, personified; it does not exist outside this particular person; it can be realised only by this particular person and by no one else. In abstraction (and this is a practical-effective abstraction, similar to such an abstraction as, say, a 'mammal'), an employee with creative potential is unique and cannot be replaced by another. Therefore, unlike the labour power that an employee sells, the creative potential – talent – is not alienable in principle. Hence, in principle, the inability to dismiss this employee with the same ease as an employee who performs reproductive labour. This is due, in principle, to the possibility and necessity of the transition to a partnership between capital and a creative worker and the impossibility of exploiting the latter.

All this means that a person's creative potential a phenomenon is like love, friendship, and honour – everything that cannot be sold or bought. But capitalism makes the object of alienation and exploitation *everything*: love, honour, conscience, and, yes, the creative potential of human being. And every actor in capitalist relations knows this.

There is a fundamental contradiction here. How exactly it is allowed and what is the nature of the exploitation of the creative worker? We will say more about this below. It is important to recall in this case that the concepts of 'labour power' and 'creative potential' are theoretical abstractions. There is no person in existence who alienates only labour power or only creative potential, just as absolutely healthy people do not exist. It is a question of degree.

There are five points which differentiate the creator and the 'normal' hired worker as 'objects' (in inverted commas, since in the case of creativity they are the creative subjects) of exploitation. In the first place, human creative potential, creative labour power, is a commodity which is always subject to dual ownership. It is inalienable from its 'bearer', who does not lose it even when it is sold to someone else. Moreover, in the process of consumption of this commodity, its use value grows. Unlike labour power, which after it is bought is consumed by capital, exhausting the worker physically and morally, the creative potential of a human engaged in the labour process (and hence being exploited) increases, and this is one of the main results of creativity. Although the 'ordinary' worker may in the course of the labour process also improve her or his qualifications, there is a substantial difference between an increase in the ability of a conveyor-belt worker to tighten nuts quickly and the progress made in the creative abilities of a researcher who starts as an assistant and advances to the status of project head. Unquestionably, there are limits to how much creative potential can grow, and after a certain time it begins to be exhausted (in physical terms even creative people, unfortunately, are not blessed with eternal youth), but this has little effect on the essential situation. In the case of the reproductive content of activity, labour is thus a burden, while in the case of creative activity it is a sphere of self-realisation, an actual need.

Secondly, and as is well known, the creative process operates not just in working time, but also in the worker's free time. This is why capital strives to acquire the human being, with all her or his personal qualities, for the whole time of the vital activity, along with all the products of her or his personal self-realisation. From this, in particular, stems the interest that the owner of capital has in securing a long-term (in extreme cases, lifelong) contract with the creator.

Thirdly, in acquiring creative human capacities, capital is obliged to pay the cost of reproducing this particular commodity. Alongside the traditional components of the value of labour power (the means of maintaining the worker and her or his family), this includes the whole totality of the costs of educating the creative worker and improving her or his qualifications (or providing retraining for a new profession); of the acquisition and constant use of cultural products; of the recreation of the individual; and of ensuring a healthy way of life, so that the worker lives longer. In addition, this value also includes certain social guarantees, providing the creator with 'the right to make mistakes' (freedom from having to suffer if her or his creativity does not yield commercial results since, as we recall, in creativity a negative result is also a result). This shows, in theoretical terms, the reasons behind a phenomenon which empirically is very familiar: human creative capacities are an expensive commodity.

At the same time, creative activity in and of itself acts as a stimulus to its existence. Financial motivations in this case are something external; hence capital can parasitically feed off the internal motivation of the creative worker, receiving part of the worker's creative potential free of charge, without paying for the stimuli which the worker provides for herself or himself through engaging in creation.

Fourthly, creative activity's above-mentioned property of yielding results that are unforeseen (and in some cases quite negative) means that the owner of capital buys a 'pig in a poke' – that is, acquires what is precisely a potential, undefined either qualitatively or quantitatively. What capital does not purchase is an ability, fixed qualitatively and quantitatively, to create a certain value (with this fixation taking the form of an hourly rate or even piece-rate payment), but a fundamentally undetermined potential; it thus pays for potential alone.

At the same time, the price of this commodity, creative potential (unlike ordinary labour power), does indicate that society (in the first instance) and the market do use certain parameters to gauge individual creative workers and their potential. The social, non-market assessment that we make here (for example, through the regard we pay to an educational diploma, a university degree, or prestige among colleagues in the case of scholars) is greater to the extent that the subject of the activity is engaged in authentic creative activity in the creatosphere (science, art, and education). The strictly market-based assessment is more important to the extent that we are concerned with the labour of professionals in the perverse (useless) sector (corporate management, finances, mass culture, professional sport). In other words, both society and the market are trying to estimate the potential of creative worker, but they use different criteria. Society pays attention to the signs of creative activity (in the case of academics, diploma, doctoral degree, and publications). Market estimations of the price of such labour are not based on the costs of reproduction of a certain worker, as with non-creative labour, but on the expected benefits the worker will bring. These observations help in particular to account for the possibility that the price of the creative worker will deviate massively from the actual cost of reproducing her or his creative qualities; as we know, the market of simulacra as a whole values a pop star or a lucky rainmaker hundreds of times more highly than a Nobel prize-winning scientist, not to speak of a rural schoolteacher.

Finally, and this is especially important, the dual nature of creative activity results in the dual nature of exploitation in the sphere of creative labour. It will be recalled that creativity is at once a profoundly individual activity, carried out by a particular subject, and also universal labour, a collaboration, a dialogue open in space and time between the creative worker and her or his colleagues, forerunners and successors, with all those whose cultural outcomes he or she has desubjectivised through her or his activity and with those who will desobjectivise the results of her or his labour. The creators of a new theory in physics are not only its immediate authors, but also their teachers, their students, and Pythagoras and Einstein. This is how new music is composed, or a 'pedagogical poem' is created, embodied in the lives of pupils. This leads to a conclusion of fundamental importance: in each individual case in which creative activity takes place, capital *exploits dually* not only the particular, individual subject of that activity, but also the entire world of culture, and all of the human species whose cultural potential it indirectly appropriates. The mediating principle in this case is the process of dialogue that occurs between the creative worker whom capital employs, and the entire world of the creatosphere.

We shall return later to this thesis, which is important for what is to follow. Here we draw an intermediate conclusion: the creator as an 'object' of exploitation is substantially different from the 'normal' hired worker, who, while also an object of exploitation, is the subject not of creative, but of reproductive labour.

The most important differences are those between the content of the exploitation in the sphere of creative activity and the exploitation analszed in *Capital*. As was shown earlier, creative activity in terms of its content is the product of the common activity of co-creators interacting in a process of unalienated dialogue, and not of the abstract labour of isolated producers. Because of this, while it does create value and surplus value for capital, creative activity does more: it also creates universal social wealth.

A digression is necessary here to remind the reader that, as shown in the works of representatives of critical Soviet Marxism (Khessin 1964b), value is a category reflecting only, and exclusively, the relations of commodity production. That is why Marx stated dozens of times that value and use value are two aspects of a *commodity*, and not of any product. Value is a historically specific category, like any other category of commodity production. Such an understanding of categories – as reflections of historically specific production relations, as shown at the beginning of the book – is the alpha and omega of the Marxist methodology; this stands in contrast to the methodology of orthodox economic theory, for which both value and capital, etc. are, as it were, eternal, extra-historic, universal categories of any economy (which, by the way, they, as a rule, identify with the market). To take the simplest example, potatoes, which Russians themselves grow in the country and eat themselves, have no value. The labour that created them is not the labour of private commodity producers operating in the system of the social division of labour and alienating the commodity on the market in exchange for another commodity produced by another commodity producer. In the same way, information obtained from Wikipedia, or another source that is publicly available and created free of charge, has no value, though it has great use value.

We can now return to the chain of reasoning begun above. In circumstances where commodity relations of production dominate – and especially in the context of the 'total market' – universal social wealth takes a perverse form, receiving a value-assessment of indeterminate size. It is important to note that this value-assessment (the price of a creative product, transformed into private (intellectual) property) can be tied only indirectly to the expenditure of labour by the creator, and may not bear any relation to it whatever. This expenditure is not in any case subject to measurement, even in terms of duration; time that is spent in creative activity is not work time, but free time.

In the case of the exploitation of workers in the sphere of creative labour, therefore, surplus value is neither created nor appropriated. What happens is, instead, the creation of universal (unalienated) cultural wealth by the worker-creator (and indirectly, by the whole world of culture) and the appropriation of this wealth by corporate capital, that is, by alienated material wealth personified. What capital appropriates in this process is not the unpaid work time of the creator, but her or his free time, since it is during this time that the above-mentioned wealth comes into being.

It is important to note that from the point of view of Marx and of most of his followers (or at any rate, of those who have worked in the Soviet or post-Soviet space), the time people have free from work is not leisure time, but time for their free, rounded development as human beings. This is why Marx wrote in the third volume of *Capital* that increases in free time represented progress for the 'realm of freedom', and that free time represented a negation of the 'realm of necessity':

> In fact, the realm of freedom actually begins only where labour which is determined by necessity and mundane considerations ceases; thus in the very nature of things it lies beyond the sphere of actual material production. Just as the savage must wrestle with Nature to satisfy his wants, to maintain and reproduce life, so must civilised man, and he must do so in all social formations and under all possible modes of production. With his development this realm of physical necessity expands as a result of his wants; but, at the same time, the forces of production which satisfy these wants also increase. Freedom in this field can only consist in socialised man, the associated producers, rationally regulating their interchange with Nature, bringing it under their common control, instead of being ruled by it as by the blind forces of Nature; and achieving this with the least expenditure of energy and under conditions most favourable to, and worthy of, their human nature. But it nonetheless still remains a realm of necessity. Beyond it begins that development of human energy which is an end in itself, the true realm of freedom, which, however, can blossom forth only with this realm of necessity as its basis. The shortening of the working day is its basic prerequisite. (Marx 1894/1998: 807)

Understood in this way, time spent on creative activity (and consequently on self-development) is free time, and hence to the degree to which the activity of the worker in the areas of education, science, art, and social innovations is creative, the time spent in this activity is free. Capital turns this time, which is free from the point of view of its content, into work time. This, however, is merely a perverse form, imposed deceptively on society by the system of production relations of late capitalism. In this sense, it is correct to say that in the case of a creative worker, the exploitation is of the worker's free time, and hence, as was noted earlier, of her or his vital activity (free time is precisely the time in which people live, that is, carry out their self-realisation). Capital also transforms the free time of all workers into commodified leisure time, redistributing their income in its favour and forcing workers to intensify their labour efforts. Thus modern capital is trying to use not only labour time but also free time to extract more profit.

The most important paradox in this case, however, is the duality not only of the object, but also of the content of the relationship of exploitation in the case of (co-)creative workers. This lies in the fact that if we proceed from the laws of the creatosphere, even the creative worker herself or himself has no basis for appropriating the value-assessment of all the cultural wealth which he or she brings into being. Under the laws of the creatosphere, a cultural value in economic terms (that is, as a resource which is used exclusively by a single party, and brings income exclusively to that party) belongs not to its creator, but to the entire world of humanity and to every member of the human species. Buzgalin (2017) has already argued that the world of the creatosphere is characterised by 'the ownership by each of everything'. A cultural value is the result of a process of co-creation, performed through a cultural dialogue between a particular creator and her or his direct and indirect colleagues. In the strict sense of the word, therefore, the exploitation in the sphere of creative activity is not only the exploitation of a particular creative worker, but also the exploitation by capital of the entire creatosphere, the appropriation free of charge of all the cultural values that have been de-objectified by a particular creative worker, employed by a corporation, in the process of creating a commercial innovation for this corporation. Moreover, since capital is not only the totality of individual enterprises, but also the concrete-universal aspects of capitalism, we can thus speak of the exploitation by capitalism in its totality of the human creatosphere in all its spatial and temporal wealth (getting ahead of ourselves a little, we might say that to the creatosphere must be added its alter ego, the earth's biosphere). This latter helps ensure the substantial differences between the exploitation in the sphere of creative activity and 'normal' capitalist exploitation.

Hence, in the case of appropriation by a particular capitalist (for example, Henry Ford) of the surplus value created by the reproductive work of some totality of hired labour (say, the workforce at an automobile plant), the quantitative aspects of the problem of ending exploitation can be resolved relatively simply: by taking away the surplus value from the capitalist involved and handing it over to the enterprise workforce. On the national level, this problem can be solved through nationalisation (provided that the state, in economic and political terms, represents the interests of the workers). Hence the socialisation (or nationalisation) of the means of production has been and remains a key question of (industrial) socialism as the negation of (industrial) capitalism.

With creative activity everything is far more complex. In this case, the alternative to capitalist exploitation cannot be the transfer of ownership of the result of activity to the creator herself or himself (whether the creator is individual or collective is immaterial here), since this result is no more than the 'final stage' of an unending common process of co-creation. The ending of the exploitation of (universal) creative activity can therefore only be the ending of (private) ownership of cultural values (intellectual property), and the latter can be realised only as the ending of the relations of alienation and appropriation (in their economic sense) in the world of the creatosphere, through the rejection in this world of property as a specific institution.

To reject (private) intellectual property is not, however, to reject relations of objectification and de-objectification, or the attribution of an author's name to the result of creative activity; the work of science or art that arises from the exertions of creator N. can bear whatever name its author gives it, and will still become a cultural phenomenon with which the other subjects of co-creation will thenceforth engage in dialogue. These relations are of the same character as the process through which a star or planet newly discovered by an astronomer is named and included in a star atlas.

From this, we can draw the important conclusion that putting an end to the exploitation in the sphere of (universal) creative activity and, accordingly, of (private) ownership of cultural values (intellectual property) is thus an authentically communist process, a vital component of the process of transforming the 'realm of necessity' into the 'realm of freedom', and not just of capitalism into socialism. In this sense, the question is not one of socialism, even postindustrial, but of communism.

In this case, the emphasis not only on the transition from capitalism to socialism, but on a larger-scale transformation, which Marx and Engels call 'the ascent of man from the kingdom of necessity to the kingdom of freedom' (Engels 1880/1998: 324; see also Marx 1894/1998: 807), is important, because the larger scale of transition is associated with more large-scale changes in social life. In the latter case, it is not only about the removal of private property relations and the appropriation of surplus value by the owner of capital: in addition, the transition to the 'realm of freedom' implies the overcoming of all, and not just capitalist alienation relations. In particular, it means overcoming the subordination of a person to the division of labour when the majority of creative functions remain only for certain social and professional groups, and the removal of commodity relations and other alienated economic forms, the state and other forms of political alienation, religion, etc. This presupposes moving much further and deeply along the path of disarray than is the case under socialism, which is usually understood as the initial stage of the 'realm of freedom', within which the subordination of the human being to the division of labour, the market, and the state is preserved. Accordingly, ending the exploitation in the sphere of (universal) creative activity cannot take the form merely of socialisation within the framework of an individual enterprise or even of nationalisation. This is an authentically communist process in which a transition takes place to other 'rules of the game', for which a new social space-time of vital activity has to be created. As such, this process is by definition open and international, and instances of it are extremely common in today's world. For example, the question of rejecting (private) intellectual property has been placed on the agendas of international social movements and networks (such as the network of supporters of free programming provision); of parties (e.g. 'pirates') and of NGOs. Some of the most interesting of today's international projects are being constructed on these principles: Wikinomics (Tapscott and Williams 2007), anarchonomics, gift-economics, the 'open access' model, social networks, and so forth.

Such are the characteristics, in terms of content, of the exploitation in the sphere of universal creative activity. It is important to note that this content falls within the parameters not only of the capitalist system of production relations (in which a qualitative characteristic of this process is the appropriation by capital of the active personal qualities of the human individual), but also in the spatial-temporal transformation of the 'realm of necessity' into the 'realm of freedom'. It is only here, in the category-field of studying the leap into the world of the creatosphere that lies beyond material production in the proper sense, that it becomes possible to fully and adequately define the content of the exploitation of creativity by capital.

A brief digression is necessary here. The liberation of creative labour from its subordination to capital implies not only the creation of new relations for creative workers proper, but also advancement along the path of changing the content of the labour of all workers and the formation of a community which we would call creative workers. It would consist of the mass stratum of working people engaged in publicly accessible areas of creative activity, which in the future may and should become the dominant type of labour. We recall that in a society where 'smart production' becomes the technological basis, the most widespread areas of employment become education for all and throughout life, shaping human health, research and development, management, the restoration of nature and society, etc. It is in these areas that the creative side becomes the determining content of human life activity.

Certainly, in the foreseeable future, most workers of the peripheral and even semi-peripheral countries will be engaged in reproductive labour. However, where a person is engaged in reproductive labour, subordinated to the division of labour and the machine, it is possible to make a new, socialist form (production relations), the development of which is ahead of the development of the content (productive forces). Here we are dealing with a situation similar to the formal subordination of labour to capital, when bourgeois production relations arose on the basis of inadequate old, pre-industrial productive forces. Secondly, when we speak of social liberation, we are talking about the future. A technological breakthrough from agrarian-industrial to 'smart' production can be accomplished in just a few decades, as evidenced by the experience of the advanced spheres of the Soviet economy of the twentieth century and the Chinese from the beginning of the twenty-first century. At the same time, it is much more difficult to solve the problem of forming social relations adequate for this new level of productive forces. The specific traits of the exploitation in the sphere of creative activity outlined above do not, however, touch as yet on the other aspect of this dual process: the exploitation by a particular aggregation of corporate capital of a particular creative worker (whether individual or collective is again unimportant). From a qualitative point of view the existence of this exploitation is beyond question; we have already shown the main mechanisms through which the creator and her or his vital activity are subordinated to corporate capital. Moreover, since creative activity is never just shared labour but also individual labour, the question arises of ending this aspect of exploitation as well. From the point of view of content, the main lines along which this question can be resolved are relatively clear: the place of capital has to be taken by a free association of creative workers (the specific forms to be taken by this organisation will not be explored in this book).

Examining the forms of exploitation in the sphere of creative activity requires us to differentiate between two aspects: the forms of the relationship of exploitation and the forms of appropriation of the results of that exploitation. Strange as it might seem, the differences in the relationship of exploitation are not particularly significant. In most cases, the creative worker employed by a corporation remains a hired worker, with a contract, a negotiated salary, and (in the case of a socially 'progressive' business) a benefits package and certain employment rights. If we compare the most typical creative workers (teachers in private schools, medical staff in private hospitals, programmers and staff of the research departments of firms) tend to be better paid than 'normal' workers (those engaged in reproductive labour), the creative workers), are more often on long-term contracts, and are subject to forms of management closer to 'personnel relations' or analogous models; their labour is more autonomous, with the process less harshly determined by capital, and more attention is devoted to improving their qualifications. The list of differences is well known, and is reiterated frequently in works on management issues in creative corporations.

Despite this, the relations of subjection of labour to capital, including even formal subjection, are undergoing significant changes in this case. In parallel with other labour in capitalism, relations are developing in which the creative worker becomes a free agent in form and/or content; no longer subordinate to capital, he or she becomes a member of the so-called free professions. The question of the form in which the results of the exploitation in the sphere of creative activity are appropriated is much more complex, since here the changes are fundamental. To depict them, we need also to try to adequately reflect the quantitative side of the exploitation in the sphere of creative activity.

### Exploitation in the sphere of creative activity: quantitative aspects

The situation from the quantative point of view is fundamentally different from that in classical capitalism. Marx's formula of exploitation, which is based on dividing the labour time of a worker into necessary labour (which replaces the cost of her or his labour power) and surplus labour (the additional labour which creates the surplus value appropriated by capital) no longer operates here. As was noted earlier, the universal cultural wealth that is appropriated by capital is created during the worker's free time.

So what is happening here? Two different qualitative parameters are involved. One is the cost of reproduction of human creative qualities under the capitalist system. The other is the value-assessment (the transferred perverse form) of the universal cultural wealth created by the exploited creator and (critically) by the whole preceding world of culture with which the given creative worker engaged in dialogue during the process of her or his activity.

To define this relationship more precisely in terms of its application to the conditions of capitalist production, it should be noted that the following must be deducted from the total income that accrues from the realisation of creative wealth ($Wcr$):

- the cost of compensating for the creative resources purchased by the capitalist ($Ccr$; unlike the elements of 'normal' constant capital, their value is not transferred to the final product, since they do not have value, but only a value-assessment);
- the cost of acquiring the creative qualities of the human individual ($Hcr$);
- the value that is newly created in the course of the 'normal' capitalist production that accompanies creative activity (the wages $V$ of the 'normal' workers and the surplus value $M$ that is created by them), and the value ($C$) represented by the 'normal' material expenditure that is transferred to the end product.

The remaining total is the value-assessment of the part of the universal cultural wealth, arising out of the labour of the creative worker and of the whole world of culture, that is appropriated by the owners of the corporation ($Wmcr$). It becomes the profit which capital receives from exploiting the creative worker and (again, critically) the whole world of culture. (This is fundamental. We emphasise that when capital uses creative factors, it always exploits not just the individual worker, but the entire world of culture. The reason is that the creative worker receives a substantial part of the 'resources' essential to her or his creativity free of charge from society. The range of these resources is extraordinarily wide, from general theoretical knowledge to exhibitions of artworks in museums and to natural beauty that stimulates the worker's creative insight. The results of this go to capital. It will be recalled also that the cost of the information purchased by capital figures among the expenses which capital incurs.)

In this case, the relationship between $Wmcr$ on the one hand, and the cost of reproduction of the creative worker (the remaining cultural goods were de-objectified free of charge by the creative worker and/or made up part of the capitalist outlays) plus the value-assessment of the creative resources obtained by capital on the other, will represent the measure of the exploitation by a given specific capital not only of its creative workers, but also of the entire world of culture ($Wmcr'$). As simple formulae, these relationships can be expressed as follows:

$$Wcr = Wmcr + Hcr + Ccr + (C + V + S) \tag{1}$$

Accordingly,

$$Wmcr = Wcr - (C + V + S) - Hcr - Ccr \tag{2}$$

The degree of exploitation is given by:

$$Wmcr' = Wmcr / Hcr \tag{3}$$

In thinking about the circuit of creative capital, the similarity between the designations ($Wmcr$ and $M$, $Wmcr'$ and $M'$) should not, as has already been explained, conceal the differences in content between the formula for the exploitation of creative labour and the formula of Marx. First, there is the difference between surplus value as the result of 'normal' capitalist production and the value-assessment of universal cultural wealth, appropriated by the owners of a corporation which makes use of creative resources (we have not yet found a brief categorical designation for this phenomenon). Second, when capital uses creative activity there is always a dual object of exploitation: the particular creative worker, and also the entire creatosphere. The duality of the process of exploitation of the creatosphere and of its individual subject has a number of important consequences. In particular, it becomes clear that formula (3) above reflects only one side of the exploitation – the one which affects creative labour as individual activity – but does not reflect the other side, relating to creativity as a dialogue with the whole world of culture, and therefore is fundamentally *incomplete*. Hence the problem: if the universal cultural wealth appropriated by the owners of a corporation that makes use of creative resources arises not only from the labour of a specific creator, how is it possible to arrive at a quantitative expression for the exploitation of a specific hired creative worker?

As was shown earlier, there can only be one answer to this question: *it is not possible* because the 'contribution' to this wealth made by a particular creative worker and by all her or his predecessors and colleagues in co-creation cannot be expressed quantitatively. In the creatosphere there cannot, as a matter of principle, be a quantitative expression of the relationship between the expenditure of labour of the participants in cultural dialogue, the process of co-creation. Under market forms of organisation of this process, the given expression is still more impossible since creative workers (and hence capital) use the basic goods of the creatosphere free of charge.

More precisely, the relationship between the creative worker's wages and the profit made by the capital employing her or him will be an index expressed in quantitative terms.

We must note that, thanks to the above-noted combination of the creative and reproductive components of activity in any labour process, the profits of a creative corporation always include not only intellectual rent but also classical surplus value, created by the reproductive component. This quantitative 'separation' of rent and surplus value presents another fundamentally insoluble task. The reason for this, we repeat, is the fact that any real activity by practically any creative worker also includes a routine reproductive element. This applies still more to the totality of hired workers who are exploited by capital. Thus the the relationship between profit and wages in a creative corporation reveals not the degree of exploitation of the creative worker, but the proportion in which intellectual rent is distributed between the owner of capital and the worker.

This conclusion seems paradoxical: *prima facie*, we are characterising a creative worker, who creates socially meaningful wealth (music, new technology, human health, or poetry) the value of which exceeds by tens or hundreds of times what he or she receives in payment, as something close to a landlord receiving parasitic income. Where is the problem? Is the hypothesis incorrect? Not at all. There is simply a genuine contradiction that creative activity is always both individual and universal. It involves the creation not of value but of universal cultural riches, and this fact derives neither from the one of its qualities nor from the other. Hence a substantive analysis conducted on the same level of abstraction found in the first volume of *Capital* yields only the one answer already set out above.

We shall now formulate this contradiction once again, distinguishing between the universal human and peculiarly capitalist attributes of this complex dialectic. In a world without capital or private ownership of cultural goods, where the latter are generally accessible and available free of charge, the creator as the subject of individual activity bestows far greater wealth on society than he or she receives from society for the (expanded) reproduction of her or his human qualities. From this angle, it seems as though society 'exploits' the creator. However, this is just, given the universality of all creative activity. The indeterminably important contribution of all the co-creators of culture is objectified in the riches fashioned by the individual creator, and her or his individual 'share' in this cannot and should not be determined, since a creator (such is her or his essence) does not work for reward.

In a world where (1) there is private ownership of cultural values, and this ownership (2) results economically in intellectual rent which is (3) appropriated by capital, the situation is substantially different. The *universal* character of creative activity is transformed under the hegemony of the market and capital into a monopoly on a particular part of the universal cultural wealth, and 'fences it off' in much the same way as a landlord fences off her or his land, excluding it from use by any other subject. Other natural riches can also be so fenced off. Cultural goods, as already explained, are 'technologically' limitless, but private (intellectual) property introduces an external restriction that takes an economic and legal form. That is how intellectual rent enters the picture. We shall return to this later, but for the moment we need to address the fact that (1) intellectual rent, like all rent, is a form of parasitic income, and that (2) in the world of the market and capital it is this *rent* which is becoming the sole source of *market* income for all creators. This is true of capitalists, and of their hired workers, and also of creators who sell the results of their activity independently, such as craft shoemakers who sell the bespoke footwear they produce.

In this world too, however, a creator is simultaneously the subject of creative activity not only in its universal but also in its individual respect. In this sense as well, the creative worker is the object of exploitation, and capital exploits not just the entire creatosphere, but also particular workers. A somewhat remote analogy can be made with hired workers in the banking sector or other areas where, Marx's labour theory of value maintains, neither value nor surplus value is created. (The third volume of *Capital* contains an explanation of the mechanism of exploitation of workers paid out of surplus value created in material production.) Just as in the case of bank nationalisations the speculative component of bank profit is liquidated, and not transferred to bank employees or society, when private intellectual property is abolished, the creative worker receives not the profit of the creative corporation (this profit disappears, along with intellectual rent) but remuneration paid by society, analogous to the salary of a professor or a teacher in the public sector.

This is merely an analogy. In the first place, a creator, unlike our bank employees, produces socially useful goods. Moreover, the speculative income of the banking sector and intellectual rent have different sources and are different in nature. In the former case, the source is value created in material production and redistributed to the advantage of speculators; in the latter, it is genuine social wealth which can only have an assessed value.

This leads to an apparently paradoxical conclusion: if the question of the exploitation of a creative worker is examined only quantatively (that is, from the point of view of the volume of income which he or she receives in value terms), the liberation of creative labour from subjection to capital does not change anything, and especially not in the position of this subject. In principle, the creative worker receives funds from society no greater than those needed for the reproduction of her or his human qualities. Since many of the goods in this case will come free of charge (education, health care, access to information), it might even be supposed that the money income of the creative worker might be less than under capitalism.

However, there are some nuances. Firstly, an inevitable outcome of the capitalist market system is a large divergence between the price of a creative worker and the cost of reproducing her or his potential. The hegemony of corporate capital establishes these divergences such that the price of the workers most closely enmeshed with capital and serving its hegemony by participating in the reproduction of the perverse (useless) sector – workers in such areas as finance, corporate management, the media, mass culture, professional sport, and so forth – greatly exceeds the cost of reproducing their human qualities. Conversely, workers in generally accessible areas of the creatosphere – teachers in state schools, social workers, and so on – are paid substantially less than the cost of reproducing their human qualities: in the US, for example, a schoolteacher in a Black ghetto is not paid enough to put her or his children through a good university.

Secondly, only in developed countries does capital pay creative workers well enough to cover the cost of reproducing their human qualities and creative potential, and often this is not the case even in those countries. Although generally accessible creative activity is crucially important from the point of view of developing the creatosphere and, consequently, the universal criteria of progress, most of the world's rank-and-file subjects of creative activity receive even less. The world's rank-and-file intelligentsia are undervalued by capital, while a circle of 'professionals' is overvalued. In this way, modern global capital sets up an internal contradiction among creative workers. The rank and file, as subjects of authentic creatosphere activity and not of work in the perverse sector, are closest to the 'realm of freedom', and are undervalued by capital even according to the standards of capitalism. Thus they have an interest in ending the global hegemony of capital. The professionals, who carry out the tasks of directly 'creating' the hegemony of capital through their employment in the perverse sector (that is, the sector which supplants and distorts the creatosphere) and whom capital overpays, are objective foes of ending this hegemony.

Thirdly, the quantitative, value-related aspect of creative workers' exploitation is the least important for them. What they value, as *homines creatores*, is the degree of freedom they enjoy in their activity. The transformation of the conditions of creative activity and of its space and time into a function of capital and, thus, of creative workers themselves into objects of exploitation constitutes the most profound basis for the antagonism between global capital and the creative human being. This basis is all the more important given that capital also introduces elements of personal dependency to this relationship, subordinating to itself, as already stated, the 'divine soul' of the human individual and turning her or him into a slave. However, here, too, there are critical details. For the professionals who serve the hegemony of capital this slavery is sweet, since it keeps them privileged, pampered, and seemingly (here we see the world of simulacra!) partners of capital in their role. Meanwhile, we should not forget that under capitalism the position of *every* subject of creative activity is dual; on the one hand such people are creators yearning for freedom in their vital activity, while on the other hand they are owners of 'human capital', sellers of creative potential with an interest in getting a good price for their commodities. Subjectively, therefore, the creator may be both an opponent of the hegemony of capital and a supporter of its retention.

A clarification is in order at this point. The profit of corporations employing creative labour can be presented as a perverse form (to be sure, from the point of view of Marxism any profit is a perverse form) of the sum of surplus value and of the value-assessment of universal cultural wealth, appropriated by the owners of a corporation that employs creative resources:

$$Pcr = f(M + Wmcr) \tag{4}$$

We can now start to examine the specific form of appropriation of the results of the exploitation in the sphere of creative activity, intellectual rent.

## Intellectual rent: the questions of appropriation and use

As noted earlier, the income of the owner of capital who employs creative resources is analogous in practice to rental income. This income is intellectual rent, defined in superficial fashion as income obtained from ownership of a product that arises out of creative or intellectual activity. Neoclassical economists are not interested in its nature, only in its quantitative determination, while Marxists are more interested in the nature of this new form of exploitation (Žižek 2009).

We begin, however, with the similarities between these types of income. It is not accidental that we define rental income from rights of ownership over creative resources like rent from any other general resource – land, oil, gas – held as private property. It is regarded as rent not only by Marxism but also by mainstream economic theory and (importantly) by economic practice. Intellectual rent is (1) linked to a monopoly exercised by a private owner such as a creative corporation or other aggregation of capital, employing creative workers over a particular fragment of the creatosphere (for example, some body of information or a work or art) in the form of private property. In addition intellectual rent, unlike natural rent, is (2) extended to goods which, in terms of their content, are boundless and whose 'fencing off' is exclusively an economic and legal figment.

This acknowledges that a cultural product ('intellectual product') is a social and not a private good. If this social good is turned into private property, what this allows its owner to obtain is not profit but rent, intellectual rent. We will use that term here, although it would be more correct to call it cultural or creatosphere rent.

From the Marxist point of view as well, this income has to be categorised as rent in terms of its form. Universal cultural wealth becomes a source of monetary income only to the extent that it acquires the form of (private) property. Just as absolute rent is no more than an obstacle inherited from the past (feudal landholding) which impedes capitalist development in agriculture, the result of artificial barriers to the development of production and an unnecessary addition to the price, intellectual rent is an artificial hindrance to the development of creative activity.

Despite these similarities between normal and intellectual rent, they have different sources. Intellectual rent results from activity which creates wealth. Natural rent, at least in its absolute form, by contrast, does not arise from any labour, and hence, by virtue of its source, has a false social value, which presupposes the redistribution of abstract social labour. Intellectual rent, we repeat, is the product of a value-assessment of universal labour.

Finally, it is important to clarify that in a capitalist context, intellectual rent is not only the source for recouping the costs of acquiring the paid creative resources and (super-)profits obtained by a creative corporation, but also the source of the income received by the creative worker. This, however, does not make the creative worker a parasite on society, as a landlord is. On the contrary, he or she is a creator of social wealth which, in its useful effect, exceeds many times over what society spends on her or his reproduction.

Returning to the quantitative determination of the exploitation in the sphere of creative activity, and introducing intellectual rent ($Rcr$) to the formulae adduced earlier, we can set out the positions defined above using the simple formula:

$$Rcr = Ccr + Hcr + Wmcr \qquad (6)$$

or:

$$Wmcr = Rcr - (Ccr + Hcr) \qquad (7)$$

The formula for the gross income of a corporation, expressed using the factor of intellectual rent, takes the form:

$$Wcr = (C + V + M) + Rcr \qquad (8)$$

From this also stems the outward difference, readily established, between *Wmcr'* and *M'*. In the case of the exploitation of the 'classic' industrial worker, Marx discusses the world of perverse forms in which surplus value acts as the product of capital as a whole. In terms of its content, surplus value is the product exclusively of the living labour of a hired worker, while profit (not as the result of hired labour but as the product of capital as a whole) is no more than a perverse form of surplus value. In the first case, capital exploits not only the creative worker, but also the entire world of culture; therefore, in terms of its content, the creation of a surplus good, having a value-assessment and appropriated by capital (*Wmcr*), is the product not only of the individual creative worker's labour, but also of her or his co-creation, in a dialogue with the whole world of culture of which he or she, as the employee of a certain capital, is only a part (*Ccr*).

Just as profit merely appears (though this appearance is also something objective) to be the product of capital and is 'in reality' the product exclusively of living hired labour, so in the case of a creative worker, *Wmcr* 'in reality', and not in the world of appearances and delusions, is a product of the *entire* creatosphere.

To complete our analysis of intellectual rent, we may therefore summarise the possible ways in which the three economic actors – the owner of a cultural good who receives the corresponding rent; the entrepreneur; and the worker – can position themselves. We leave to one side (1) the relations which apply in the public sector, where cultural goods are universally available and belong to everyone, and where there is no rent. Earlier, we focused our attention on the situation in which (2) the owner of an intellectual product and the entrepreneur are one and the same (for example, a creative corporation), while the creator acts as a hired worker who has no rights over the intellectual goods he or she creates. A further variant is also possible: (3) capital acquires an intellectual product (say, a patent for the production of a new medicine) from a third entity. In this case, the owner of the capital must either limit itself to the 'usual' surplus value obtained from the exploitation of 'ordinary' hired workers (in this example, the workers of a pharmaceutical firm) or strike a deal with the owner of the patent for part of the intellectual rent obtained by that owner. In principle, case (3) is of little interest to us, since it does not bring any new subtleties to the relationship between owner and worker; the changes affect only the distribution of intellectual rent between two types of exploiters (just as in the case where the owner of land and the capitalist who uses it may or may not be the same person). Finally, there is another possible variant: (4) the creator, the entrepreneur, and the owner may be a single individual or a group of people, such as a creative collective or cooperative.

This latter variant might seem at first glance to be very widespread in creative business, but if we examine not only the form (self-employment, start-ups) but also the content, it turns out that in most instances we are dealing with nothing more than creative 'dispersed manufacturing', that is, the same basic case (2). Nevertheless, variant (4) is of interest to us from the perspective of exploitation in the creatosphere under circumstances in which the (private) owner of a cultural value is the creator herself or himself.

Here, it turns out, the question of the exploitation of the creatosphere is also applicable. While this does not involve the exploitation of the creative worker by a third person, the creatosphere is used by the creative worker as a private owner. In appropriating the value-assessment of the cultural value which he or she creates in collaboration with the whole world of the creatosphere, the creator-owner acts as an exploiter of humanity. If (private) intellectual property is renounced – that is, if all the components of the creatosphere are socialised (turned into a free, generally available public resource) – the creator-owner stands to lose the significant part of her or his wealth based on the extraction of the intellectual rent. In this case, no one takes away the creator-owner's cultural wealth, but her or his income will not depend on intellectual rent.

We thus arrive at a theoretical grasp of the now-familiar duality of the creator-owner in the capitalist world, which differs from the internal contradiction in the position of the wage worker and the 'normal' petty bourgeois. The independently working creator differs from the 'normal' petty bourgeois, (for example, a farmer) in that the creator appropriates free of charge publicly available cultural goods, and receives as income money that does not represent new value which he or she has created, but a value-assessment of the universal wealth which he or she, along with (it should be noted) her or his co-authors in open dialogue and co-creation, has brought into being. Unlike the 'normal' petty bourgeois, the independently working creator is also a subject of the exploitation of the world of culture, and of every one of us. But (to recall the starting-point of our reasoning), as a worker, the creator, while appropriating intellectual rent, was originally, is, and will remain a scientist, a writer, an engineer. The cultural significance of her or his being belongs to the creatosphere, whatever economic or legal form that being might assume.

The conclusion that intellectual rent is the source of the wages paid to the creative worker casts a *prima facie* doubt on the conclusion, drawn by our predecessors and reaffirmed here, concerning the parasitic nature of intellectual rent. The essence of the matter is that the very relationship which lends the form of cost to social wealth (which has no cost), and which transfers this wealth not to each member of society who is capable of desobjectifying it ('ownership by each of everything'), but to certain private owners, is parasitic. The fact that these private owners include the

...rect creator of this wealth does not change this essence; under the laws of the creatosphere the creator does not work for the sake of reward, but receives from society or its representatives (a creative association, the state, an NGO) free benefits and a socially guaranteed income that ensures the reproduction of her or his human qualities. However, there is also another side to this coin.

### 'Cultural' capitalism: the possibilities for delimiting the market from the creatosphere

The fact that market agents and, above all, creative corporations appropriate, free of charge, part of the goods of the world of culture (the results of the preceding development of science and culture, the fruits of generally accessible education and fundamental science) poses the problem of the demarcation and interaction of the two worlds – the free and generally accessible world of culture, and the world of the market, paid for and restricted by private property – as a fundamental theoretical and practical question in relation to the period of transformation of the 'realm of necessity' into the 'realm of freedom', of 'late' capitalism into 'early' communism.

For 'mainstream' economic science there is no problem here at all; free goods are created using the money of market agents (corporations, hired workers) who pay taxes and make sacrifices, and these goods are appropriated free of charge on the basis of general availability or of government norms. Private goods are created by market agents and are appropriated by them on a paid basis. The different nature of the goods, restricted or unrestricted, is conditioned by the different modes of their appropriation.

For a Marxist, as we set out to show above, this situation conceals the fundamental question of the exploitation by capital of the world of the creatosphere: the appropriation by capital, either free of charge or partially paid for, of the cultural values ('creative resources') of humanity. The existence of this exploitation also allows us to pose a hypothesis concerning the transitional forms of its partial ending – a sort of 'acculturation' of capitalism. If we proceed from the fact that (1) capital in its commercial activity appropriates without payment the social goods of the creatosphere, as a way of increasing profits (using a portrait of Mozart on a box of sweets, for example, might allow more sweets to be sold for a higher price than if the box carried some more common picture), and that (2) this additional income is a particular form of rent (in this case, we shall call it cultural), then the conclusion follows logically: this rent, like any other, should be taken from the capitalist and given to the owner. Since the owner of culture is everyone (as is demonstrated within the framework of the Marxist paradigm), then rent from the use of cultural phenomena by capital should be used for the development of the area in which every phenomenon belongs to every subject, that is, the creatosphere. To simplify, business should pay no less for using a portrait of Mozart in an advertisement than for using a photograph of a model, and the money which the firm makes from using the public goods of culture should go into international funds for the development of the creatosphere.

This suggestion violates a fundamental principle of market economics: public goods, since they are public, are available equally free of charge to everyone. Here, we suggest 'excommunicating' the commercial sector from what people create free of charge. An analogy in this case might be with free museums, libraries, internet sites, and so forth, which are not used for profit in private interests. The same is proposed in this given case, and the principle behind the discrimination also prohibits the free use of cultural phenomena that are in the public domain for commercial purposes. If it is for the production of objects of private property, then the goods of the creatosphere should be paid for. If it is for the production of generally accessible objects, then the goods should be free. Certain cultural phenomena might be banned altogether from commercial use.

The questions of how this might be done technically, how much business entrepreneurs should pay and to whom, how the cultural goods that are to be paid for should be demarcated from those available for use free of charge (such as, for example, language or the rules of arithmetic) are a task for a subsequent theoretical and practical excursion. As a first step one might suggest the creation of international expert commissions charged with 'patenting' public cultural goods, determining the parameters for the commercial use of artworks, and so forth. These parameters might range from prohibition to the payment of rents into international funds for the support of the arts, on the basis of a model such as the ban on commercial showings of video recordings that are sold for viewing by private citizens. A mechanism of control (bearing in mind that this would extend only to commercial firms) might also be organised by analogy with the controls on the use of patented intellectual products. These forms would be imperfect, like any palliative measure aimed at shaping transitional relations while remaining within the bounds of the capitalist system and the 'realm of necessity'. This control mechanism would apply only to transitional forms that will wither away altogether with the overcoming of capitalism itself.

We should note briefly here that similar decisions are possible in the area of 'ecologising' capitalism, using natural rents for the benefit of all humanity. As global environmental problems become more acute, nature (particularly land) is being transformed into a universal cultural value, a 'social good'. This suggests that it should be generally accessible, as an element of the creatosphere and subject to desobjectification. In this respect, private property can only act as a perverse form, impeding the use of the natural world as a cultural phenomenon – a value open and available to everyone.

It is also particularly appropriate to note that since the natural resources of planet Earth were created by the natural development of the biosphere, then we may regard the thesis of humanity's universal ownership of natural resources as proven (discounting for now the factor of human activity, which has either increased – as in the case, say, of agricultural land in developed countries – or lowered the productivity of these resources). We stress that it is not particular firms, states, or even international organisations that are the owners, but humanity. How and to whom humanity entrusts the realisation of its general interests here is a practical matter, though a very important one.

The fact that ownership of natural resources is universal means that rent from the use of all these resources (or more precisely, of those put to commercial use) should be appropriated by humanity for the purpose of solving global problems: ensuring that all citizens in every country have a socially guaranteed minimum living standard, while global environmental, social, humanitarian, and other programmes are implemented. Here, it should be stressed, none of the principles of capitalism is violated. Humanity, as the owner of the earth (the biosphere), receives rent by right of ownership just like any other actor, such as a landlord. Capital, in the case of private use of natural resources, receives its usual profit, just as happens, in our example, with the use of land belonging to a landlord.

In concluding this chapter we should note that, in our view, this highly abstract study of the exploitation of creative labour is important not only because it substantially updates Marx's theory of surplus value, but also because of its socio-political resonance. In our previous writings about social creators as subjects of the struggle to advance towards the 'realm of freedom' we left the nature of the exploitation of the creators to one side. In the present text we have hoped to demonstrated that in the future process of social liberation, the major gains made by workers engaged in creative activity will not take the form of increases in their personal money incomes, and that those whose living standards improve markedly will be only those 'rank and file' members of the intelligentsia, mostly in poor countries, whose incomes are below the level needed for the expanded reproduction of their human qualities. In money terms, a section of the 'elite' intelligentsia will even lose. Most important is what creators will acquire as they advance towards the 'realm of freedom': free, unlimited access to knowledge and information, education, and culture; the possibility of passing on their work and its results to everyone, forever; freedom from subjection to commodity and money fetishism for themselves and their descendants; the possibility of working wherever and however their personal goals demand, rather than being subject to the market conjuncture and, when they work, being forced by the power of capital to use their talents to invent new lies about some toxic soft drink. Instead, they will be able to consider the interests of humanity, society, and nature and, by the way, to take account of their own self-realisation as well.

## Notes

1  The main sources on which this chapter is based, and in relation to which we propose qualitatively new solutions, include works by Atkinson and Bourguignon (2015), Florida (2005), Kotz (2015), Piketty (2014), and Sen (1992, 1997).

2  'A spider conducts operations that resemble those of a weaver, and a bee puts to shame many an architect in the construction of her cells. But what distinguishes the worst architect from the best of bees is this, that the architect raises his structure in imagination before he erects it in reality' (Marx 1867/1996: 188).

3  'The prehistory of human society accordingly closes with this social formation' (Marx 1859/1987: 264).

4  Desobjectivisation is that interaction of subject with object which provides the understanding of the essense and qualities of the object which make it possible to use the object in accordance with its nature and properties.

# 9

# Twenty-first-century reproduction: inequality and the 'useless economy'

This chapter is necessarily brief and exploratory since we have yet to complete our elaboration of this category of questions. If we nevertheless make so bold as to place the chapter before the reader, it is because these questions form an integral, though yet unfinished, part of our study of the categories of twenty-first-century capital.

## Reproduction under the conditions of late capitalism: the new quality of the general law of capitalist accumulation

Any economic system is structured by relations that extend well beyond the relation of the worker with the means of production and the relations of coordination (the ties that connect the producer with the consumer). These include a complex of other relations, chief among which are the *relations of reproduction* that complete the unity of the essential production relations characteristic of a particular social system. We henceforth use the term 'reproduction' in the sense that Marx gave it:

> Whatever the form of the process of production in a society, it must be a continuous process, must continue to go periodically through the same phases. A society can no more cease to produce than it can cease to consume. When viewed, therefore, as a connected whole, and as flowing on with incessant renewal, every social process of production is, at the same time, a process of reproduction.

> The conditions of production are also those of reproduction. No society can go on producing, in other words, no society can reproduce, unless it constantly reconverts a part of its products into means of production, or elements of fresh products. (Marx 1867/1996: 565; see also Marx 1885/1997: 71–88, 390, 469, 480, 488, etc.)

We regard as a fundamental methodological proposition that the theory of the reproduction of the relations of late capitalism has a substantially richer and more complex structure than that of the reproduction of classical capitalism set out in *Capital* (which is by no means simple). The theory of the reproduction of late capitalism includes, in particular, several additional levels beyond 'classical' reproduction. These are:

- the specific patterns that become evident in the 'sunset' of this system, which not only reproduce the relations of the system but also represent the genesis within the old (capitalist) system of the relations of the *new* (post-capitalist) order;
- these relations reproduce not only the relations of capital, but the 'realm of necessity' more generally, even as they create and sustain emergent features of post-capitalist relations that are also relations of an emergent 'realm of freedom';
- the growing significance of the creatosphere makes the material basis of this reproduction inadequate to the nature of the relations of capital.

Each of these three parameters substantially complicates the question of the reproduction of late capitalism. We will apply this approach below.

### The 'sunset' of capitalism and of the 'realm of necessity': how the reproduction of production relations is transformed

A distinguishing feature of Marx's *Capital* is that it studies economic dynamics on the basis of their content. This is true of the reproduction of production relations, of the law of accumulation that characterises this reproduction, of the patterns of employment that are conditioned by it, and so forth. The structure of reproduction is examined only in the second volume of *Capital*, and only minimal attention is devoted to the question of rates of economic growth and to the functional dependencies of its various parameters.

Since the beginning of the twentieth century, practically all non-Marxist currents in economic theory (and from the second half of the century the majority of Marxists as well) have acted differently. They have focused mainly on quantitative questions and modelling, conjuring with figures for GDP, growth, inflation, unemployment, and the like in all sorts of ways. The examination of fundamental functional economic dynamics has been subordinated to these quantitative concerns. As suggested by the title of one of our books,[1] we follow a different path, giving pride of place to questions relating to the reproduction of production relations and to the law of accumulation, in the forms these assume in the late capitalist context.

In *Capital*, Marx showed how the relations of simple commodity production are transformed into relations of capitalist appropriation:

> At first, the rights of property seemed to us to be based on a man's own labour.
> At least, some such assumption was necessary since only commodity owners

with equal rights confronted each other, and the sole means by which a man could become possessed of the commodities of others, was by alienating his own commodities; and these could be replaced by labour alone. Now, however, property turns out to be the right, on the part of the capitalist, to appropriate the unpaid labour of others or its product, and to be the impossibility, on the part of the labourer, of appropriating his own product. The separation of property from labour has become the necessary consequence of a law that apparently originated in their identity. (Marx 1867/1996: 583)

Thus Marx explained how the reproduction of the relations of commodity production resulted in the transformation of relations of commodity production into capitalist production relations. Here we will try to solve another problem: to show how the reproduction of late capitalism production relations resulted in the trends of self-negation of capital.

The general law of capitalist accumulation, we recall, established that the concentration and centralisation of capital means that, simultaneously, 'all methods for the production of surplus value are at the same time methods of accumulation; and every extension of accumulation becomes again a means for the development of those methods. It follows therefore that in proportion as capital accumulates, the lot of the labourer, be his payment high or low, must grow worse' (Marx 1867/1996: 639). Marx adds: 'Accumulation of wealth at one pole is, therefore, at the same time accumulation of misery, agony of toil, slavery, ignorance, brutality, mental degradation, at the opposite pole, i.e., on the side of the class that produces its own product in the form of capital' (Marx, 1867/1996: 640).

It is no secret that the twentieth century has demonstrated the presence in the capitalist economy of significant *counter-tendencies*. Their presence explains the form that the law of accumulation assumes during the 'sunset' epoch not only of capitalism, but also of the 'realm of necessity'. Summing up the laws of this dual 'sunset' as set out earlier, we argue that other processes are under way, in addition to the reproduction of peculiarly capitalist production relations and the processes, characteristic of these relations, of both the accumulation of capital wealth under the control of increasingly complex forms of capital at the one extreme and, at the other extreme, the reproduction of the hired worker as the sole owner of her or his labour power.

*First*, the process of the accumulation of capital is transformed into an extensive and intensive expanded reproduction of its hegemony. The extensive expanded reproduction of the hegemony of corporate capital extends the process of accumulation outside the borders of the purely economic world to include spheres beyond the production of material goods and utilitarian services: not only such non-economic areas as foreign and domestic state policy (as also the case in earlier times), but also large parts of the creatosphere today figure as sources, participants, and outcomes of the reproduction of capital. The same is becoming increasingly true of the human individual as the main actor within the creatosphere, and also of the perverse sector, the world of simulacra.

The intensive expanded reproduction of the hegemony of corporate capital occurs through constant qualitative change in its structure and dynamics. It now includes new forms and methods (1) of creating 'fields of dependency' (market power) and of unification with the national state and transnational institutions; (2) of intensifying the processes of financialisation and deepening the channels of financial power; (3) of the formal and real subordination of labour and the human individual to capital; and so forth.

We will now proceed to examine how the relations of reproduction transform themselves when qualitative changes in the content of labour occur as a result of the birth of the creatosphere. This process is conditioned by the beginning of the process of transformation of the 'realm of necessity' into the 'realm of freedom', and is characteristic of the present-day stage of the 'sunset' of late capitalism. This is the *second* process involved in the transforming of the relations of accumulation. The progress of the productive forces, the birth of the creatosphere, and especially the increasingly broad use of intellectual and creative labour as a type of wage labour employed on a mass scale bring about a change in the quality both of capital and also – importantly – of the worker. These changes modify patterns of accumulation and condition of reproduction. What is involved here is much more than an increase in the cost of labour power. The intertwining of the processes of reproduction of capital and reproduction of labour, as a result of which capital becomes, to a degree, the source of the reproduction of a new type of worker, and the worker's wage becomes the source of the accumulation of capital; this comes to represent a principle introduced by the new content of labour.

On the one hand, capital, along with the worker, becomes the direct agent of the reproduction of the worker and of her or his professional and personal capacities. The reason for this lies in the fact that progress in the content of labour (including the birth of the creatosphere) conditions the need of capital to make large-scale use of professional workers and, to a somewhat lesser degree, of creative workers, and also furthers the interest that capital has in shaping and subsequently employing precisely this type of labour. Capital is thus forcing the state to finance the development of the 'human capital' of firms, by improving the qualifications of workers, by providing credits for education, and in many other ways. Capital also participates in this process at least partially, both through taxes and directly (through corporative education systems, etc.).

A further aspect of the intertwining of the process of reproduction of capital and hired labour is the transformation of the incomes of hired workers into a source for the accumulation of capital. The specific forms taken on by this process are well known and have been described above, they consist of the complex system of savings and investments made by the people concerned in pension and investment funds, and also of their consumer credits, which constitute one of the main sources for the present-day accumulation of capital. Involving the wages of hired labour in the process of capitalist accumulation, capital is increasing the frameworks of capital reproduction. In reality, this involvement is not limited only by the incomes of highly skilled and highly paid workers, but this social layer becomes the significant participant in savings in favour of capital accumulation.

The 'sunset' of capitalism and of the 'realm of necessity' stimulate not only substantial changes in the content of labour, but also the development of transitional production relations, in which the relations of capitalist accumulation and elements of the genesis of new, post-capitalist relations are combined in a contradictory way. These factors condition the *third* process of transformation of the relations of reproduction under the conditions of late capitalism. This process will be familiar from Chapter 5, where we described it in characterising the transition from the imperialist to the social-reformist stage in the evolution – or *in*volution – of late capitalism. At the heart of the process is the fact that the birth of the relations of *counter-hegemony* (that is, social creativity) of working people brings with it the emerging fresh shoots of post-capitalist relations of the appropriation and distribution of income, and thus leads to the restriction and partial undermining of the formal and real subordination of labour and humanity to capital. The category of working people includes all workers, not only hired employees, since workers who are formally independent entrepreneurs are also subject to exploitation.

This relatively complex way of formulating the essence of the process, though stringent in theoretical and methodological terms, conceals its well-known forms. These forms consist of the transitional relationships (featuring early manifestations of post-capitalism) that impose limits on working time, provide for job safety, and allow for partial participation by workers in management. Also in this category are the relationships that provide for partial redistribution of income from capital to labour (progressive income taxes, social welfare payments, guaranteed minimum wages, and so forth), and that allow citizens access free of charge to a range of benefits (particularly areas of education, health care, culture, and so forth). These transitional production relations are summoned to life on the one hand by the activity of the socio-economic subject that is counterposed to capital – that is, by the struggles of trade unions, left political parties, and other social organisations and movements – and, on the other, by the objective need for a partial reform of capitalist relations. This need results from changes in the content of labour, and from the evolving world-economic configuration (the rise of the socialist alternative, and so on). These processes constitute the field of class struggle between workers and capitalists, and the measure of the development of transitional forms of capitalist production relations is dependent on the balance of class forces. After some concessions in favour of working class in the post-war period, the past three decades have demonstrated the counter-attack of capitalists.

The arguments above lead to a conclusion on the dual nature of the social functions of the bourgeois state. On the one hand, we find state support of different channels for involving wages in the process of the accumulation of capital, and on the other, we find the use of part of capitalist profit for the reproduction of the creative labour force. Thus we see simultaneously the deepening of subordination of labour to capital and some features of the self-negation of capital. In the context of researching the relations of reproduction, this duality is important, especially since it conditions a significant transformation of the *law of capitalist accumulation under the conditions of late capitalism* which will be formulated below. First, however, we need to pursue further our study of the transformations that late capitalism brings to the relations of reproduction.

The *fourth* aspect of the expanded reproduction of the hegemony of corporate capital is a direct outcome of the previous three. Its essence lies in the fact that the process of accumulation of capital occurs increasingly through extensive and intensive expansion in areas located beyond actual material production.

As the process of accumulation extends beyond material production, it involves new sources of the accumulation of capital, new actors, and new results. This has been discussed in Chapters 6 and 7, especially with regard to the market of simulacra, the process of financialisation, and so forth. With this extension of accumulation, the mechanisms of hegemonism undergo constant qualitative improvement, using a continually expanding range of non-economic methods – psychological, cultural, ideological, and so forth. The hegemony of capital relies on new forms of its economic power of capital: (1) the formation of 'fields of dependency' (market power) for achieving unification with the national state and transnational institutions; (2) the intensification of financialisation and the deepening of the channels of financial power; (3) the formal and actual subordination of labour and humanity to capital; and so on.

One consequence of these processes is a substantial change to another pattern of reproduction, in this case associated with the appearance and continuous (though not uniformly intensive) growth of transaction costs. Under the conditions of expanded reproduction of the hegemony of capital, the growth of transaction costs becomes an unavoidable consequence of each of its components, and is multiplied by their integration. Any significant step     ls increasing the control of capital over the process of reproduction in the contemporary economy (both capital itself and the labour force) requires new institutional elements. For example, the control of big capital over the production and distribution of knowledge requires a very expensive system for the defence of private intellectual property rights; the suppression of the resistance of working people requires greater expenditure on police, lawyers, etc.

As a result, we are able to formulate as a hypothesis the presence of a tendential law of the growth of transaction and (anti-)social costs in the process of the expanded reproduction of the hegemony of capital. The more capital tries to involve the human potential in the process of reproduction of capital, the greater its transaction and social costs. From the accumulation of savings of working people in the financial system to the control over the creative process during the labour time, these new requirements do not come cheap. Moreover, all capital's attempts to displace the rising costs of its reproduction onto the shoulders of working people only increase social costs, such as impoverishment, unemployment, growth of illiteracy, illness, etc.

We regard this assertion as a hypothesis because it is so difficult to provide statistical proof of the pattern. However, some evidence of its correctness may be found in of statements by experts and certain statistical data which show that the levels of bureaucratisation, corruption, and criminalisation in countries with a greater degree of socialisation are not higher than in countries with more liberal economic structures (see Moreira 2019; Baden-hausen 2018). The large-scale survey of statistical correlations between social equality and mental and physical health, criminalisation, social mobility, drug use, education, etc., contained in the book *The Spirit Level* (Wilkinson and Pickett 2010) strongly confirms that countries with higher levels of inequality have higher levels of negative social trends.

The *fifth* crucially important feature of the expanded reproduction of production relations at the current stage of late capitalism has to do with its attempts to 'go global' and subordinate the whole world to its role in both extensive and intensive fashions. What this involves, in the first instance, is the fact that the entire world is becoming a field for struggle for this hegemony and for resistance to it, something that is best expressed by the French word *mondialisation* ('world-isation'), which conveys the essence of the phenomenon better than 'globalisation'. In the second instance, we note the penetration of this expanded reproduction into all areas of the life of society, a situation that has given rise to a whole system of global problems.

## The transformation of the law of capitalist accumulation

We can now propose a hypothesis for a law of accumulation in the late capitalist epoch. In this context, the classical law needs to be augmented with a proposition to the effect that the processes of the accumulation of capital at one extreme, and of the impoverishment of workers at the other, are characteristic of late capitalism to the extent that they are not countered by the social creativity of working people, which has the effect of reducing socio-economic inequality. A strengthening of activity by anti-capitalist and reformist forces narrows the scope and reduces the impact of the law of capitalist accumulation, while a weakening of activity by these actors leads to the reverse tendency. The law of capitalist accumulation of the 'sunset' epoch of capitalism and of the 'realm of necessity' can then be formulated as follows: there is an inversely proportional relationship between the expansion of the hegemony of capitalism on the one hand, and the degree of progress of the creatosphere and of the social creativity of working people on the other.

The reverse side of this law is a contrary relationship: the degree of socialisation of capitalism is greater to the degree that the social creativity of workers and citizens and fresh manifestations of the creatosphere develop, leading ultimately to an ever-greater exclusion of essentially capitalist relations by manifestations of the 'realm of freedom'. The socialisation of capitalism is the field of struggle between different political and social forces. The result of this struggle is that in various fields of socio-economic space and time we find different models taking shape: a Scandinavian type with a high degree of socialisation of capitalism, or more liberal (less socialised) models of the system, or intermediate models featuring a social market economy (see Buzgalin and Kolganov 2005: 287–98).

As indirect quantitative indicators of the degree of socialisation of capitalism, we can use such indices as the share of social benefits (distributed wholly or partially without payment) in GDP, and the relationship between Gini coefficients before and after payment of taxes. We name these, accordingly, the coefficients of social benefits ($Ks$) and of the equalisation of incomes ($Ke$). Hence,

$$Ks = Qs / Q$$

where:

$Q$ is the volume of GDP

$Qs$ is the volume of social benefits

$$Ke = G/Gt$$

where:

$G$ is the Gini coefficient before payment of taxes

$Gt$ is the Gini coefficient after payment of taxes

Their integration with definite values can provide us with a coefficient of the socialisation of capitalism (Ks):

$$Ks = f\{Ks, Ke\}$$

For the present, we leave to one side the last integral coefficient, since we are not yet ready to offer a finished model for the combination of the above coefficients, and would note that even the simplest statistical illustrations make it possible to show the validity of the formulations proposed earlier.

Thus empirical evidence confirms that, firstly, the coefficient of social benefits in modern developed countries is quite high and ranges from a fifth to a third. Secondly, this coefficient varies significantly, depending on which model of late capitalism – closer to the social-democratic or to the neoliberal – is realised in a given country. Thus the coefficient of social benefits differs significantly between countries such as the US and Sweden (see Table 4). The role of income redistribution, measured by the difference between the Gini coefficients before and after taxation and government transfers, also differs significantly between countries with a socially oriented the economy and countries with predominantly liberal state economic policies (see Figure 7).

All this testifies to the possibility and importance of carrying out not only a qualitative but also a quantitative study of the level of socialisation of capitalism. This relationship is the alter ego of the alleged contradiction between economic efficiency and social justice. The usual account of the opposition between the two is based on numerous 'inexactitudes'. First, this interpretation proceeds implicitly from a market-centric model of

**Table 4** Social benefits as a share of GDP for Sweden and the US, 2018

| Government spending on social benefits | % of GDP | |
|---|---|---|
| | Sweden | US |
| Social protection | 19.6 | 7.5 |
| Education | 6.9 | 5.9 |
| Recreation, culture, and religion | 1.3 | 0.3 |
| Health | 7.0 | 9.3 |
| Housing and community amenities | 0.72 | 0.47 |
| Environmental protection | 0.5 | 0.0 |
| Total (coefficients of social benefits) | 36.02 | 23.73 |

Source: Authors' calculations on the basis of OECD, 'General government spending', 2018, doi: 10.1787/a31cbf4d-en (accessed 4 February 2021).

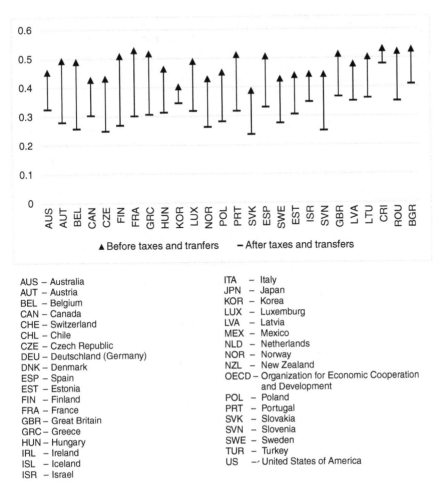

**Figure 7** Gini coefficient before and after taxes and transfers, 2018.

economic theory, suggesting that the sole measure of efficiency is the rate of profit and of justice, the redistribution of income from the richest to the poorest strata of society. However, modern-day economies also feature relations that are transitional to post-market forms, so the results of economic activity will include progress in human qualities, and not merely profits.

Second, the progress of social justice assumes not only redistribution of income, but also, and above all, the growth of equally accessible conditions for development – education, health care, and, most important, interesting creative activity. In this more precise understanding of the categories, it is clear that more equal access to the conditions for development is not an obstacle to increased efficiency in the economy, but a condition of it, if we consider economic efficiency to include progress in human qualities.[2]

Reviewing work by Peter Drucker (1996), Vladislav Inozemtsev and Ekaterina Kuznetsova write that this author

> draws on a wealth of statistical material that confirms such well-known facts as the successes of the European social welfare system in reducing the proportion of citizens who live below the poverty line; in providing high unemployment benefits (when the head of a family with two children loses his or her job, the family's standard of living falls by only 10 per cent in Sweden and the Netherlands, by 11 per cent in France, and by 26 per cent in Germany, while in analogous circumstances in the USA the standard of living falls on average by half); in pension provisions (in the main European countries, the proportion of pensioners living below the poverty line ranges from 4.4 to 7.7 per cent, compared with 19.6 per cent in the USA); in health care (in the USA, where 14 per cent of GDP is spent in this area, 43 million people lack medical insurance, and life expectancy remains lower than in any of the present countries of the European Union). (Inozemtsev and Kuznetsova 2002: 42–75, 275–8)

In any case, the system of production relations described earlier provides for the reproduction of the total hegemony of capital even it it is primarily based in the economic sphere. Crowning the system of relations of total hegemony is the sum of the non-economic resources and methods that serve the hegemony of capital, and that render it total in terms of the 'vertical' aspect of the social structure as well. This system may appear absolute and eternal, but alternatives to it are also growing in its depths.

## The new structure of social reproduction

The study of the structure of social reproduction that appears in volume II of Karl Marx's *Capital* has become a fundamental source for Marxists. In our view, however, the substantial changes that have taken place in the forces of production and in production relations over almost a century and a half require that this model be developed further. Before we outline how we propose to develop it, a few methodological remarks are necessary.

### *Reproduction under conditions of the 'sunset' of capitalism and the 'realm of necessity': progress of the creatosphere vs. expansion of the perverse sector*

Volume II of *Capital* rests on the fundamental distinction between Department I (production of the means of production) and Department II (production of the objects of consumption). In Marx's theory, this distinction explains the mechanism through which surplus value is realised.[3] Does the new structure of production require altering this framework? If so, how?

This question does not arise if we accept the principles of modern-day econometrics, which notoriously follows the well-known principle: 'Look under the street-lamp, not where you lost it'; they research the phenomena that are reflected in the statistical handbooks, and in the way the handbooks indicate. The handbooks contain only the information needed to optimise the extracting of the profits of capital and to ensure the stability of this process on the macro-level. (Inasmuch as everything else is (virtually) left out of the resulting economic indices, it *seems* not to exist so far as economic theory is concerned.)

Meanwhile, the most significant proportions (and disproportions) in the world economy are associated with more complex processes that are not to be found on the surface of events. They exist and operate at a fundamental level. What is involved here is not simply the relationship between sectors, such as the financial and non-financial sectors or goods and services. Many critically important questions of the contemporary economy are reflected only obliquely in today's statistics, and in numerous cases information about them is not to be had there at all. This is true, in particular, of measurements of the role and degree of development of the creative content of labour, and of the amount of free time (i.e. not leisure time, but time spent on the free and harmonious development of the individual). Nor are statistics to be found on the degree of expansion of simulacra.

Marxist economic theory, unlike its neoclassical counterpart, maintains that research must be conducted precisely *here*, in the field of profound structural shifts in social reproduction. Just because, for the present, everything in these areas is 'dark', since there are no 'street lamps' (that is, data in sufficient volume and of adequate structure), we cannot abandon study of the questions concerned. This is where the 'instrument', which (to use Marx's vivid expression) can replace the telescope, the microscope, or other equipment for the political economist, comes in and makes it possible to discern things that are invisible to the 'naked eye' of the ordinary individual and her or his scholarly colleague. This instrument is the power of scientific abstraction. Its most developed form is the method of ascent from the abstract to the concrete. Before we can apply it, however, we must perform a protracted labour of critical analysis, of synthesising empirically accessible practical phenomena while also 'cleansing' them of all the 'deformations' that the world of perverse forms and fetishes introduces to them.

Without immersing ourselves in the subtleties of these methodological and theoretical concepts, we are able to present the results of our previous research, which in turn rests on elaborations by our teachers and colleagues.

Let us continue our brief commentary on the multi-dimensional question of the reproduction of late capitalism.

In Chapter 1, we stated that the epoch of the 'sunset' of capitalism and of the 'realm of necessity' was giving birth to two new and fundamentally important structural shifts. The first of these is the transformation of the sphere of culture, once relatively unimportant for the economy, into the creatosphere, which (through its influence on the progress of the content of labour, of technology, of demand, and so forth) comes close to determining the quality and dynamic of material production. The second shift consists of the development, almost at breakneck speed, of the sphere that we have characterised as the perverse (or useless) sector.

As noted earlier, there has been nothing accidental about the expansion of this sector. Resulting from contradictory trends, it has brought about a radical shift in the structure of the social reproduction process during the 'sunset' of the 'realm of economic necessity'. The expansion has been conditioned by growth in the productivity of industrial labour and by the birth of the post-industrial sphere. Together, these factors have made it possible to free up significant resources from material production. The rise of the perverse sector, on the other hand, has resulted from structural shifts in material production becoming bound up with trends and forms advantageous to modern global capital, leading to the use of these resources in a sector that does not create material products and services that fulfil productive and/or personal needs, and that does not create cultural values either.

The thesis that curtailing the perverse sector is an absolutely indispensable condition for progress seemed highly debatable until quite recently (that is, until the financial crisis of 2008). The failure to identify the sector as an obstacle was associated above all with the growth of the sphere of transactions (mostly in the financial market) in the developed countries of the West, where this growth had become one of the dominant trends of the second half of the twentieth century, though it had begun much earlier. In today's conditions of near-universal criticism of financialisation, however, our hypothesis identifying the financial sector as useless, which we advanced in the late 1990s, appears more and more convincing.

In any case, world economic practice bears witness that such areas as finance and the movement of fictitious capital, corporate and state management, the military-industrial complex, and mass culture are becoming prime targets of big business. The most prosperous groups within the working class (so-called 'professionals') increasingly orient their activity towards these areas, since it is here that the best-paid jobs are concentrated. The greatest exertions of modern economic thought are focused on the study of these spheres, along with research by sociologists, psychologists, specialists in the field of information technology. and many others. The assertion that the perverse sector acts as a powerful brake on socio-economic progress, and especially on the process of transition from the dominance of material production to the creatosphere seems, at the very least, to be well worth discussing. However, finding a detailed answer to the question of how this assertion can be substantiated is a task for future research.

Nevertheless, the trend towards re-industrialisation that has emerged since the world crisis of 2008 (even in such parts of the developed world as the US and Western Europe)[4] shows that the expansion of the financial transaction sector, however profitable, hinders the normal reproduction of national capital as a whole, and cannot replace material production. There is, of course, also the danger that the eventual exit from the dead ends of the perverse sector will not lead in a progressive direction but in a regressive one: not forward, to the creatosphere, but backward, to the past of classical industrial production.

We stress that in the perverse sector, activity with a creative content is not directed towards the growth of utilitarian consumption and material production, but towards carrying out tasks linked to the progress of forms of this production and consumption that are false in their essence, and that are characteristic of modern corporate capitalism. Here, a sort of 'doubling of the transformation' is taking place. Material production in the market is no longer the gravitational centre of social relationships, of the attraction of resources, of the receipt of incomes, and so forth. The first transformation here is that of the useful good into a commodity, a value: an activity devoted to the servicing and mediation of market transactions themselves. This latter activity consists predominantly of the production of simulacra. So the second transformation is that of the commodity into a simulacrum.

We further stress that transactions between different institutions (for example, between firms and legal structures, between the state and corporations, between the state and ideological structures, and so on) also contain a productive component. This latter, however, shrinks as time goes on, while the parasitic, simulative component expands (among the instances of this is the process of financialisation, discussed earlier). This expansion will continue unless countervailing forces (for example, regulatory action by society) put a brake on it.

Between material production and utilitarian consumption, between producer and consumer, between owner and worker, huge masses of fictitious capital, bureaucracy, mass culture, and so forth thus arise and mediate the lives of the people concerned. It is these phenomena that swallow the vast resources set free by the progress of material production that occurred during the twentieth century, resources that might have been used to develop the creatosphere.

As noted earlier, activity in the perverse sector, which is the most prestigious sector under the conditions of modern global capitalism, cannot fail to attract a significant proportion (probably the majority) of the most able and creative people, those who have potential as innovators. Accordingly, this activity becomes the most important field for the application of the newest technologies (above all, information technologies), and it is here that the main creative and innovative potential of humanity is being concentrated. Here, in the perverse sector, in the areas of the science and innovative activity that service it, the creative content of labour and the perverse forms described earlier are becoming intertwined. The people employed in this area, who possess high creative and innovative potential, have been won over extensively by the business interests concentrated in the sector. For these gifted people, tearing themselves away from the perverse sector and making the transition to a different sphere of creative activity is extraordinarily difficult, since their motivation, the results of their activity, and its very character are dictated by the perverse forms of this sector. Indeed, their entire lives must in this case be qualitatively changed. This leads us ineluctably to conclude that in the perverse sector, the contradiction between the advance of labour that is creative in its content, and the perverse forms represented by the market and power relations that mediate creative activity, appears in its harshest form.

However, we have got ahead of ourselves somewhat. Let us return to questions of the structure of social reproduction. Changes in the structure of actual material production make up the principal structural component of the genesis of the creatosphere. Nevertheless, the most significant structural changes associated with the birth of the creatosphere are, in fact, related to the progress of creative activity and, accordingly, of the areas in which cultural goods are produced and in which the process of forming, raising, educating, and developing human beings as free, many-sided individuals goes ahead.

Education and training (involving people of all ages, not just children and young people) are becoming such areas, as are all those in which the individual develops through creative activity itself and through social contact that stimulates innovation. Strictly speaking, creative labour is the sphere that gives rise to a free personality, developing in a multifaceted manner. Here we are able to confirm the conclusion formulated in the preceding section: since the creatosphere also has its Departments I and II, respectively producing the means of production and those of consumption, 'Department I' of the creatosphere, linked to the formation of the creative individual, may in the near future become the main, dominant growth point for societies that wish to follow the direct path of the sublation of material production and of the development of the creatosphere, instead of the piling up of perverse forms of this process.

In such areas as science, artistic culture, and so forth purely creative activity may, as already noted, appear as a sort of 'Department II' of overall social activity. This 'department' must also progressively force out mass culture, ecclesiastical production, and other substitutes for the creatosphere, at the same time as actual material production declines in parallel.

## Changes in the structure of social reproduction

Before we dwell on the particular nuances we have introduced, it should be stressed that the economy of late capitalism also reproduces the traditional structures of any economic system. These are the sectoral divisions emerging from the specific nature of the objects produced and/or results of labour, and also the distinction between various technological systems that is based primarily on the particular character of the instruments of labour. Nevertheless, the study of the reproduction of what are, above all, productive relationships allows us to introduce other refinements as well.

In this case we are able, *first*, to employ the criteria of socio-economic progress (the progress of the human individual and of other components of the productive forces), and to distinguish (1.1) the areas of social production that conduce to the progress of these parameters (most of the sectors of material production and of the creatosphere), and also (1.2) the areas in which phenomena arise that serve exclusively the aims of extracting profit and other alienated objectives (geopolitical expansion, and so forth). As noted earlier, the first of these areas is the real sector, in which useful goods are produced. The second is the useless sector, which may more strictly be described as perverse, since it does not produce goods that are useful for the progress of the economy, society, and the individual, but perverse forms that for the most part are simulacra.

From a theoretical point of view, the criterion for distinguishing these two spheres is simple, and has been formulated in Chapter 6: the creation, or non-creation, of components of the progress of the human individual, of the productive forces, and/or of cultural values. In practice, this criterion can be applied only indirectly, since only in theoretical terms are we are able to determine that the creation of these components of progress plays the greater role in one of the sectors chosen in practice (for example, in industry, education, or health care), while their non-creation plays the greater role in others (finance, mass culture, and so forth). Both in industry and in education, however, more than a few simulative pseudo-goods are being created. Meanwhile, the sphere of finances is essential for enhancing the investment process, for carrying on what may be described, somewhat picturesquely, as 'public accounting', and so forth.

Second, by employing so basic a criterion as the content of labour and of (productive) technologies within the framework of the actual real sector, the following major areas can be distinguished:

(2.1)	production based on reproductive manual labour and employing pre-industrial technologies (this includes a proportion of material production and of the area of services);

(2.2)	production based on reproductive machine labour and employing industrial technologies, excluding the most modern ones;

(2.3)	the creatosphere, in which the leading role (not necessarily dominant in quantitative terms, but determining the character and mission of the area) is played by creative activity; the creatosphere comprises most of education (including child care), health care, culture, and activity devoted to the recreation of nature and society, as well as that part of material production that is based on post-industrial technologies, in which the human individual, as Marx put it, acts primarily as a controller and regulator.

*Third*, within the framework of the creatosphere we are able to distinguish analogues of Departments I and II. We may recall that in the industrial economy, whose basis was, naturally, industry, the production of machines (production of the means of production) was specifically designated within the Marxist discourse as Department I. The production, with the help of these machines, of objects of consumption was, accordingly, Department II. By analogy, we may assume that within the framework of the creatosphere, the role of Department I is fulfilled by the areas that witness the production of the main 'resource' of development: human creative potential; these are such 'branches' as education, health care, social work, and so on. The use of this principal resource for the production of the most important results of the functioning of the creatosphere – cultural values and, in particular, innovations, expertise, works of art, and so forth – proceeds in such fields as fundamental and applied science, engineering and social creativity, management, artistic culture, and so on. These areas, consequently, fulfil the role of Department II of the creatosphere.

In the economy where the creatosphere plays the leading role acting as the locomotive of development, actual material production and the sector of useful services (useful, that is, for the progress of human qualities, and for the solving of environmental problems) will play a role that derives from the development of the creatosphere. Accordingly, within the framework of material production it is possible in this case to distinguish (by following Marxist tradition while developing it slightly) a Department III of the creatosphere (production of the means of production); a Department IV (the production of objects of consumption); and a Department V (production of useful services). Beyond this real sector there will lie a sphere of

**Table 5** The structure of social reproduction of the market economy under the conditions of the birth of mass creative activity

(a) The two main sectors of social reproduction

| Social reproduction | |
|---|---|
| Real (useful) sector | Perverse (useless) sector |
| Creatosphere | Material production and the sector of useful services |
| (Departments I and II of social reproduction) | (Departments III, IV, and V of social reproduction) |

(b) The structure of the creatosphere, including Departments I and II of social reproduction

| Creatosphere | |
|---|---|
| Formation of human qualities | Employment of human qualities to create cultural phenomena |
| (Department I of social reproduction) Education, art, health care, sport, etc. | (Department II of social reproduction) Research and development and other areas that create new technologies, works of art, etc. |

(c) The structure of material production and of the sector of useful services, including Departments III, IV, and V of social reproduction

| Material production and the sector of useful services | | |
|---|---|---|
| Production of the means of production (Department III of social reproduction) | Production of objects of consumption (Department IV of social reproduction) | Production of useful services (Department V of social reproduction) |

*Source*: developed by the authors.

the production of simulacra and other useless (and even simply harmful) phenomena: the perverse sector (see Table 5).

Of course, inserting statistical information into this table would be fraught with methodological and practical difficulties, since the available statistical data are grouped in a fundamentally different fashion, and only with great difficulty can they be identified with the structural groups presented above. Nevertheless, the theoretical model set out in Table 5 makes it possible to show (though, naturally, not to prove) that, from the point of view of content, the structure of social reproduction under present-day conditions must take on a substantially different appearance from what is now accepted. Within it, from the point of view of content, it would be appropriate to distinguish all the main categories noted above (material production and utilitarian services, the creatosphere, and the perverse sector) and their specific 'branches'. This structuring would not only be correct in theoretical terms, but also fundamentally important from the point of view of practice. The practice concerned, however, would not be that of doing business and of calculating profits and losses from any activity whatever (from the point of view of content), but that of advancing society towards a world in which social reproduction was subordinated to environmental, social, and humanitarian priorities.

In the latter case, we might, on the basis of the grouping of resources suggested above, and also of the outcomes of social reproduction, assess in quantitative terms the degree to which society has advanced from the world of satisfying utilitarian requirements to that of developing human qualities. We might also assess the degree of useless (harmful) expenditure of the resources of society and nature on achieving fictitious results. In this case, the efficiency of social reproduction will be greater to the extent that goods essential for the development of human qualities (production in the creatosphere) account for more, and goods created in the perverse sector for less, per unit of the material goods produced in society. As a quantitative expression of the efficiency of social reproduction, we propose the following formula:

$$Ef = (Cr - Ir) / Q$$

where:

$Ef$ is the efficiency of social reproduction,

$Cr$ is the volume of production of values in the creatosphere (per head of population),

$Ir$ is the volume of production of useless phenomena in the perverse sector (per head of population)

$Qm$ is the volume of production of material goods and services (per head of population)

*For reference:* the overall volume of production of all goods and services ($Q$) is equal to the sum of the volumes of production of material goods and services, of values in the creatosphere, and of useless phenomena in the perverse sector ($Q = Qm + Cr + Ir]$).

Unfortunately, we cannot offer a numerical illustration of this model. The main reason for this is not the limited nature of our research capabilities, which include a subjective component, but the objective peculiarities of the existing quantitative data and above all of national and international statistics. These are gathered to fulfil tasks related to capital as a totality, and their focus is thus on direct phenomena of economic life that, as has been pointed out repeatedly, are perverse forms that create an appearance quite different from the actual content. To try to judge the quantitative parameters of meaningful processes on the basis of statistics that reflect perverse forms is exceedingly difficult.

We can, however, argue that concealed behind the concepts of the 'services sector' and 'material production' in the modern capitalist economy is an extremely heterogeneous array of categories. If we take the degree of progress away from material production and towards the creatosphere as the criterion for selecting structures to be studied, then numerous theses that now are all but universally accepted appear very doubtful, especially when the formation of the perverse (useless) sector is taken into account.

First, the partial (and at times direct) identification of the post-industrial sector with the sphere of services, something typical of many of the authors mentioned earlier in this book, appears essentially *incorrect*. The service sector includes a huge stratum of pre-industrial and industrial types of activity: the work of dishwashers, drivers, hotel staff, cleaners, salespersons, etc. Further, it must not be forgotten that in the sectors of material production (industry, transport, and so forth), post-industrial technologies are now highly developed. Industrial robotics with artificial intelligence, computer numerical control machines, the industrial internet of things, and genetic engineering are only a few of many examples.

Second, it is becoming clear that the criterion of 'post-industrialism', as a vaguely applied measure of the degree of development of societies and, in particular, as one of the criteria used to distinguish the 'first world' from the rest of humanity is at best inadequate. This is the case even if the term is used quite strictly, as a synonym for technologies on a higher plane than that of industry. Its inadequacy reflects the fact that it fails to take account of so crucially important a parameter as the sphere (and hence the motives, goals, and social, environmental, and humanitarian *results*) in which these high technologies are employed. Meanwhile, to identify the post-industrial sector with the perverse sector is particularly inappropriate.

Third, the branches of the services sector that are most important from the point of view of progress (economic, social, and humanitarian) are those that provide the greatest scope for fresh manifestations of the creatosphere (the two criteria coincide only in part). The branches in question are not those in which advanced information and other high technologies are employed to the greatest extent, and certainly not those in which the perverse sector has experienced its broadest development.

It would not be difficult to pursue these threads further, but most important for us at present is the fact that they are all conditioned not by the classification we have drawn up somewhat arbitrarily and employed in Table 5 (which, we repeat, is only an illustration), but by the theoretical hypothesis that is to follow. This hypothesis, it will be recalled, maintains that it is the creatosphere, and not the multitude of perverse forms referred to earlier, that is the progressive heir to the development of material production.

## Notes

1  We have in mind *My poydem drugim putem: ot 'kapitalizma Yurskogo perioda' k Rossii budushchego* [We shall follow a different path: from 'Jurassic capitalism' to the Russia of the future] (Buzgalin and Kolganov 2009a).
2  For a more detailed treatment of this point, see Grinberg 2013 and Buzgalin 2013. The global aspect of the question appears in Aitova 2014.
3  As Marxists know, resolving this question did not prove to be as simple and straightforward as the standard Soviet textbooks on the political economy of capitalism used to suggest. Early in the twentieth century the question aroused heated discussion between legal Marxists, Populists, V.I. Ul'yanov, Rosa Luxemburg, and others. In the present work we shall not take up the issues concerned.
4  'The idea of an initiation of reindustrialisation within the US is supported by the growing number of employees in the manufacturing sector. After a low point, in March 2010, with approximately 11.4 million employees, the number had increased to 12.6 million by April 2018. ... In 2017, the total number of manufacturing jobs due to reshoring since 2010 reached 576,000' (Gharleghi 2018). From 2010 to 2014 a slight increase in the share of the manufacturing industry was noted in Germany, Great Britain, Denmark, the Netherlands, Hungary, the Czech Republic, and Poland, whereas in 2000–10 in almost all these countries except Poland, there was a continuous decrease in its share (see Młody 2016: 457).

# Conclusion
# Capital and capitalism: what has changed in the twenty-first century

Any conclusion that undertakes to summarise the main ideas of a book must necessarily oversimplify. For the attentive reader, the conclusion is thus in a sense a redundant fragment. After more than forty years of reading and writing conclusions, we have therefore decided, in this conclusion, to concentrate on systematically outlining the new phenomena that are characteristic of the capitalism of the early twenty-first century as compared with that of the nineteenth, and on showing what our understanding of the nature of commodities, money, and capital introduces that is new in comparison with what the greatest work of political economy of the modern era, Marx's *Capital*, bestowed on humanity.

At the same time, we lay no claim whatever to being the authors of a new *Capital*. While standing on the shoulders of giants (not only of Marx, but also of dozens of great Marxists of the twentieth century and of our contemporaries), we have merely tried, as far as our powers permit, to carry out the work of systematising the studies involved and, as authors, of interpreting, developing, and supplementing them. In this conclusion, therefore, we summarise the various 'novelties' to be found in our book, which, we remind English-language readers, constitute only a few fragments of the fifth, two-volume Russian edition of our *Global'nyy capital* (Global capital).

## Methodology does indeed matter

One of the simplest but also (as we see it) most important tasks faced by the authors in preparing this book has been to 'open up' to English-language readers the world of Marxist studies in Russian – a world that until now has in most cases been unfamiliar to such people. The analysis is based on a general summary of more than 100 major works published by Russian-speaking Marxists over the past twenty-five years. Taking our lead from these traditions – critical Soviet, and post-Soviet – we have begun with a thesis that is not especially fashionable nowadays, but that in our view is of fundamental importance: 'methodology does indeed matter'. We separate the elements in the methodology of Karl Marx that remain valid and need re-actualising from those that are obsolete and require critical updating. The systematising of these provisions, together with a discussion of the main trends of research in post-Soviet Marxism, provides a starting point for our elaborations.

As we develop the traditions of critical Soviet Marxism (in post-Soviet left circles this legacy is referred to increasingly often as 'Ilenkovist'), key provisions of the method of ascent from the abstract to the concrete and of the historical-genetic approach are being re-actualised in our work. In particular, applying the historical-genetic method to the study of 'late capitalism' allows us, by proceeding from the abstract to the concrete, not only to show how the nature of commodities, money, capital, and the relations of reproduction has changed under conditions of twenty-first century capitalism. It also allows us to demonstrate the interconnectedness and dialectical unity of these changes.

Naturally, this amounts to a critique of recent works of social analysis that assume as self-evident a reliance on the methodology of positivism and postmodernism. We have set out to show that these methods do not permit an understanding of the modern market and capital, and doom scholars to achieving no more than descriptions of external forms. The foundation for this critique is provided by research into the causes and consequences of the dominance of positivism and postmodernism in the modern social sciences, and on this basis, we make a constructive criticism of these trends. As we show, these currents emerged as a result of objective changes in the material, technical, and socio-economic bases of modern capitalism, becoming products of the development of the total network market and of the hegemony of capital. They have furthered the progress of the fictitious sector and the expansion of simulacra. The dominance of these approaches has led to a rejection of fundamental methodological and theoretical research, reflected in a general spread of pragmatism, narrow-mindedness, and, ultimately, economic imperialism in the social sciences. This situation has resulted not only in a rejection of 'grand narratives', but also in an identification of the 'narrative' of methodological individualism and other attributes of the neoliberal trend as the supposedly 'natural' foundation for social enquiry.

## From the 'realm of necessity' to the 'realm of freedom'

Our critique of positivism and postmodernism led us, logically, to a critique of the general spread of economics and of its extension, so-called economic imperialism. We have sought to reveal the causes of its emergence and